Library of
Davidson College

CAMBRIDGE CLASSICAL STUDIES
General editors: M.I.Finley, E.J.Kenney, G.E.L.Owen

AN ESSAY ON ANAXAGORAS

An essay on Anaxagoras

MALCOLM SCHOFIELD
University Lecturer in Classics and Fellow
of St John's College, Cambridge

CAMBRIDGE UNIVERSITY PRESS
Cambridge
London : New York : New Rochelle
Melbourne : Sydney

Published by the Press Syndicate of the University of Cambridge
The Pitt Building, Trumpington Street, Cambridge CB2 1RP
32 East 57th Street, New York, NY 10022, USA
296 Beaconsfield Parade, Middle Park, Melbourne 3206, Australia

© Faculty of Classics, University of Cambridge 1980

First published 1980

Printed in Great Britain at
Redwood Burn Ltd, Trowbridge and Esher

Library of Congress Cataloguing in Publication Data

Schofield, Malcolm.
    An essay on Anaxagoras

    (Cambridge classical studies)
    Bibliography: p.
    Includes indexes

    1. Anaxagoras. 2. Aristoteles. I. Title.
II. Series.
B205.Z7S36   182'.8   79-10348

ISBN 0 521 22722 4

For Elizabeth

CONTENTS

Preface	page ix
Abbreviations	xii
INTRODUCTION	1
1 MIND	
Anaxagoras's dogmatism	3
Anaxagoras's ambiguity	10
The archaic sage	22
Appendix: Anaxagoras's floruit	33
2 PRIMORDIAL MIXTURE	
The beginning of the book	36
The status of the primordial mixture thesis	40
Textual evidence	40
Aristotle's interpretation	43
Reflections on Aristotle's interpretation	52
A problem for Aristotle's interpretation	59
An alternative interpretation	61
Conclusion	64
3 UNLIMITED SMALLNESS	
The constituents of the primordial mixture	68
The irrelevance of size	79
(a) Anaxagoras and Zeno	80
(b) Fragment 3	82
(c) Fragment 6	89
Conclusion	94
4 SEEDS, PORTIONS AND OPPOSITES	
Anaxagoras's defence of his central doctrine	100
Portions and opposites	107
Seeds	121

The scholiast's question	133
Conclusion	143
Notes to Chapter 1	145
Notes to Chapter 2	151
Notes to Chapter 3	155
Notes to Chapter 4	161
Bibliography	169
Index of passages	174
Index of Greek terms	178
General index	180

PREFACE

In the writing of this small book I have incurred many debts of gratitude. First I am glad of an opportunity to express deeply felt thanks to the Master and Fellows of Balliol, who by electing me to the Dyson Research Fellowship in Greek Culture gave me the time and the stimulus to write – among other things – first drafts of much of the material of Chapters 1, 2 and 4 in 1970-2. Versions of Chapter 1 were read to several learned societies in Oxford and Cambridge. An invitation to address the Triennial Meeting of the Roman and Hellenic Societies in Oxford in 1975 prompted a first version of some of the matter in Chapter 3, and resulted in many enjoyable conversations about Anaxagoras.

I am grateful to my College, Faculty and University for two terms' leave in 1976-7 which enabled me to write a penultimate draft, read subsequently by a number of friends. I thank for their criticism and encouragement Myles Burnyeat, Edward Hussey, Tony Long, Colin Macleod, David Sedley, and especially Geoffrey Lloyd, who wrote and discussed with me detailed comments on the whole manuscript. John Ackrill made me a loan (later converted into a gift) of his copy of Jöhrens. Others kindly let me see unpublished work of their own: David Sider, Michael Gagarin, Jonathan Barnes, whose sections on Anaxagoras in his now published new book were a constant stimulus and pleasure, and once again Geoffrey Lloyd, who has been pursuing researches much more broadly based than mine on dogmatism and argument in early Greek philosophy and science. The limitations of this book will all too readily be perceived to be my own: if it has virtues, they reflect those of my friends.

I have also had the good fortune to find in Jan Chapman the ideal typist. There cannot be many people who combine her command of Greek with the exemplary speed, accuracy and elegance of her typing. I thank her for her work on two successive drafts of the manuscript.

It seems fitting to conclude with a word or two in homage to the *genius loci*. In the grounds of St John's College, Cambridge (in whose library I am writing these words) there stands an ancient stone building, until recently the property of Merton College, Oxford, which rejoices in the name of the School of Pythagoras. It may once have been called after another Presocratic:

> 'In the earliest deeds belonging to Merton College the house is merely described as a messuage. In the deeds relating to the transfer of the property in 1270 from the Dunnings to that college it is referred to as "the stone house in which Eustace, father of Richard Dunning, formerly dwelt". The masons' contract of 1375 describes the house as being "commonly called Mertonhall". The same name was given to it in a lease of 1503. In the reign of Henry VIII, Leland called it the Schola de Merton, thus suggesting a transitional stage in the change to its modern appellation of the "School of Pythagoras". The last name first appears on Richard Lyne's plan of Cambridge made in 1574, but I do not think he is responsible for this change of name. The reason for the adoption of the present name takes us back to what Professor Maitland called "the oldest of all the inter-university sports", to wit, the "lying match" regarding the relative antiquity of the rival universities. In 1464 a certain doctor of medicine named John Herrison, who was Chancellor of Cambridge University from 1465 to 1468, made a transcript of a chronicle attributed to Nicholas Cantelupe and entitled *Cronica Fundacionis Destruccionis et Renouacionis Universitatis et Civitatis Cantabrigg*. At the end of his transcript Herrison added a few notes of his own regarding former eminent persons who had flourished at Cambridge. Amongst the alumni thus claimed by him was Anaxagoras, who according to him was buried at Cambridge. Herrison was sufficient authority for subsequent writers to accept the connection of Anaxagoras with Cambridge as undisputed. In 1535 John Lidgate wrote of the days
>
> > When Cantebro, as it well knoweth,
> > At Athenes scholed in his yought,
> > All his wyttes gratelye did applie,
> > To have acquayntance by great affection
> > With folke experte in Philosophie.

> From Atheines he brought with hym downe
> Philosophers most sovereigne of renowne
> Vnto Cambridge, playnlye this is the case,
> Anaxamander and Anaxagoras.

The "lying match" reached its climax in 1568 when John Caius took up the cudgels against Key of Oxford. Herrison's manuscript was in Caius's own college and was drawn upon for the *De Antiquitate Cantabrigiensis Academiae*. Caius cited Herrison in the following passage in that work:

> If John Herrison, a grave and learned author, is to be believed, Anaxagoras was buried in Cambridge. This I neither affirm nor deny. I only say this - that it is as possible that Anaxagoras died at Cambridge in the houses, which are called by the name of Anaxagoras (*in aedibus quae nomine Anaxagorae appellantur*) as that your University was sprung from Alfred or born of the Greeks, as your history boasts.

In 1568, therefore, when *De Antiquitate* was written, there was a building in Cambridge which was known to Caius as the "House of Anaxagoras" and it can hardly be doubted that this was the same building as that which Lyne described in 1574 as "Domus Pythagorae". The change to the better known name of Pythagoras was an easy matter. The appellation received official recognition in the reign of Charles I, who in his confirmatory grant to Merton of their manor at Cambridge describes it by the title "Pythagoras's Farm".' (J.M. Gray, *The School of Pythagoras*, Cambridge Antiquarian Society, Quarto Publications, N.S.4 (Cambridge 1932), 37-8)

Cambridge   M.S.
October 1978

ABBREVIATIONS

References to ancient authors are given in standard forms of abbreviation, mostly those adopted in the latest edition of Liddell and Scott's Lexicon. Modern authors are cited by name and (if more than one of their writings is mentioned) a number, which corresponds with that assigned to the work in question in the bibliography, where full particulars of all secondary literatures are given. In addition note the following acronyms:

DK   H. Diels and W. Kranz, *Die Fragmente der Vorsokratiker*, sixth edition, Berlin 1951-2

FGH   *Die Fragmente der griechischen Historiker*, by F. Jacoby, Berlin 1923-30 and Leiden 1940-58

LSJ   *A Greek-English Lexicon*, compiled by H.G. Liddell and R. Scott, revised by H.S. Jones (with Supplement 1968), Oxford 1968

OCD   *The Oxford Classical Dictionary*, second edition by N.G.L. Hammond and H.H. Scullard, Oxford 1970

RE   *Paulys Realencyclopädie der classischen Altertumswissenschaft*, edited by G. Wissowa, W. Kroll and K. Mittelhaus, Stuttgart 1893-1972

SVF   *Stoicorum Veterum Fragmenta*, collected by H. von Arnim, Leipzig 1903-5

INTRODUCTION

Anaxagoras is probably most widely known as the fifth-century author whose book rekindled hopes of philosophy in the breast of Socrates. But it is no secret to students of ancient Greece or of philosophy that nothing survives of that book but a few miserable fragments, which, like all such survivals from the classical and preclassical ages of Greece, have attracted the frequent and exhaustive scrutiny of learned and sensitive critical scholarship. What room, then, for another book about Anaxagoras?

As it so happens, there is no authoritative book written in English that is devoted wholly to Anaxagoras. The last thirty years have seen a succession of fine shorter essays, some published as journal articles, others as chapters of general books on the Presocratics. But there seemed to be scope for a longer study, in which author and reader could at their leisure mull over the very texture of Anaxagoras's writing and reflect upon their own expectations of a philosopher so distant in time and in idiom and so disjointedly preserved. This book suggests that there is a considerable gap between what we hope for and what we find in the case of Anaxagoras. A Pythagorean table of opposites will flatten any subtleties in the argument but introduce some of the main contrasts which it explores:

Ideal philosopher	*Actual Anaxagoras*
argumentative	narrative
enquiring	dogmatic
cooperative	didactic
reason	authority
common sense	special insight
clear	ambiguous
determinate	indeterminate
classical	archaic
fluent literate	early literate
epistemological	metaphysical

So the book is an essay, and an essay particularly on the problems which the dogmatism and ambiguity of Anaxagoras's fragments pose for the philosophical interpreter. It makes no attempt to discuss the important and often influential views which Anaxagoras appears to have expressed on many topics - particularly in cosmology, perception and physiology - that are not mentioned in the fragments. Nor does it examine all the fragments, nor scrutinise with equal care each that it does take up.

We begin with the longest and most important of all the fragments, Fragment 12 on the cosmogonical activity of mind. We set aside some of the hoarier questions which Anaxagoras's account has provoked, in the hope of exploiting our best chance of seeing what a continuous stretch of Anaxagoras was actually like. We shall find that it poses very sharply many of the interpretative issues which have already been adumbrated. Chapter 2 turns to Anaxagoras's thesis of primordial mixture, expounded at the very beginning of his book: for this is presumably where Anaxagoras wanted us to begin upon the task of understanding his physical theory. The chapter asks what status the thesis has in his system: axiom or theorem. With the assistance of Aristotle a speculative answer is worked out in rather more *a priori* fashion than anything else in the book. Chapter 3 continues the exploration of Anaxagoras's primordial mixture, and in particular pursues in the detail of three fragments (Fragments 1, 3 and 6) his pioneering conception of the infinite smallness of things in the mixture. Finally, in Chapter 4 we launch our assault on the central doctrine of Anaxagoras's system, the thesis that in everything there is a portion of everything, which poses formidable problems of ambiguity even if it is the one major element in the system upon which its author appears to have brought argument to bear at a fundamental level. Every interpreter feels the desire to improve upon the rather divergent evidence of the fragments and of the secondary sources about what Anaxagoras actually meant by this doctrine. The chapter, and indeed the monograph as a whole, aims to give him a finer understanding of the prospects of success and failure.

Chapter 1
MIND

ANAXAGORAS'S DOGMATISM
τὰ μὲν ἄλλα παντὸς μοῖραν μετέχει, νοῦς δέ ἐστιν ἄπειρον καὶ
αὐτοκρατὲς καὶ μέμεικται οὐδενὶ χρήματι, ἀλλὰ μόνος αὐτὸς ἐφ'
ἑαυτοῦ ἐστιν. εἰ μὴ γὰρ ἐφ' ἑαυτοῦ ἦν, ἀλλά τεῳ ἐμέμεικτο
ἄλλῳ, μετεῖχεν ἂν ἁπάντων χρημάτων, εἰ ἐμέμεικτό τεῳ· ἐν
παντὶ γὰρ παντὸς μοῖρα ἔνεστιν, ὥσπερ ἐν τοῖς πρόσθεν μοι
λέλεκται· καὶ ἂν ἐκώλυεν αὐτὸν τὰ συμμεμειγμένα, ὥστε
μηδενὸς χρήματος κρατεῖν ὁμοίως ὡς καὶ μόνον ἐόντα ἐφ'
ἑαυτοῦ. ἔστι γὰρ λεπτότατόν τε πάντων χρημάτων καὶ
καθαρώτατον, καὶ γνώμην γε περὶ παντὸς πᾶσαν ἴσχει καὶ
ἰσχύει μέγιστον, καὶ ὅσα γε ψυχὴν ἔχει, καὶ τὰ μείζω καὶ τὰ
ἐλάσσω, πάντων νοῦς κρατεῖ. καὶ τῆς περιχωρήσιος τῆς
συμπάσης νοῦς ἐκράτησεν, ὥστε περιχωρῆσαι τὴν ἀρχήν. καὶ
πρῶτον ἀπό του σμικροῦ ἤρξατο περιχωρεῖν, ἐπὶ δὲ πλέον
περιχωρεῖ, καὶ περιχωρήσει ἐπὶ πλέον. καὶ τὰ συμμισγόμενά
τε καὶ ἀποκρινόμενα καὶ διακρινόμενα πάντα ἔγνω νοῦς. καὶ
ὁποῖα ἔμελλεν ἔσεσθαι καὶ ὁποῖα ἦν[1] καὶ ὅσα νῦν ἔστι καὶ
ὁποῖα ἔσται, πάντα διεκόσμησε νοῦς, καὶ τὴν περιχώρησιν
ταύτην ἣν νῦν περιχωρεῖ τά τε ἄστρα καὶ ὁ ἥλιος καὶ ἡ σελήνη
καὶ ὁ ἀὴρ καὶ ὁ αἰθὴρ οἱ ἀποκρινόμενοι.

The other things share in a portion of everything, but mind is
unlimited and self-controlling and has not been mixed with
anything, but exists alone itself by itself; for if it were
not by itself but had been mixed with something else, it
would share in all things, if it had been mixed with any (for
in everything there is a portion of everything, as I have
said earlier); and the things mixed together with it would be
preventing it so that it would not control any thing in the
same way as it actually does being alone by itself. For it is
finest of all things and purest; and moreover it harbours
every discerning judgement about everything, and [so] harbours
greatest strength; and moreover all the things that have soul,

both the greater and the smaller, all of them mind controls.

And mind controlled the whole revolution, so that it started to revolve at the beginning. And first it began to revolve in a small way, but it is revolving more, and it will revolve more. And the things that were being mixed together and separated off and distinguished, mind knew them all. And whatever things were to be - both those which were and those which are now and those which will be - all these mind ordered, and also this revolution in which now revolve the stars and the sun and the moon and the air and the aither which are being separated off.[2]

The extract I have quoted and translated constitutes the greater part of what is by far the longest fragment of Anaxagoras surviving to us (Fragment 12).[3] And although this cannot be shown to have had anything to do with its survival,[4] it is easily the most striking and memorable of all the fragments - and indeed among the most powerful passages in all Greek prose in its intensity and slow-moving grandeur. Anaxagoras has chiselled out a style perfectly fitted to the expression of a profoundly synoptic vision of the nature of things. This is no mere academic philosophy, occupied with logic chopping or abstruse technical theory, we say to ourselves; it is more like a hymn[5] to the remote yet familiar power of νοῦς.

That, at any rate, is what one might feel in a sympathetic mood. In another, Fragment 12 might strike one as dogmatic, highfalutin poppycock. It is just the sort of speculation Aristophanes in the *Clouds* held up to ridicule as tedious, silly and unnatural. Sir Kenneth Dover thinks we might find Aristophanes's attitude hard to comprehend. 'It is difficult for the modern reader', he claims, 'to understand how a writer as sensitive and subtle as Aristophanes could have taken the field with such vigour on the side of the philistines against that spirit of systematic, rational inquiry which we regard as an essential ingredient of civilization.'[6] I do not myself see the difficulty, for humorists and satirists are often conservatives distrustful of ideas. But even if we do not feel a need to defend Aristophanes, it is worth quoting Dover's concluding observation on the matter: 'Exciting though some Greek philosophical and scientific speculations now seem to have been, viewed as an early stage in the intellectual history of Europe, they were not always expressed in a way which would necessarily make them appear, even to a rational man, more plausible than Hesiodic myths.'[7] Does not Anaxagoras's Fragment 12 look like a case in point? It is usually taken to be not so much a virtue as the duty of a philosopher both to argue for his assertions and to make evident the vast importance he attaches to argument. But in most of our passage Anaxagoras seems to try to win our assent by the methods of the hierophant, not the dialectician.

Contrast Parmenides. Anaxagoras appears to have been deeply impressed by the arguments of Parmenides. It is probable that some of the basic theses of his own physics were worked out in the spirit of a demonstration that, although Parmenides was right to rule the ideas of coming to be and perishing meaningless, nonetheless change and plurality were still possible.[8] Now Parmenides's Way of Truth is hard, terse argument - the word deserves repetition - throughout, despite its presentation as a religious revelation. And its author bids us discount the expectations of indisputability aroused by revelation when he has his goddess say: 'Judge by reason (λόγος) my much-contested refutation (ἔλεγχος).'[9] So if Anaxagoras tacitly acknowledged that, precisely by the force of argument, Parmenides had necessitated a radical revision of the terms in which physical speculation was conducted, why did he argue so little himself?

Or contrast Diogenes of Apollonia. Diogenes, like Anaxagoras, was in the business of cosmological theory, not of metaphysical paradox. In philosophy and literary style alike he was heavily influenced by the older thinker. And he followed Anaxagoras in giving a fundamental place in his scheme of things to mind, or more strictly to intelligence or understanding (νόησις). He differed from Anaxagoras in predicating intelligence of matter (he was a monist), but also in his willingness to argue the case for ascribing a crucial role in physics to intelligence. Thus Simplicius reports that he presented the following consideration in support of the claim that the single basic stuff has much intelligence in it (B3):[10]

>οὐ γὰρ ἄν, φησίν, οἷόν τε ἦν οὕτω δεδάσθαι ἄνευ νοήσιος ὥστε πάντων μέτρα ἔχειν, χειμῶνός τε καὶ θέρους καὶ νυκτὸς καὶ ἡμέρας καὶ ὑετῶν καὶ ἀνέμων καὶ εὐδιῶν· καὶ τὰ ἄλλα, εἴ τις βούλεται ἐννοεῖσθαι, εὑρίσκοι ἂν οὕτω διακείμενα ὡς ἀνυστὸν

κάλλιστα.

For, he says, it would not be possible without intelligence for it so to be divided up that it has measures of all things - of winter and summer and night and day and rains and winds and fair weather. The other things, too, if one wishes to consider them, one would find disposed in the best possible way.

It seems that this was not Diogenes's only argument for his thesis. For Simplicius tells us that he went on to say (B4):[11]

ἔτι δὲ πρὸς τούτοις καὶ τάδε μεγάλα σημεῖα. ἄνθρωποι γὰρ καὶ τὰ ἄλλα ζῶια ἀναπνέοντα ζώει τῷ ἀέρι. καὶ τοῦτο αὐτοῖς καὶ ψυχή ἐστι καὶ νόησις, ὡς δεδηλώσεται ἐν τῆδε τῇ συγγραφῇ ἐμφανῶς, καὶ ἐὰν τοῦτο ἀπαλλαχθῇ ἀποθνήσκει καὶ ἡ νόησις ἐπιλείπει.

Further, in addition to those, there are these important indications too. For men and the other living creatures live by means of air, through breathing it. And this is for them both soul and intelligence, as will get clearly shown in this treatise; and if this is removed, they die and intelligence fails.

Diogenes evidently thought it was not good enough simply to assert (as Anaxagoras had done) that mind ordered all things: from the presence of order he *inferred* intelligence. And in general, he took the place of mind in nature to be a topic on which evidence (σημεῖα) should be brought to bear. Not a whisper of evidence in Fragment 12 of Anaxagoras, where it would surely not have come amiss. Yet Diogenes is usually and rightly held to be an inferior thinker.

Of course, our extract from Fragment 12 is not dogmatic throughout. In a fine but neglected article of 1933 Karl Deichgräber argued that in it two quite different styles can be distinguished.[12] It was his main purpose to draw attention to the style of solemn predication, as he called it, in which attributes are heaped upon their subject, νοῦς, in clauses of the simplest possible form, linked by nothing but the reiterated particle καί. Although these and other features of the style are found outside the archaic period, in Anaxagoras they must count as characteristic marks of the archaic nature of his prose. Indeed, this passage provides a classic example of the paratactic syntax, and of the verbal repetitions needed to organize a paragraph from such simple units,

which the labours of Norden, Fränkel and others have taught us
(following Aristotle's description of the archaic λέξις εἰρομένη,
'strung-together style') to associate with the period,[13] which
lasted longer in prose than in poetry.[14]

The dominant style of our extract, then, is that of solemn
predication. But there is a stretch running from εἰ μὴ γὰρ...ὡς καὶ
μόνον ἐόντα ἐφ' ἑαυτοῦ which is altogether more complicated in syntax, and has two features in particular which set it off from the
rest of the extract. First, it is a complex piece of argument.
Anaxagoras here argues for his claim that νοῦς is not mixed with
anything by showing that the consequences of denying that claim are
unacceptable; in other words, by an indirect proof:[15] if νοῦς were
mixed with anything, it would be mixed with all things; but if it
were mixed with all things, they would prevent it from controlling
anything in the way that it actually does unmixed, on its own. The
second distinctive mark of this passage is its cross-reference to an
earlier part of Anaxagoras's book. As Deichgräber says, this is
very much in the manner of a treatise or text-book, not appropriate
in hymn-like writing. In a deeper sense, this whole argumentative
section is a piece of cross-reference. Its function is to show the
place of νοῦς in the ontology of Anaxagorean physics, to substantiate in physical detail the contrast with other things adumbrated
at the beginning of the fragment. Argument is used to explain the
internal consistency of Anaxagoras's views, not to defend his basic
theses.

It should not be thought that this more complex argumentative
style is without archaic features. Notice the artless economy of
ὁμοίως ὡς καὶ μόνον ἐόντα ἐφ' ἑαυτοῦ. Anaxagoras could have written, more mechanically, ὁμοίως ὡς καὶ νῦν κρατεῖ vel sim., and then
added by way of conclusion: νοῦς is therefore *not* mixed with all
things, and so not mixed with anything. As it is, by writing μόνον
ἐόντα ἐφ' ἑαυτοῦ he indicates the moral without laboriously rehearsing it. He thus manages both to avoid losing his reader or hearer
in the toils of his logic and to achieve an anaphoric return to his
point of departure (and, as it turns out, to the style of solemn
predication): as beautiful an example of that favourite device of
archaic style, ring composition, as one could hope to find. One
might feel that the repetition of εἰ ἐμέμεικτό τεῳ (recalling εἰ...

τεῳ ἐμέμεικτο ἄλλῳ) is less happy: it is logically otiose, and the
sentence which it concludes is so short that Anaxagoras cannot have
intended it as an *aide-mémoire*, which is at any rate one of the
functions of the similar (but not so exactly repetitious) words εἰ
μὴ οὕτω συνίστατο ὥστε ταὐτὸ εἶναι at the end of the penultimate
sentence of Diogenes B2. But it does help the reader - and still
more the hearer (if we imagine the fragment read aloud) - to focus
on the premiss of the argument, i.e. on the consideration which
governs all that follows. The emphatic clarity achieved by this
sort of repetition, particularly of subordinate clauses, is primitive but effective: compare Hesiod, *Theogony* 65-7 (where the iteration of the succulent phrase ἐρατὴν/ἐπήρατον ὄσσαν ἱεῖσαι is designed to convey the dreamlike seductiveness of the song of the
Graces), the Berezan lead letter of *c*. 500 B.C.[16] (where iteration
expresses desperate urgency), and P.Oxy. 3070 of the first century
A.D. (where an iterated conditional clause helps the recipient of
the letter - although its illustrations admittedly do the job
already - to concentrate on its indecent proposal).[17]

So it has to be allowed that there *is* argument in our extract.
But the argumentation is clearly subordinate in emphasis and substance to the declarations which Anaxagoras makes in his style of
solemn predication. It is almost as if he had inserted a footnote
after μόνος αὐτὸς ἐφ' ἑαυτοῦ ἐστιν, to explain the physical rationale for the claim he has just made to readers interested in the
fine print of his ontological theory. But, of course, it is *not* a
footnote. It is carefully welded into the text at beginning and end
(notice ἔστι γὰρ λεπτότατον κτλ.). It seems to gain in importance from the weight which attaches to the phrase μέμεικται...ἐφ'
ἑαυτοῦ ἐστιν within the clause νοῦς δέ...ἐφ' ἑαυτοῦ ἐστιν. And its
very length and prominence cause it to have a very decided effect on
the tone of the whole fragment. Deichgräber is quite right to argue
that there is much about the style of solemn predication here to
remind us of monotheistic hymnody.[18] He points to the simple mass-
ing of attributes of νοῦς, to the reiteration of πάντων...περὶ
παντὸς πᾶσαν...πάντων...συμπάσης κτλ., to the reiteration of
περιχωρεῖν and its cognates, to the recurrent νοῦς at the end of
clauses and sentences, repetitions which, as Denniston remarked,
'flood and permeate, rather than strike, the ear'.[19] There is no

doubt that these elements of the solemn style dominate our extract. But the presence of the argumentative passage surely cannot but suggest that even if, as they stand, they are only affirmations, Anaxagoras's grandiose statements about νοῦς are the product of subtle ratiocination, and could be justified by it if need be.

It might also be argued that the structure of the extract as a whole implies a form of argument, despite the absence of inferential particles in the greater part of it. For the extract seems to fall naturally into two paragraphs. The first of these runs from τὰ μὲν ἄλλα to πάντων νοῦς κρατεῖ. It hangs together both in content and as a syntactic unit. This is easily demonstrated. We have already seen how the argumentative passage εἰ μὴ γὰρ...ἐόντα ἐφ' ἑαυτοῦ is subordinated grammatically and logically to καὶ μέμεικται...ἐφ' ἑαυτοῦ ἐστιν. No less clearly ἔστι γάρ...πάντων νοῦς κρατεῖ attaches grammatically to what precedes (although the logic of the attachment is more obscure); the reiterated καὶ...γε ties each clause to its predecessor ('and what is more').[20] The whole paragraph constitutes a description of the nature of νοῦς, beginning with its most general characteristics and moving to a consideration of its relations with other things. Contrast the section which runs from καὶ τῆς περιχωρήσιος to οἱ ἀποκρινόμενοι. This is much less obviously a syntactic unit, although its end at least is clearly marked (the next sentence begins ἡ δὲ περιχώρησις - a change of subject, emphasized by initial δέ). But it is evidently concerned with a single topic, namely, the role of νοῦς in cosmogony. All the verbs predicated of νοῦς are aorists. The first sentence, καὶ τῆς περιχωρήσιος...τὴν ἀρχήν, gives a general account of νοῦς's activity; καὶ τὰ συμμισγόμενά...οἱ ἀποκρινόμενοι is more detailed, specifying separately νοῦς's knowledge and its ordering of the process of περιχώρησις. Now it is evidently quite attractive to see the claims of this second section as meant to be supported by those of the first paragraph. For the attributes ascribed to νοῦς in its cosmogonical role - control, knowledge, ordering - are precisely those ascribed to it in the first paragraph. It is as though Anaxagoras were seeking to justify his choice of νοῦς as what controlled the cosmogony by reference to properties of νοῦς which can be more directly seen to belong to it.[21] Perhaps this is his way of arguing that νοῦς uniquely possesses those powers which are required to initiate and control the coming into being of a world.

But, of course, Anaxagoras's manner here is not that of a writer attempting any sort of justification. His second paragraph is surely presented more as amplification of the praises sung to νοῦς in the first than' as an inference drawn from them. The most we are entitled to claim, I think, is that Anaxagoras adopts the natural logical order of exposition for one who is in fact if not professedly deriving a cosmogonical hypothesis from features of the world as it is at present. No doubt the logical order is also rhetorically effective.

We shall resume discussion of Anaxagoras's dogmatism in the third section of the present chapter. It is now time to turn our attention to the other main feature of his work which this book will explore: his ambiguity.

ANAXAGORAS'S AMBIGUITY

Ambiguity is pervasive in Fragment 12. Consider Anaxagoras's very first assertion about νοῦς, the claim that it is ἄπειρον. Zeller was so puzzled by it that he wanted to emend the text, offering ἄμοιρον or ἁπλόον instead of ἄπειρον.[22] Context seems to indicate that νοῦς differs from other things in its possession of this, as of the other attributes ascribed to it. But that does not get us very far. Perhaps Anaxagoras means that νοῦς is not constrained by any physical boundaries or limitations[23] - both in the negative sense that it is not confined to a definite location, and in the more positive sense that it is able to range, in Epicurus's fashion, throughout the whole of the infinite universe:[24]

> Ergo vivida vis animi pervicit, et extra
> processit longe flammantia moenia mundi
> atque omne immensum peragravit mente animoque.

Or perhaps the point is that whereas, if you examine any other thing, you will (or could in theory) find portions of everything else in it, the opposite is true of mind: the further you investigate, the more mind - just mind - you discover, whether because its capacity for initiating action and acquiring knowledge is inexhaustible, or because when you have investigated everything there is still your own investigation to be investigated. On this interpretation, Anaxagoras would presumably have been thinking of

Heraclitus's dark saying:[25] ψυχῆς πείρατα ἰὼν οὐκ ἂν ἐξεύροιο, πᾶσαν ἐπιπορευόμενος ὁδόν· οὕτω βαθὺν λόγον ἔχει ('the limits of soul you would not discover by going places, not if you travelled every road: so deep a *logos* does it have'). Or perhaps he has a syllogism at the back of his head: νοῦς knows all things; but the sum of all things is infinite; therefore νοῦς is infinite. Then we would have to construe νοῦς as either the divine Mind or mind as it ideally is, surveying all time and all being, as Plato says of the philosopher.[26] No doubt ingenuity could multiply possibilities still further. But it seems doubtful whether it could establish solid ground for preferring one above the others.

Consider next the clause: ἔστι γὰρ λεπτότατόν τε πάντων χρημάτων καὶ καθαρώτατον. Obscurity begins with the γάρ, as I shall show later. But perhaps that is of no particular significance. Aristotle's γάρ is not always perspicuous. Much more intriguing is the question: does Anaxagoras mean that mind (or Mind) is an especially fine and pure stuff or matter? or are these words an attempt to formulate the idea that it is not corporeal at all? or are they meant to express the notion that mind has no specific characteristics of its own - in the sense that if it is conceived on the analogy of a tablet or of a constituent stuff in one's head, then the stuff is featureless, the tablet not made of anything and with no physical properties (except, perhaps, spatial ones). This last interpretation was Aristotle's, but the others also have their protagonists. They are not all logically exclusive interpretations: the third could be read as consistent with the first or the second. None can be argued with anything approaching conclusiveness. Scholars who are predisposed to think of all Presocratic philosophers as capable at best of struggling out of the shackles of a crude materialism will probably incline to the first alternative; as will those who press the implication of Fragment 14 that νοῦς is spatially distributed ('it exists where all the other things do, in the surrounding multiplicity and in the things which have been assimilated and in the things which have been separated off'), and who suspect that Anaxagoras generally thinks of the word as Quine does of mass nouns, as an expression denoting all the mind there is.[27] They will naturally point to the probability that Anaxagoras used at any rate λεπτότατον in a physical sense elsewhere, in discussing sea water.[28] The second alternative will appeal to scholars who are impressed above all by Anaxagoras's clear determination to insist that νοῦς is a radically different sort of entity from flesh, gold, air, etc. They will produce parallels for λεπτός in the sense 'subtle', and as applied to the mind.[29] And they will feel that Anaxagoras's adoption of spatial vocabulary elsewhere with respect to νοῦς need not prove very much for the interpretation of the present passage, since any ontology which includes mind – particularly any dualist ontology, such as his – will face somewhat uneasily the problem of its relation to body.[30] I myself incline to Aristotle's interpretation, as making a good philosophical point.[31] All three views of the clause have their attractions. And not only is there no obvious way of legislating between them, but there is nothing to exclude the possibility that Anaxagoras, with a clear head, intended *both* the third *and* one of the others, or alternatively that he simply failed to distinguish between them, or, if he succeeded in that, to make up his mind which he intended.

So far I have produced just two examples of irremediable ambiguity (or perhaps, in the first case, vagueness). Now I turn to a more deep-seated, if less intractable, problem of equivocation, which runs through at least the first paragraph of the fragment.

It is usual practice to translate νοῦς in this fragment as 'Mind' with a capital 'M'. An analogy with 'God' is intended: as God is the supreme or unique god, so the νοῦς of which Anaxagoras speaks is the supreme or unique mind. Sometimes scholars go further and hold explicitly that Anaxagoras made God a mind.[32] Certainly he writes about νοῦς in such a manner as to encourage this interpretation. As we have seen, he adopts the solemn religious style of doxology so familiar in ancient texts (and so exhaustively studied by Norden).[33] Omniscience is already ascribed in this manner to the Sun by Homer (*Il*. III 277) and to Zeus by Hesiod, who also sings of his power in the same way (*Op*. 267, 5-8). Xenophanes (B24) had employed the style in describing his one god: οὖλος ὁρᾷ, οὖλος δὲ νοεῖ, οὖλος δέ τ'ἀκούει ('all of him sees, all understands, all hears'). In Aeschylus there are passages which express a broadly philosophical conception of Zeus as supreme or only god, sometimes in the style of solemn predication (e.g. *A*. 149ff., Fr.70 Nauck[2]). After Anaxagoras we can cite from the fifth century alone

Sophocles (*El.* 175), who has his chorus speak of 'Zeus, who sees and rules all things' (Ζεύς, ὃς ἐφορᾷ πάντα καὶ κρατύνει); Democritus (B30), who talks - to us obscurely - of a few of the learned raising their hands to the place where now we Greeks speak of air, and calling it all Zeus in mythical language, and saying: 'he sees and gives and takes away all things, and he is king of all' (καὶ πάνθ' οὗτος οἶδε καὶ διδοῖ καὶ ἀφαιρέεται καὶ βασιλεὺς οὗτος τῶν πάντων); and Diogenes of Apollonia, who in B5 associates the divinity of the principle which in his own philosophy is 'the possessor of intelligence' (τὸ τὴν νόησιν ἔχον, viz. ὁ ἀὴρ καλούμενος ὑπὸ τῶν ἀνθρώπων) with its 'reaching everywhere and disposing all things and being in everything' (ἐπὶ πᾶν ἀφίχθαι καὶ πάντα διατιθέναι καὶ ἐν παντὶ ἐνεῖναι), attributes which in turn justify the claims that by it 'all men are governed' and that it 'controls all things' (πάντας καὶ κυβερνᾶσθαι καὶ πάντων κρατεῖν). Having once adopted this style, Anaxagoras would have needed to take very explicit measures had he wished to discourage his reader or hearer from construing νοῦς in familiar Greek fashion as a personification (for as Dover says:[34] 'The Greek tendency to personification of natural phenomena and abstractions ensures that a man who is regarded as rejecting the traditional gods is assumed to worship gods of his own choice, not to reject worship as such'). That he failed to achieve any such discouragement is shown by the language and thought of these later fifth-century passages, which are surely at least in part inspired by him.

On the other hand there is a good deal of evidence in the fragments which suggests that Anaxagoras did not mean to be talking of one supreme Mind so much as about mind in general. In many contexts νοῦς seems to work not like a proper name or a definite description but - to quote Jonathan Barnes - 'as a mass noun, like "gold" or "flesh"' or Heraclitus's 'sea-water'. Consider Fragment 11:

'In everything there is a portion of everything except νοῦς,
and there are some things in which there is νοῦς too.'

It is clear that 'everything' in 'a portion of everything' means 'every *kind* of thing'. So it would seem likely that Anaxagoras means a kind of thing by νοῦς, too. This also looks the right way to take νοῦς at the end of Fragment 12:

'But no thing is altogether separated off nor distinguished

> from anything else except νοῦς. And all νοῦς is alike, both
> the greater and the smaller.'

It is obviously very much easier to take νοῦς in 'all νοῦς' as functioning like a mass noun (compare 'all cheese' or 'all flesh') than as analogous with 'God'. But if these two passages are taken together, their gist is very like what we have at the beginning of Fragment 12, where Anaxagoras says:

> 'The other things share in a portion of everything, but νοῦς
> is unlimited and independent and not mixed with anything, but
> exists alone on its own.'

So there is a case for thinking that here, too, Anaxagoras means to be contrasting other sorts of thing with νοῦς (in general). This was certainly how Aristotle interpreted him. He frequently reports Anaxagoras as having said of νοῦς that it is unmixed, pure, etc., plainly with Fragment 12 in view. But the contexts in which he does so (in particular *de An.* III 4) show that he takes him as having meant that these were characteristics of νοῦς in general.[35] Moreover, if there is any sign of the personification of νοῦς in our extract from Fragment 12, this need not count against Aristotle's interpretation. When St Paul said: 'Charity suffereth long and is kind; charity envieth not; charity vaunteth not itself, is not puffed up, etc.', he was thinking of charity in general - the charity you or I might hope to exemplify - not the goddess Charity. He meant: 'If someone is charitable, then *eo ipso* he is long-suffering and kind, does not envy, etc.'

Upon this interpretation it is easy enough to account for Anaxagoras's initial contrast between νοῦς and other things. νοῦς, he says, is ἄπειρον, unlimited; αὐτοκρατές, autonomous or independent; and μέμεικται οὐδενὶ χρήματι, not mixed with anything. He will mean that *no* mind is mixed with anything else; that is, no mind contains within it portions of other things, as bread and water contain (according to the doxographical account of his theory) portions of hair, flesh, nails, etc. He will mean that *all* our minds are autonomous, in that what we think is mostly up to us, in our power and in that of no other thing or person. What is involved in the thought that νοῦς is ἄπειρον is, as we have seen, less plain. But none of the constructions we considered putting upon it was incompatible with the possibility that Anaxagoras meant that *no* mind is limited.

We now run into difficulties, however, with the concluding part
of the first paragraph, ἔστι γὰρ λεπτότατον κτλ. The first clause
presents no problem for the interpretation, although its connexion
with what precedes is obscure, and despite disagreement whether the
predicates 'finest' and 'purest' carry physical or metaphorical
meaning. It is perfectly natural to read the clause as holding that
mind in general is a very pure and fine thing. But what are we to
make of the next clause: καὶ γνώμην γε περὶ παντὸς πᾶσαν ἴσχει καὶ
ἰσχύει μέγιστον? The obvious way to take this is as an assertion of
omniscience; and Anaxagoras requires νοῦς to be omniscient in its
cosmogonical role: it knew all the things which were being mixed
together and separated off and distinguished. Yet it is *prima facie*
highly implausible to maintain that mind in general is omniscient,
although Neoplatonists and other monists about the mind have been
ready enough to do so. Should we suppose that Anaxagoras here
slides from consideration of the general character of mind to an
assertion about the supreme Mind? Certainly supreme Mind would fit
the part of cosmogonical agent so soon to be described.

The translation of the clause runs as follows: 'And, what is
more, it harbours every discerning judgement about everything, and
[so] harbours the greatest strength.' This statement is ambiguous.
It certainly can be read as an attribution of omniscience to νοῦς.
But equally it can be read as saying that if anyone makes any
discerning judgements about anything, it is nothing else but mind
(i.e. his mind) which houses them; and this is taken to be a source
of great strength to mind - presumably because its unique capacity
for knowledge and for initiating action upon the basis of knowledge
gives it also a great ability to control and plan.[36] On this construction of the Greek we can save καὶ γνώμην γε κτλ. as an assertion, like all its predecessors in the first paragraph of Fragment
12, about mind in general. It may be felt to be an implausible or
unnatural reading of the Greek. But before we acquiesce in that
feeling, we should consider the very next clause in Anaxagoras's
text: καὶ ὅσα γε ψυχὴν ἔχει καὶ τὰ μείζω καὶ τὰ ἐλάσσω, πάντων νοῦς
κρατεῖ ('and moreover all the things that have soul, both the
greater and the smaller, all of them mind controls'). This clause,
too, is ambiguous: it could mean that some single supreme Mind controls the behaviour of all animals (or, indeed, all animate things);

or it could mean that if something is animate, then it has a mind, or some mind in it, directing what it does. Nor is it at all clear in this case which way the ambiguity should be resolved. It is, then, worth our while to contemplate giving the following consistent interpretation of the scope of the quantifiers in each of the last two clauses of Anaxagoras's paragraph: for any judgement about anything, there is some mind which has it; for anything animate, there is some mind which controls it.

Most readers, however, will still prefer to believe that in the clause with which we are primarily concerned Anaxagoras has omniscience in view. How decisively does this supposition count against the idea that he is still preoccupied with mind in general?

Let us suppose that we were able to put to Anaxagoras the question of how one man's mind (e.g. Plato's) differs from another's (e.g. Xenophon's). Now Anaxagoras is an unequivocal dualist about the mind and the body, as the opening sentence of Fragment 12 shows. So he would not be prepared to *individuate* minds as functions of the bodies in which they find themselves. Perhaps he would suggest that Plato has one bit of mind stuff (whether this were conceived of in physical terms or not), Xenophon another bit, and that you could tell these were distinct by their locations in different bodies. But even if we accepted an answer from him on this point, he would still have to explain why Plato's mind *differs in character* from Xenophon - and in particular, why Plato was so much more intelligent than Xenophon. It is not easy to guess at his reply to this question. Aristotle tells us disapprovingly that he held that it was man's possession of hands which made him the most intelligent of animals.[37] We might gloss this as the view that it is simply or chiefly in the physical equipment which mind has at its disposal for executive action that man is superior. But it is hard to see a way of extrapolating an answer to our question about Plato and Xenophon from this interpretation of Aristotle's report (not least because we had in mind a difference between them in *theoretical*, not practical, intelligence: as a practical man Xenophon wins hands down). One thing, however, does seem clear: Anaxagoras is probably committed to holding that all mind is qualitatively alike (by his general theory of the relation of νοῦς to other things); and as we saw, he explicitly assents to this proposition at the end of Fragment 12, when he says: 'All νοῦς is alike, both the greater and the smaller.' So whatever explanation he might attempt of the superiority of Plato's intelligence to Xenophon's, it could not be that Plato had a better or a purer or a subtler mind than Xenophon.

It is tempting to push this line of interpretation further, and to say that if a person manifests limitations of knowledge or understanding, these could not for Anaxagoras constitute or express intrinsic limitations of their minds, except insofar as mind is of its very nature limited in its powers of understanding. We need not in fact take the qualification 'except...' very seriously. For it is likely enough that Anaxagoras has already denied any intrinsic limits to mind's powers of knowledge and control when he said: νοῦς is unlimited'. And it is surely significant that nowhere in the first paragraph of Fragment 12 (or indeed elsewhere in this or any other fragment) does he show any sign of being exercised by the possibility that mind is limited either in its powers of knowledge or in the exercise of those powers. Contrast his treatment of mind's powers of control or executive action. His indirect proof that νοῦς is not mixed with anything else attempts to show that, if it *were* mixed with something, it could not exercise the control it actually does exercise. And he does not ascribe to it control over all things, only over those which have soul. This suggests that even though mind is not hampered by mixture with other things, its control over them is limited, not indeed by any intrinsic deficiency of its own nature, but for some other reason. There is not much profit in speculating what that reason might be. Perhaps it has something to do with mind's regard for the providential economy of nature. Perhaps, for example, mind comes to be in things and intervenes to exercise direct and immediate control over them only when - as in the case of human hands - it can *exploit* the way matter is disposed in the natural world to achieve effects beyond the reach of purely physical causation, not when its intervention would *disrupt* the normal processes of nature or bring about the sort of effects they could produce any way.

If, then, no mind is limited by intrinsic or extrinsic factors either in its power of knowledge or in the exercise of that power, it is a short step to the conclusion that mind - i.e. any mind - is omniscient. Anaxagoras's general theory of mind, at any rate as we have reconstructed it in the last two paragraphs, leaves him with no alternative to it, provided only that he would deny that a mind may quite inexplicably just fail to exercise a power which nothing prevents it from exercising. In the next chapter we shall notice a reason for supposing that Anaxagoras did indeed subscribe to the principle (of which this assumption is a specific version) that every event has a cause.

It remains counter-intuitive to hold that every mind is omniscient. But perhaps our rendering of νοῦς as 'mind' is not quite right. Although Anaxagoras talks of νοῦς as though it were a substance or agent, perhaps he conceives of it as *understanding*, i.e. as what we would think of as a mental state or faculty (comparable with Diogenes of Apollonia's νόησις). If he does, then it is much easier for us, recalling the doctrine of νοῦς as understanding in Plato's *Republic*, to imagine why he may have thought that all understanding, wherever it occurs, is total understanding or omniscience. For, like Plato, he may have believed that in order fully to understand any one thing, or to know why any one event will happen, it is necessary, because of the coherence of all reality, to understand all things and to know why every event will happen as it does. Of course, there remains the difficulty that according to Anaxagoras some finite beings actually possess νοῦς (cf. Fragment 11, quoted above). It looks as though he would have to explain the fact that they do not *appear* to possess total understanding by saying (with the Neoplatonists) that their minds or souls are not sufficiently receptive of this understanding or (with Leibniz) that they express understanding of the world only from a particular point of view.[38]

To sum up: the clause καὶ γνώμην γε περὶ παντὸς πᾶσαν ἴσχει καὶ ἰσχύει μέγιστον is naturally read as attributing omniscience to νοῦς. But it is *prima facie* implausible to hold (as the line of interpretation we have been pursuing commits us to construing the Greek thus read) that *any* νοῦς is omniscient. Anaxagoras, however, may have been ready to uphold this view, because of his belief that all νοῦς is separate, unlimited, and alike. Nor, if we interpret νοῦς as *understanding* or as *mind inasmuch as it possesses understanding*, is the view so strange or indefensible after all.

It is, therefore, possible without straining credibility to

construe the first paragraph of Fragment 12 as enunciating a number
of claims about mind in general. On this account Anaxagoras affirms
that mind (or *a* mind, as we might say, using the word as a count
noun) is not limited; that it is autonomous; that it does not contain mixed within it portions of other things, but exists independently of them. This last assertion he supports by an argument: if
it were mixed with other things, it could not control anything as it
does control them on its own. He then adds that a mind is purer and
finer than anything else; that it has understanding of all things
and so is strong; and that it is what controls an animal (or indeed
the behaviour of any animate thing). The logic of the addition is
not entirely clear. This is one place where Anaxagoras's predilection for a grandiloquent paratactic style is maintained at the cost
of perfect argumentative clarity: he goes for the effect of three
simple balanced clauses linked by καί...γε, without sufficiently
indicating how their content supports what precedes. But I think
the connexion is straightforward enough. Anaxagoras wants to butt-
ress the claim made right at the end of the argumentative passage
that mind in fact controls things [sc. to a high degree] through
being alone on its own. The statement that νοῦς is finest and purest of things is most naturally taken simply as positive evidence,
additional to the negative proof offered in that passage, that νοῦς
is unmixed, and independent. It supports μόνον ἐόντα ἐφ' ἑαυτοῦ.
The last two clauses of the paragraph, containing statements of the
strength and control of νοῦς, are in turn most easily construed as
supporting the claim that νοῦς does exercise a great degree of control. They bear on the κρατεῖν which we have to understand with the
clause ὡς καί...ἐφ' ἑαυτοῦ. More sophisticated and speculative
explanations of Anaxagoras's train of thought have been offered, but
their sophistication and ambition count against them.[39]

But if we can make coherent, consistent sense of the first
paragraph upon this interpretation, what of the second paragraph?
Must not the statements made there about νοῦς as cosmogonical agent
be statements about a supreme Mind? Evidently in some sense the
author of the cosmogony *is* conceived of as a supreme mind. But this
need not mean that νοῦς in the second paragraph is thought of as a
proper name or definite description *meaning* 'the supreme Mind' from
the outset. When in the first paragraph Anaxagoras says that νοῦς

is unlimited, autonomous, unmixed, pure, fine, omniscient, we have been taking him to mean by νοῦς 'any mind'. When he says that whatever has soul is controlled by νοῦς, we have had to shift the sense to 'some mind', in the light of the construction of the scope of the quantifiers required by the interpretation. But the shift leaves Anaxagoras still talking of νοῦς in general terms. Now when he follows πάντων νοῦς κρατεῖ at the end of the paragraph with the words καὶ τῆς συμπάσης νοῦς ἐκράτησεν at the beginning of the cosmogonical section, we must evidently take νοῦς in the same way again. Upon the present interpretation, he will have meant that some mind controlled the whole περιχώρησις - or, in more idiomatic English, the whole process was controlled by a mind. This seems a perfectly natural and appropriate reading of the Greek. And it is then easy to explain the way the two references to νοῦς later in the second paragraph work. Anaxagoras writes: καὶ τὰ συμμισγόμενά τε καὶ ἀποκρινόμενα καὶ διακρινόμενα πάντα ἔγνω νοῦς, καὶ ὁποῖα ἔμελλεν ἔσεσθαι, καὶ ὁποῖα ἦν καὶ ὅσα νῦν ἔστι καὶ ὁποῖα ἔσται, πάντα διεκόσμησε νοῦς. We may take Anaxagoras to mean that what was being mingled and separated off and distinguished was known by a *mind*; and that the ordering of what was to be was performed by a mind. Of course, he would want to hold, and want us to understand, that the knowledge and the ordering belonged to the *same* mind as controlled the περιχώρησις. But his emphasis, on this reading, is that all alike are to be ascribed to mind ἁπλῶς; and that mind, not any other thing, was the power responsible for the whole cosmogony.

It is time to draw some conclusions. From the beginning it was clear that we *could* understand νοῦς in our extract from Fragment 12 as *meaning* 'the supreme Mind', and that we could translate and interpret throughout accordingly. I hope it is now no less clear that we could equally well understand it as meaning simply 'mind' in general throughout. It follows that the identity of the subject of the fragment is systematically ambiguous.

How much does this ambiguity really matter? Certainly the passage carries different nuances according as it is read now one way, now the other. Indeed, so far as the second paragraph is concerned, the difference between the two interpretations scarcely amounts to more than that. But even as regards the first paragraph they diverge very much less in real substance than might at first have appeared.

Consider first the interpretation according to which νοῦς means just 'mind' in general. At various points in our exposition it has proved difficult to keep this interpretation distinct from the alternative interpretation. Take, for example, the question of the individuation of minds. Anaxagoras's doctrines of the separation of νοῦς from other things and of the likeness of all instances of νοῦς make it unlikely that he was much interested in the problem of how we individuate minds or indeed of how we differentiate between them in any way whatever. It is very natural to interpret him as a monist about the mind: whether a strong monist, who believes that it is just one and the same mind which inhabits your body and my body (but not the pen with which I am writing), or a weak monist, who believes that there is one bit of mind stuff in you and another bit of identical stuff in me. One's inclination to take him as a monist is reinforced by the discovery that he holds mind to be omniscient, since total understanding is not a condition to which your mind and mine do anything but dimly approximate at best. Again, when he says that νοῦς controls all animate things, this statement can (as we have seen) be read as implying that Plato is controlled by *his* mind, Xenophon by *his*, and so on. But now try the thought that this slug or cabbage[40] is controlled by *its* own mind, that slug or cabbage by *its*: these minds are not different, but one and the same immanent mind — as it were the Stoic λόγος σπερματικός.[41] Of course, if mind in general is so hard to distinguish from the supreme Mind, it is not surprising that Anaxagoras employs the periods of hymnody in describing it. His attitude is perhaps akin to that evinced in Euripidean passages which identify the human mind with divinity; as in Fr. 1018 Nauck² (A48):

ὁ νοῦς γὰρ ἡμῶν ἐστιν ἐν ἑκάστῳ θεός

mind is the god in each of us

and in the famous passage[42] reminiscent of Diogenes from the *Orestes* (884ff.):

ὦ γῆς ὄχημα κἀπὶ γῆς ἔχων ἕδραν,
ὅστις ποτ' εἶ σύ, δυστόπαστος εἰδέναι,
Ζεύς, εἴτ' ἀνάγκη φύσεος εἴτε νοῦς βροτῶν,
προσηυξάμην σε...

> O thou stay of earth, thou who hast thy seat upon the earth,
> whoever thou art, difficult to know despite all our guesses,
> Zeus - whether necessity of nature or mind of mortals - I pray
> to you...

If, on the other hand, Anaxagoras means to be speaking of 'the supreme Mind' throughout Fragment 12 and the other fragments which refer to νοῦς, what he says clearly bears upon and reflects what he would want to say about mind in general. Thus when he says (in Fragment 11) that in some things there is νοῦς, then on this interpretation we shall have to take him as indicating that the mind in me and the mind in you are bits or manifestations of the supreme Mind. And if he is confident that the supreme Mind is supreme specifically in knowledge and control of the world and its contents, free from mixture with material elements, how does he come to associate these characteristics with it except by reflection upon what human minds in general are like?

Here, then, is an ambiguity which, for all its pervasiveness, does not in the end seriously muddy our understanding of what Anaxagoras is saying in Fragment 12. But his proneness to ambiguity, like his predilection for dogmatism, deserves further consideration in the next section.

THE ARCHAIC SAGE

> *Soc.* I am inclined to think, my good friend, that it was
> not surprising that Pericles became the most finished exponent
> of rhetoric there has ever been.
>   *Phdr.* Why so?
>   *Soc.* All the great arts need idle talk and high-flown
> speculation about nature. It seems to be from that source that
> such mental elevation and thoroughly finished execution come.
> And those are the qualities Pericles acquired to supplement his
> inborn capacity. He came across a man of that sort, I fancy,
> in Anaxagoras; and by filling himself with high-flown speculation and by arriving at the nature of understanding (νοῦς) and
> of folly - topics, of course, to which Anaxagoras devoted most
> of his discourse - he drew from that source and applied to the
> art of speeches what was suitable for it. (Plato, *Phaedrus*
> 269e-270a)

Anaxagoras of Clazomenae, when asked: 'Who is the happiest man?' said: 'None of those you suppose – he would seem to you an odd sort of person'... They say that Anaxagoras replied to someone who persisted in raising difficulties of this sort and went on asking for what purpose one should choose to be born rather than not: 'For the sake', he said, 'of contemplating the heavens and the order throughout the whole world.' (Aristotle, *EE* 1215b6-8, 1216a10-14)

When someone brought him [sc. Anaxagoras] the news that his son was dead, he said with the utmost composure: 'I knew he was mortal when I begot him.' (Galen, *De Plac. Hipp. et Plat.* IV 7)

Mussolini could not have been more false to the spirit of these anecdotes when 'in his last, grotesque speech before the Anglo-American landing in Sicily, [he] said: "The Greek philosopher Anaxagoras (pardon my erudition) said that man is the measure of all things"'.[43] Indeed, the Anaxagoras of these passages is the very model of the true philosopher whose portrait Plato drew in the digression of the *Theaetetus* as counterweight to the Protagorean conception of man and of philosophy. How much literal, historical truth they contain is naturally open to doubt. The *Phaedrus* text, in particular, suggests that these and the numerous similar stories about Anaxagoras arose partly because of a popular tradition about the sort of man he was and the character of his relationship with Pericles, and partly because of the impression his book made upon people. The book and its author were plainly felt to be noble, strange, not quite human.

Holger Thesleff judges that 'Anaxagoras's philosophy is fundamentally a visionary proclamation which has been fitted into a simple intellectual scheme'[44] (as we shall see, Anaxagoras's *thought* attains a considerable degree of complexity: but Thesleff is thinking of the simple literary structure and largely paratactic syntax of the fragments). 'Visionary proclamation' is the form which other Presocratics besides Anaxagoras gave to their philosophical utterances, treading in the footsteps of Hesiod in the *Theogony*. It can fairly be said to be the form adopted by philosophers so diverse (and in particular so diverse in their choice of literary genre and in their own professed relationship to their λόγοι)[45] as Parmenides, Heraclitus, and Empedocles. It is a form

naturally appropriate for thinkers (as for 'holy men') who lay
claim, tacitly or otherwise, to an authority derived from knowledge
that the truth about the world is not as the ordinary man supposes,
but can be achieved only by the use of powers which either he cannot
attain or he does not tap. A contemporary philosopher, at any rate
one working in the analytic tradition, is bound to attach great
importance to avoiding dogmatism and ambiguity of utterance. For
the archaic sage, intent on assaulting and overturning the assumptions and beliefs of ordinary people, it was a positive advantage
that an aura of mystery should attach to his words; and if he
claimed the right to challenge common opinion, he needed to sound
as if he did so from a position of strength, indeed of certainty: an
effect which might be achieved as well by confident assertion as by
the presentation of argument. We need not suppose that Anaxagoras
meant to be mysteriously ambiguous (as presumably he chose to be
dogmatic). Philosophers of the mainstream Ionian tradition probably
prided themselves on the simplicity with which, unlike the poets,
they spoke;[46] and no doubt they would have found the verses of
Parmenides and Empedocles and the oracular and proverbial styles of
Heraclitus repugnant in their opacity. But the terseness and preg-
nancy of Anaxagoras's prose in practice produce a mysterious effect,
as above all in the case of his central doctrine: 'In everything
there is a portion of everything.'

We have seen, however, that Parmenides made argument central to
his visionary proclamation. Indeed, the main message he proclaimed
was that argument, and argument alone, is the way to discover the
truth - the unexpected truth - about things. Did Anaxagoras reject
this message? Plainly, in view of his confidence in the possibility
of natural philosophy, he could not have accepted that argument
alone was necessary and sufficient for the discovery of truth. He
evidently took our common experience of the world as a structure
containing a plurality of changing things to be the necessary basis
for all fruitful enquiry into truth. And, of course, we possess one
fragment in which he explicitly asserts the epistemological value of
phenomena, which had been rejected as worthless by Parmenides.
Sextus attributes to him the dictum: ὄψις τῶν ἀδήλων τὰ φαινόμενα
('Things that are apparent are the vision of things that are unclear').[47] Unfortunately, although we can be confident that

Anaxagoras is here saying something with which Parmenides would have
disagreed, neither the meaning of this remark nor its role in his
thought are at all clear. It may well have been invoked not in
connexion with the main tenets of his philosophy, but with reference to inferences about particular natural phenomena.[48]

Anaxagoras's resistance to Parmenides's enthronement of argument as queen of philosophy may conceivably have gone even further.
Perhaps he did not see the need to give argument any more than a
subordinate place in philosophy. Certainly such a view is what his
practice (in Fragment 12 and, as we shall see, elsewhere) suggests.
And it is a view which would fit with the very slight interest in
epistemological issues which he shows in the Simplician fragments,
and with the possibility that the slogan Sextus records may have
been given limited and localized application. Moreover, it is
possible to conceive of reasons why Anaxagoras should have rested
content with such a view.

In the first place, he was writing in an Ionian tradition of
philosophy whose standard mode of exposition was the cosmogonical
narrative. The writings of Anaximander and Anaximenes seem to have
taken the form of a description of what was there in the beginning,
and of how a world or worlds came into being, and of the way all
sorts of 'meteorological' phenomena like eclipses, earthquakes, and
thunder and lightning come about.[49] There is little evidence that
these writings contained arguments; and it seems likely enough that
their central claims were, like Anaxagoras's basic theses about
mind, just blankly asserted. Insofar as we follow the Greeks in
counting the Milesians philosophers, we do so because we infer from
the doxographical evidence that their cosmogonical narratives satisfied certain standards of generality, non-arbitrariness, economy and
explanatory power which we find wanting in Hesiod or Pherecydes of
Syros. In their adoption of a mainly descriptive form of exposition, the Milesians perhaps set the precedent which was to be
followed not just by later philosophers but by authors of early
Ionian prose treatises in general. Of much of this literary activity nothing survives: for example, we have none of the early architectural manuals or treatises mentioned by Vitruvius.[50] But the
meagre remains of the first geographers and logographers are largely
descriptive in character. And the same is true of *Airs, Waters,*

Places, perhaps the earliest extant Hippocratic work which can be classified as a treatise (rather than a manual or case book); indeed, this work presents both its basic conceptual scheme (i.e. its analysis of the various environmental factors which affect health and disease) and the detailed application of the scheme as straightforward facts, when in reality it is elaborating a highly *a priori* speculative theory.

It would be wrong to suggest that any of these authors eschewed explicit argument altogether. On at least five occasions[51] the writer of *Airs, Waters, Places* offers τεκμήρια, 'proofs' or 'signs' or 'evidences' of the truth of his assertions. But the assertions in question are all concerned not with basic principles, but with fairly specific matters, such as the 'fact' that the sun draws off the finest and lightest part of the humours of the human body (Ch.8), or that Scythian women tend to be infertile because they are fat and flabby (Ch.21). Similarly, Herodotus's predecessors, like the historian himself, appear sometimes to have supported the choice of a particular version of a story with an appeal to εἰκός, what is 'likely'.[52] And, of course, Aristotle tells us that, according to Anaximander, the earth stays still (at the centre of the universe) διὰ τὴν ὁμοιότητα, 'on account of indifference': an explanation which Aristotle, at any rate, spells out in the form of an argument from sufficient reason, to the effect that it is not 'fitting' (προσήκει) for something in the middle of the universe which is related similarly or indifferently to its extreme parts to move in one direction rather than any other, nor can it (ἀδύνατον) move in opposite directions at the same time.[53] For all its interest, however, this explanation is brought to bear, not on a fundamental tenet of Anaximander's scheme of things, but on an important detail in it. Argument (if we can go so far as to call it that) has no less subordinate a role here than it has in Anaxagoras.

Ionian ἱστορίη, 'enquiry', flourished as never before in the fifth century - in history, geography, medicine, mathematics, and astronomy, no less than in philosophy. When Anaxagoras sat down to write his treatise, he could do so in the confidence that the world was beginning to yield more and more of its secrets to the methods pioneered by the sixth-century Ionians. Parmenides's logic had

undoubtedly presented a radical challenge to the Ionian conception
of the world and of our understanding of it. But it is not to be
wondered at that Anaxagoras should have absorbed some of the things
Parmenides had to say about being (for example, that what is cannot
strictly speaking be destroyed or come into being), without feeling
obliged to abandon or alter radically the traditional style which he
had inherited as proper for cosmological speculation. We should see
him as a self-confident Ionian, taking Parmenides's criticisms of
cosmology in his stride.

We need not suppose that the self-confidence of his relatively
unargumentative presentation of his cosmology masks a failure to
reflect deeply on those criticisms. Anaxagoras may very well have
observed with interest that when Parmenides himself turned to cosmology, in the second part of his poem, he too employed a much more
descriptive style than in the Way of Truth, both in laying down at
the outset his views on the basic constituents of the universe as it
is conceived by mortals, and (it would seem) in his cosmogony.
Parmenides had good reason to make this change. It corresponds to
his promise to provide nothing more nor less than the most 'likely-
seeming ordering' (διάκοσμον ἐοικότα) of things, having abandoned
'trustworthy argument and thought about truth' (πιστὸν λόγον ἠδὲ
νόημα/ἀμφὶς ἀληθείης).[54] All that he can do, on his own repre-
sentation of the case, is to forget about reasoning from first principles, and to be content with an attempt to construct the simplest,
most general and most plausible hypothesis by which to account for
the content of the universal human belief in a changing and varie-
gated world. This idea of Parmenides that cosmological explanations
can be expected to satisfy only very modest criteria of rationality
and truth, and require and can accommodate only an inferior sort of
discourse, was notoriously taken over, in a less radical form, by
Plato in the *Timaeus*.[55] Now Anaxagoras is unlikely to have agreed
with either of them in rating pure *a priori* ratiocination higher
than cosmology. But perhaps attention to Parmenides's distinction
between the two paradoxically reinforced in him a proper Ionian conviction that it was better in cosmology to rest one's case on a
simple appeal to the sense of what is reasonable or what is likeli-
est to be true, rather than to pretend that he could clinch the
issue with reasoning of Parmenides's adamantine strength. In short,

Anaxagoras's failure in Fragment 12 to argue many basic points may spring not so much from an un-Eleatic distaste for argument as from an un-Eleatic respect for common sense and common reasonableness, from confidence in the verdict the reasonable man would pass on its thesis, and from an appropriate feeling for the difference between a cosmological hypothesis and a metaphysical paradox.

It is true that in the next generation Diogenes of Apollonia thought it necessary to present explicit arguments for his basic theses in physics. Similarly, Hippocratic treatises such as *On the Sacred Disease* and *On Ancient Medicine* devote a great deal of space to critical argument on the fundamental issues with which they are concerned, although (as Geoffrey Lloyd has said) the positive explanation of the 'sacred disease' offered by the writer of the first treatise is 'a highly dogmatic, speculative and schematic construct', and 'the actual theories we find in *On Ancient Medicine* on such topics as the constituents of man or the origins of diseases turn out to be much closer to the ideas of [the author's] opponents, which he says are based on arbitrary postulates, than one might expect in view of his apparent total rejection of such postulates'.[56] But all these thinkers are writing at a time when epistemological problems had begun to push themselves into the foreground of philosophical and scientific discussion, in part no doubt because of the work of Protagoras and other Sophists. This development is one which was surely fostered by a deeper consideration of the epistemological dimension of Parmenides's thought (and perhaps of Heraclitus's) than we can postulate in Anaxagoras's case. But that need not mean that Anaxagoras did not see that the Eleatic had forced cosmology to take stock of its epistemological, as of its ontological, foundations. He may simply have concluded that the stock-taking revealed that the business was in good order.

So far we have been making inferences about Anaxagoras's attitude to argument on the assumption that his conception of philosophy is adequately conveyed by his book. But books, as experience teaches and as Plato complained, seldom capture everything that is important in a man's philosophizing. And there is a set of obvious differences between modern philosophy books and articles and the writings of the earliest Greek philosophers which makes it all the more dangerous to rely solely on the written word in this connexion.

A contemporary philosopher will propound his views both by the pen
and by word of mouth. The relative importance he attaches to the
two methods will differ from individual to individual. But if he is
ambitious he will probably expect to write many books and articles
which will represent to the interested student of philosophy his
position - conceivably his developing position - on a range of
topics. He will very likely think of his written works as con-
tributions to a cooperative effort to advance thought now on one,
now on another of those topics. And his writing will constitute a
major part of his philosophical activity, as, indeed, will his
reading. Contrast the early Greek philosopher. He lived in a predominantly oral culture, and must have expected to persuade people
of the truth of his views mainly by oral teaching and discussion.
In order to make an impact, immediate and enduring, on his contemporaries he would need to reiterate a single message, on a very
general theme: 'a metaphysical doctrine intended to explain, at one
blow, as it were, the universe and its course, including human
life'.[57] In this situation it is not surprising that those who seem
to have made most impact made their messages paradoxical: Heraclitus, Parmenides, Zeno, Pythagoras - and even Anaxagoras in his
claim that in everything there is a portion of everything.[58] The
mention of Parmenides and Zeno is sufficient to remind us that Presocratic philosophers had some notion and experience of philosophical cooperation. Anaxagoras probably felt himself to be part
of an Ionian philosophical tradition; and he certainly had his
followers, who may have constituted something like a cooperative
circle of students.[59] But by and large the Presocratics give the
impression one would expect of thinkers who had to create their own
audiences (in the literal sense of the word), without the aid of
such institutions as the university or the publishing industry, and
without the possibility of relying upon a practice of book reading:
each was an example of purely individual and local enterprise. If
he took up the pen, then, he did so in a cultural setting and in a
frame of mind quite different from those of his modern counterpart.
Until the end of the fifth century, when in Athens at least literacy
became widespread and book production multiplied,[60] no philosopher
wrote more than one or two short treatises.[61] It seems reasonable
to suppose that a philosophical book would therefore have been a

much more special and polished object than we expect today. For presumably it was designed to represent the considered distillation of years and decades of thinking, discussing and teaching; to offer a final statement of its author's doctrine, and indeed of the truth about the world.

What was the point of making that statement if it were reduplicated in only a very small number of copies in communities without booksellers? Several answers have been proposed to the question; and there is no reason why several at once should not be correct. But two in particular deserve our attention, both for their own inherent plausibility and for the conflicting supplements which they may suggest that we should add to our diagnosis of Anaxagoras's attitude to argument.

One possibility is that a philosopher (or at any rate one who wrote in prose) would compose his treatise for use as a written basis for oral performance, which might then be followed by discussion with the audience. This view is advanced by Hermann Fränkel:[62]

> 'It seems likely that these books [sc. early Greek philosophy books] were not intended to be read in private, but aloud before an audience, after which they would be explained and discussed section by section: the content of these very compressed books could not have been properly understood and appreciated in any other way than by examining and discussing with one's hearers ideas which must at first seem strange. Thus at the beginning of Heraclitus's work, he refers to discussions with others on his *logos* (with a characteristic remark that his instruction made the hearers no wiser).'

A likely consequence of this theory is that a philosopher would revise his text over the years in the light of such discussions, as indeed Fränkel implies:[63] 'This confrontation with his public could hardly fail to help the author himself to clarify his thought and improve his presentation.' A further consequence, and the one of most importance for our enquiry, is that even if Anaxagoras's book contained little in way of argument for its basic theses, it need not follow that its author saw no need for such argument. It might be that he thought the proper place for *defence* of his basic ideas was in oral discussion, whereas the job of the treatise itself was simply to expound his position.

But if the philosopher's book was designed to serve him as a score serves the musician, its primary purpose was surely to preserve for posterity (or for anyone who could come by a copy of it) a record of its author's thought.[64] At any rate, it is hard to believe that an early Greek philosopher who talked in prose *needed* to write a treatise to lecture from: notes or memory (so extensively relied upon in an oral culture) would have sufficed. He *had* to put something in writing, on the other hand, if he wanted his philosophy to survive very long - as Anaxagoras had good reason to appreciate: how else could he have known, except in vague and general terms, what his intellectual progenitors, Anaximander and Anaximenes, had said? And if a philosopher wanted to persuade a critical unseen readership,[65] he would take pains to compose more than a bare summary or memorandum of his views. Like Anaxagoras, he would construct a treatise, with all the philosophical care and literary art at his command. What inference should we draw if such a treatise contained no argument for some of its fundamental theses, as Anaxagoras's appears to have contained none for some of its major claims about νοῦς? Presumably that its author (unlike a Diogenes of Apollonia) expected to persuade his readers without resort to explicit argument on these points, and that (again unlike Diogenes) he did not strive to convey the impression that the presentation of such argument was indispensable to his philosophy or his conception of philosophy.

This conclusion suggests an attitude to argument on Anaxagoras's part somewhat at odds with that mooted at the end of the previous paragraph. It is possible, however, to find an explanation which accommodates both conclusions. We may simply imagine that Anaxagoras not only thought it appropriate to the nature of a cosmological hypothesis to present it in the form of a statement about how things are, but also took this to be the most persuasive way of presenting it. He might find that, in discussion following a reading of his treatise, argument was required of him on points he had not argued in it. But the fact is that he was offering an explanatory hypothesis, and such hypotheses win credence according as the explanations they offer are satisfying, not because the inferences on which they are based are made as explicit as possible. So he might very well have sensed that the inclusion of additional arguments in his text, or the imposition upon it of a more inferential structure, might bring gains in clarity only at the cost of a less convincing communication of the simple and comprehensive vision which Fragment 12, especially, conveys: the loss in fact incurred by Diogenes.

Much of this section has been unavoidably speculative. Without the exercise of a little historical imagination we could not make much headway in understanding Anaxagoras's dogmatism. There is perhaps less scope for speculation about the reasons for the other main feature of his writing which has preoccupied us in this chapter, viz. his ambiguity.

It is plain that the ambiguity is partly a consequence of the dogmatism, and of the visionary intensity which lies behind it. If Anaxagoras had been prepared to stop and explain himself a little more, he would very likely have left less room for doubt about what he meant by saying that νοῦς is unlimited, or that it is the finest and purest of things - or indeed about the intended application of the word νοῦς itself. As it is, he writes like a man who has lived long with his profound thoughts and is so convinced of their truth and importance that he is prepared to sacrifice something of ready and precise intelligibility in the urgency of his attempt to communicate their essence.

But it may be that we should see Anaxagoras's ambiguity not only as a consequence of his own philosophical and literary priorities, but also as a phenomenon to be expected in early prose writing. I do not mean to suggest that we should equate earliness with crudity. There is something absurd in the idea that a philosopher who could argue so lucidly as in the indirect proof in Fragment 12, and write so magnificently as he does there in his solemn style, was impeded by the limitations of a crude instrument. His Greek was perfectly adequate to give sufficient expression to the distinctions which would have clarified what he wanted to say about νοῦς (for example, in order to distinguish between the supreme Mind and mind in general, he could have spoken like Plato of ὁ ἐν τῷ παντὶ νοῦς and ὁ παρ' ἡμῖν νοῦς). And in general the work of Hermann Fränkel, van Groningen and others has made it abundantly clear that archaic Greek literary style must not be viewed as an awkward adolescent stage in the growth of classical Greek, but as 'ein durchaus in sich gefestiger, eigenartiger Stil'.[66] Nonetheless the ambiguity of Anaxagoras's style is something which it is tempting to associate with a stage in prose writing when authors did not yet envisage the detailed, rigorous and systematic study of their words[67] which the use of writing for the first time made possible.[68] Classical scholars are predisposed to assume that the texts they study were designed to withstand minute scrutiny of this sort. But in Greece it was perhaps the Sophists who first discovered (and the Alexandrian grammarians who fully exploited) the possibility of analysing texts in this way.[69] And there is no reason to suppose that an early writer like Anaxagoras would ever have dreamed that every phrase of his which survived would be examined with a fine-tooth comb, in the hope that his thought could thus be discovered to be absolutely determinate in meaning. Nor, if he had, would he necessarily have shared that hope, which is a legacy of Prodicus and Aristotle to philosophy.

APPENDIX: ANAXAGORAS'S FLORUIT[70]

In the previous section I have implied that the formation of Anaxagoras's thought antedated the rise of the Sophistic movement, and that his book must be dated significantly earlier than the treatise of Diogenes of Apollonia and the oldest treatises in the Hippocratic corpus (I mentioned *On the Sacred Disease* and *On Ancient Medicine* in this respect, but the same goes for *Airs, Waters, Places*[71]). This is not a controversial opinion. But it is worth while adducing some reasons for putting the date of the composition of his book, as I incline to put it, at roughly 470-460 B.C.

The chronology of Anaxagoras's life is, as is well known, confused. There is quite a lot of evidence about his birth, residence in Athens, association with Pericles, prosecution for impiety, exile and death.[72] But some of it is garbled and a good deal of it is inconsistent. With most scholars I suppose that Anaxagoras was born in Clazomenae in about 500, and died at the age of seventy-two in Lampsacus; it is not easy to be confident about much else.[73] The evidence of prosecution for impiety is particularly troublesome, and arouses very different interpretative instincts: some assume that there is solid truth behind most of the historical reports, and take their task to be like that of a man who has to reconstruct a vase from an inadequate selection of corroded potsherds (of these J. A. Davison is the most ingenious); others infer from the divergences between the reports that they contain more fantasy than truth, and therefore incline to agnosticism:[74] 'If we look in turn at Ephoros, at the Hellenistic writers cited by Diogenes Laertius, and at Plutarch, one thing emerges clearly: not one of them actually knew what happened to Anaxagoras, though unfortunately this did not prevent them from writing as if they did.' I shall not attempt to engage fully equipped in this or any other chronological controversy. My concern in what follows is simply to draw attention to the evidence for Anaxagoras's *floruit*.

Consider the following points. (1) When about the year 467 B.C. a large meteorite fell at Aegospotami in Thrace, people saw in this the fulfilment of a prediction by Anaxagoras that rocks would fall from the sun.[75] (2) In the *Supplices* (? 463 B.C.), as also in a fragment, Aeschylus adopts the view of the cause of the summer flooding of the Nile which our sources attribute to Anaxagoras.[76] (3) In the *Eumenides* (458 B.C.) he makes Apollo, in his defence of Orestes against the Furies' charge of matricide, resort to the biological idea, ascribed to Anaxagoras by Aristotle, that the mother contributes nothing to the generation of offspring but a place (i.e. the womb) in which the father's seed may grow.[77] (4) Our sources often describe Pericles as the 'pupil' of Anaxagoras.[78] Even if we do not (as we should not) take this designation very seriously, it is obviously likely that it was in his youth that Pericles first fell under Anaxagoras's influence. We first hear of Pericles in 472 B.C., as choregus for Aeschylus's *Persae*; and it was in the late 460s that he began to make a name for himself in politics, with his attack on Cimon in 463 and his alliance with Ephialtes against the Areopagus in 462/1.[79] (5) Plato perhaps indicates that by about 450 Anaxagoras was no longer in Athens. In the *Phaedo* he represents Socrates (b. 470/69) as recalling a reading from Anaxagoras's book, presumably given in his youth, which first elated and then disappointed him with its talk of νοῦς.[80] This is not supposed to be Socrates's first encounter with natural philosophy by any means.[81] So the suggestion that Socrates had studied natural philosophy in

Athens without ever coming upon Anaxagoras's thought, and then only in a book, seems to imply that Anaxagoras was already a figure of the past, at least so far as the Athenians were concerned.

None of these points constitutes on its own anything so strong as firm evidence that Anaxagoras's direct impact as a philosopher was made mostly in Athens in the decade 470-460. But taken together they make a fair cumulative case for that conclusion, particularly since there is no comparable evidence which suggests that the impact came later. Indeed, there is good reason to think that Anaxagoras was *not* a philosophical force active in the Athens of 440-430. Plato certainly gives the impression that that decade was dominated by the Sophists; and in the *Hippias Major* Anaxagoras is contrasted with Hippias and his contemporaries as the last of the old philosophers.[82] Again, when Aristophanes mocks natural philosophy, the ideas he has in view are ones more readily associated with Diogenes of Apollonia than with Anaxagoras.[83] If Anaxagoras continued to philosophize in his later years, then probably he did so mainly in Lampsacus, where he appears to have founded a flourishing school.[84] He may have returned to Athens on one or more occasions; and conceivably it was during such a visit that Diopeithes in c. 433 proposed the decree against impiety which Plutarch took to be the occasion of Anaxagoras's withdrawal from the city.[85]

A *floruit* of 470-460 B.C. fits well enough with what little we can say of the relation between Anaxagoras's thought and that of other fifth-century philosophers. It is late enough for him to have taken profit from the reflection he evidently devoted to Parmenides's work. It is early enough for his book to have antedated, as it probably did, the physical poem of Empedocles[86] and the work of Leucippus. It leaves the temporal relation of his thought with that of Zeno[87] and Melissus appropriately obscure.

Chapter 2
PRIMORDIAL MIXTURE

THE BEGINNING OF THE BOOK
Anaxagoras's book began with the famous words:[1] ὁμοῦ χρήματα πάντα
ἦν, ἄπειρα καὶ πλῆθος καὶ σμικρότητα (Fragment 1 *ad init.*), 'All
things were together, unlimited both in multitude and in smallness.'
He plunges straight into exposition, and his very first phrase contains *in nuce* the theme of his whole natural philosophy.

Contrast the logographer Hecataeus, Anaxagoras's elder contemporary. His genealogical treatise began as follows:[2] Ἑκαταῖος
Μιλήσιος ὧδε μυθεῖται· τάδε γράφω, ὥς μοι δοκεῖ ἀληθέα εἶναι· οἱ γὰρ
Ἑλλήνων λόγοι πολλοί τε καὶ γελοῖοι, ὡς ἐμοὶ φαίνονται, εἰσίν
('Hecataeus of Miletus speaks thus: I write these things as they
seem to me to be true; for the discourses of Greeks are, as they
appear to me, many and absurd'). The author tells us his name and
his city, and he then launches into what we might call an epistemological exordium, in which he explains the status of his work, with
much use of the first person and of demonstratives, and attacks
other versions of its as yet undisclosed subject-matter on broadly
epistemological grounds. Hecataeus's procedure was favoured by
many other early prose writers.[3] It was followed, for example,
although in briefer form, by Herodotus:[4] Ἡροδότου Ἀλικαρνησσέος
ἱστορίης ἀπόδεξις ἥδε ('This is the setting forth of the enquiry of
Herodotus of Halicarnassus'), where the status of the work is linked
with an indication of its method (Ionian ἱστορίη); and by the West
Greek logographer Antiochus:[5] Ἀντίοχος Ξενοφανέος τάδε ξυνέγραφε
περὶ Ἰταλίης, ἐκ τῶν ἀρχαίων λόγων τὰ πιστότατα καὶ σαφέστατα
('Antiochus son of Xenophanes wrote these things about Italy,
[taking] the most reliable and the clearest [accounts] from the old
discourses'), where father is substituted for city and an immediate
indication of the topic of the work is given. Philosophers, too,
began their books in this fashion. Thus Alcmaeon wrote:[6] Ἀλκμαίων
Κροτωνιήτης τάδε ἔλεξε Πειρίθου υἱὸς Βροτίνῳ καὶ Λέοντι καὶ Βαθύλλῳ·
περὶ τῶν ἀφανέων [περὶ τῶν θνητῶν] σαφήνειαν μὲν θεοὶ ἔχοντι, ὡς δὲ

ἀνθρώποις τεκμαίρεσθαι καὶ τὰ ἑξῆς ('Alcmaeon of Croton, son of
Peirithos, said these things to Brotinos and Leon and Bathyllos:
about what is unapparent, the gods have clear vision, but for men to
infer from signs etc.'). And it is plausibly conjectured that Fragment 1 of Heraclitus was prefaced by words such as: Ἡράκλειτος
Βλόσωνος Ἐφέσιος τάδε λέγει ('Heraclitus of Ephesus, son of Bloson,
says this').[7] It is reasonable to infer that Antiochus and Alcmaeon
went on to refer to themselves in the first person, as did the other
three (although Heraclitus characteristically invests such reference
with contrary resonances).

The formula: '*X* son of *Y*/citizen of *Z* says this', followed by
references to the author in the first person, was probably in origin
epistolary.[8] It is certainly a natural form of introduction to a
communication not being made face to face: witness its similarity to
the formulae used to initiate telephone conversations, news
announcements, etc. Its use therefore constitutes good evidence
that its author conceived of a book thus introduced as a record of
his thought or as a means of propagating his views not dependent on
the whereabouts of his own person, although this naturally does not
exclude the possibility that he might give readings from his book to
an audience, presumably omitting the opening formula on such occasions. What inference should we draw from the fact that the
employment of such a formula is not attested for Anaxagoras?

It may be that he *did* begin in that way, but that this was
later forgotten, as probably occurred in the case of Heraclitus.
The telephone formula is most useful as a *Titelersatz* in an era when
books are not furnished with titles, as prose books very likely were
not until the Sophistic age at the earliest.[9] But once titles
established themselves it would have been very easy for such formulae to have been forgotten, or even omitted in copying; and in any
case most readers of a philosophical doxography in Hellenistic or
Roman times would be much more interested in knowing the first
philosophical statement in Anaxagoras's book than in being informed
of his authorial preamble.

An alternative possibility is that, while beginning as we are
told he did begin, Anaxagoras may have used something like the telephone formula, but at the *end* of his book: as we might conclude a
recorded message; or as in antiquity the author of the *Hymn to*

Delian Apollo identifies himself at the end of his poem, or Ion of
Samos appends his σφραγίς at the bottom of his epigram celebrating
the victory of Lysander at Aegospotami, or Thucydides concludes his
annual record: καὶ ὁ χειμὼν ἐτελεύτα οὗτος, καὶ τρίτον ἔτος τῷ
πολέμῳ ἐτελεύτα τῷδε ὃν Θουκυδίδης ξυνέγραψεν ('And this winter
ended, and there ended the third year of this war which Thucydides
wrote of').[10] There is a reason for preferring this alternative,
beyond the consideration that it does not involve attributing an
error to those ancient writers who report ὁμοῦ χρήματα κτλ. as
Anaxagoras's opening sentence. For as we have seen, authors who use
the initial telephone formula invariably couple it with an epistemological exordium, or at any rate with a hint of their methodology or
a statement of their intentions. Yet Anaxagoras omits any such
exordium.

There is a natural, if not a necessary, connexion between the
initial telephone formula and the epistemological exordium. The
formula is in all cases a personal declaration of personal author-
ship. It is accordingly well matched with an exordium designed to
stress the status of the work which follows as the disclosure of the
author's superior insight (? Hecataeus, Heraclitus), or as the results of his own enquiries (? Hecataeus, Herodotus), of his own
rational selection from the reports of others (Antiochus), or of his
own use of evidence to discover truths not plain to men (? Alcmaeon). Formula and exordium together exemplify the individualistic
tone, hostile or indifferent to tradition, which is found in much of
the literature of the archaic age. But there is scant trace either
of personal tone or of epistemological concern in Anaxagoras. His
comparative lack of explicit interest in epistemological issues we
have already noticed; and it is confirmed by the contrast between
his opening sentence and those of Heraclitus and Alcmaeon (and, of
course, of the prefatory matter in Parmenides and Empedocles). As
for personal tone, there are only two recorded instances of his
using 'I' or 'me', both enclitic in the colourless phrase 'has been
said by me'.[11] When Anaxagoras wishes to recommend a thesis, rather
than to summarize his statement of it, he employs impersonal formu-
lations such as χρὴ δοκεῖν ('it is necessary to think') or γινώσκειν
χρή ('it is necessary to recognize').[12]

An initial use of the telephone formula, then, would not have fitted particularly well with the impersonal tone and the general disinclination to discuss epistemological issues evidenced elsewhere in Anaxagoras's fragments. We may conclude that he probably did begin his book with the words: ὁμοῦ χρήματα πάντα ἦν.[13] And we may imagine that he decided to begin in this style because he thought a philosophical account of the world, implicitly claiming as it did to state general, publicly available truths, *ought* to be written in as solemn and impersonal a manner as possible, without the intrusion of the individual accents of the author. This may have been the style chosen by the Milesians to begin their cosmogonies; it is certainly the style of beginning which, as we are told, Pherecydes adopted: Ζὰς μὲν καὶ Χρόνος ἦσαν αἰεὶ καὶ Χθονίη ('Zas and Time and Chthonie always were').[14] In starting with a *Kennwort* or *Kernwort* which enunciates his main theme Anaxagoras was in any event following an old tradition, whose most celebrated exponent was, of course, Homer in both the *Iliad* and the *Odyssey*; and a very effective tradition it was: just as everyone remembered and remembers that the *Iliad* is about the wrath of Achilles and the *Odyssey* is about the wily, much-travelled Odysseus, so antiquity knew, if it recalled little else about him, that Anaxagoras said: 'All things were together' (indeed, his phrase was quickly converted into the more memorable: ὁμοῦ πάντα or ὁμοῦ πάντα χρήματα ἦν). Contrast, once again, Diogenes of Apollonia, who in the next generation began his cosmological treatise, written very much in the old Ionian vein, with the sentence:[15] λόγου παντὸς ἀρχόμενον δοκεῖ μοι χρεὼν εἶναι τὴν ἀρχὴν ἀναμφισβήτητον παρέχεσθαι, τὴν δὲ ἑρμηνείαν ἁπλῆν καὶ σεμνήν ('It seems to me that at the beginning of every account one should make the starting-point indisputable, and the mode of expression simple and solemn'). The personal tone and the epistemological character of these unexceptionable sentiments are typical of Ionian ἱστορίη. Diogenes's preoccupation with secure starting-points is more especially typical of the Sophistic age, and may be compared with the similar attitude of the author of *On Ancient Medicine*[16] and with the motive which we may presume to underlie the composition by Hippocrates of Chios of the first mathematical *Elements*.[17] We may applaud him for his sensitivity to the need for a theorist to justify his method. But we must recognize that his first sentence was immediately forgotten, whereas Anaxagoras's wholly dogmatic beginning caught the ear of posterity.

THE STATUS OF THE PRIMORDIAL MIXTURE THESIS
Anaxagoras chose to give his statement of the primordial mixture thesis the most prominent place in his book just as Protagoras was to put at the start of his Ἀλήθεια (*Truth*) the famous maxim:[18] 'Man is the measure of all things' (πάντων χρημάτων μέτρον ἐστὶν ἄνθρωπος: is this meant to echo and so to impugn Anaxagoras's beginning?).[19] We should therefore give it a more prominent place in our reflections than it receives in many accounts of his thought, including one of the latest and best, by Jonathan Barnes, which I shall exploit in what follows. I propose a question about it that is most crisply formulated in anachronistic terms: is the proposition which it expresses an axiom or a theorem of Anaxagoras's system? Or to pose the problem in a more informal way: does the thesis of original mixture represent an absolutely fundamental, irreducible belief about the nature of things, or is it an inference or extrapolation from some further thesis or theses which occupy a more central and fundamental place in Anaxagoras's physical theory? My answer - to express it as briskly and crudely as the question - is: an axiom, an irreducible belief.

TEXTUAL EVIDENCE
We are lucky to possess in Fragment 12 an extensive account of the role of νοῦς in initiating cosmogony; and it is quite likely that that fragment constituted the greater part of what Anaxagoras said on the subject, although Fragments 13 and 14 evidently belonged to a section which extended discussion of some aspects of it. What is significant for our purposes is that the fragment contains very little argument, and that what argument there is does not defend the ascription of properties and powers to νοῦς nor support the thesis that it initiated cosmogony. Argument is confined to explaining the relation of νοῦς to other substances as it must be conceived in the light of Anaxagoras's general physical theory, on the one hand, and of the power to control things which Anaxagoras ascribes to it, on the other. It is not difficult to *construct* arguments for holding νοῦς to have the properties and powers Anaxagoras says it has, or for holding that it must have initiated cosmogony (if

there was a cosmogony), on the basis of what he asserts about it.
But so far as we can tell such arguments were not supplied by Anaxagoras himself. Perhaps, then, something similar was true of his
account of the primordial scene.

Examination of Fragment 1 reinforces this view of the matter,
although it requires us to make a modification which actually
strengthens the case for thinking that the doctrine of an original
mixture was not argued. The Fragment as a whole reads thus:

ὁμοῦ χρήματα πάντα ἦν, ἄπειρα καὶ πλῆθος καὶ σμικρότητα· καὶ
γὰρ τὸ σμικρὸν ἄπειρον ἦν. καὶ πάντων ὁμοῦ ἐόντων οὐδὲν
ἔνδηλον ἦν ὑπὸ σμικρότητος· πάντα γὰρ ἀήρ τε καὶ αἰθὴρ
κατεῖχεν, ἀμφότερα ἄπειρα ἐόντα· ταῦτα γὰρ μέγιστα ἔνεστιν ἐν
τοῖς σύμπασι καὶ πλήθει καὶ μεγέθει.

All things were together, unlimited both in multitude and in
smallness. For the small was indeed unlimited. And all things
being together nothing was manifest on account of smallness.
For air and aither contained all things, both being unlimited.
For these are the greatest things present among the totality of
things, both in multitude and in magnitude.

These few lines contain no less than three instances of the inferential particle γάρ ('for'); and the first, at least, of the propositions introduced by γάρ is perhaps linked by another γάρ to a
further explanatory proposition in the bit of text now counted as
Fragment 3. But although from the very outset of his book Anaxagoras thereby reveals himself to be intent upon arguing, or at any
rate explaining himself, none of his inferences bears on the fundamental thesis that all things were together. The two explanations
which he offers fasten upon matters of secondary (which is not to
say not very considerable) importance. In the first he explains why
he has said that originally things were unlimited in smallness: καὶ
γὰρ τὸ σμικρὸν ἄπειρον ἦν, 'for in fact the small was without
limit', a thesis for which he perhaps provides metaphysical support
in Fragment 3. In the second he defends the claim that in the original mixture nothing was manifest on account of smallness. He explains that air and aither dominated all things, and then explains
this in turn by observing that these are greatest in the totality of
things. Anaxagoras here clearly appeals to what purports to be an
evident truth about the constitution of the world as it is at

present (viz. the predominance in it of air and aither) in defence of his characterization of the original mixture. So plainly he was prepared explicitly to argue from the present to the primordial scene. But the fact remains that, at least in Fragment 1, he does not attempt to derive the central thesis of an original mixture in this way. One might have expected such a derivation in the first paragraph of his book, if anywhere, particularly since that paragraph *does* contain arguments. This expectation is disappointed.

Is there any sign elsewhere in the fragments of an argument for the central thesis that all things were once mixed together? There is one text only where I detect a piece of reasoning which might have been designed to do that job. This is the sentence which Fränkel isolated as Fragment 4c,[20] rightly thinking it to be too tenuously linked with the paragraph (Fragment 4b) which it is made to conclude in Diels-Kranz: τούτων δὲ οὕτως ἐχόντων ἐν τῷ σύμπαντι χρὴ δοκεῖν ἐνεῖναι πάντα χρήματα ('Since this is so, one must suppose that all things were present in the totality'). I have translated with a past indicative,[21] since it is hard to believe that Anaxagoras would have presented an argument for the tautology that the totality of things in the universe as it is at present includes all things. It looks as though he was here concluding an argument for the thesis that whatever distinct things (or kinds of thing) there are in the world at present, just the same things (or kinds of thing) were there in the totality constituted by the original mixture. I imagine that this train of thought, hinted at - if I am right - in Fragment 4c, should be associated with that contained in Fragment 5:

> τούτων δὲ οὕτω διακεκριμένων γινώσκειν χρὴ ὅτι πάντα οὐδὲν ἐλάσσω ἐστὶν οὐδὲ πλείω (οὐ γὰρ ἀνυστὸν πάντων πλείω εἶναι), ἀλλὰ πάντα ἴσα ἀεί.
>
> Since these things have been dispersed in this way, one must recognize that all things are not in any way less or more (for it is impossible for there to be more than all), but all things are always equal.

The point of Fragment 5 is presumably that, whatever changes occur in the world, the number of things (or kinds of thing) must remain constant.[22] The clause in which Anaxagoras gives his reason for this conclusion - 'Since these things...in this way' - is unfortunately full of references to argumentation which is now lost. But it does not seem very hazardous to interpret it as appealing to the idea that whatever distinct individual objects there are in the world as it now is have come into being by a process of dispersal and separation which involves nothing more radical than the rearrangement of matter. However that may be, it is clear that from Fragment 5 it is a trivial inference to the thesis which (on my reading) is adumbrated in Fragment 4c, that whatever the number of things (or kinds of thing) in the world as it is now, there was the same number in the original mixture.

Fragment 4c may, then, provide evidence for an Anaxagorean argument which bears, more directly than any inference in Fragment 1 itself, on the central thesis of Fragment 1 that all things were together. Even so, it is not an argument for the claim that there *was* once an original state of things, nor for the claim that in that original state things were together in such a way that nothing was manifest or distinct. All Fragment 4c can be arguing is that, given the assumption of an original mixture, that mixture must contain just those things (or kinds of thing) which there are in the world as it is at present.

ARISTOTLE'S INTERPRETATION

Aristotle twice maintains that Anaxagoras's belief in an original mixture is to be explained in terms of his commitment to more fundamental physical and metaphysical beliefs. The first of these texts is *Phys.* I 4, 187a26-31:

> ἔοικε δὲ Ἀναξαγόρας ἄπειρα οὕτως οἰηθῆναι διὰ τὸ ὑπολαμβάνειν τὴν κοινὴν δόξαν τῶν φυσικῶν εἶναι ἀληθῆ, ὡς οὐ γιγνομένου οὐδενὸς ἐκ τοῦ μὴ ὄντος (διὰ τοῦτο γὰρ οὕτω λέγουσιν, ἦν ὁμοῦ πάντα, καὶ τὸ γίγνεσθαι τοιόνδε καθέστηκεν ἀλλοιοῦσθαι, οἱ δὲ σύγκρισιν καὶ διάκρισιν)·

Anaxagoras seems to have thought [the elements of things] were infinite [in number] in this way [sc. as consisting of τὰ ὁμοιομερῆ, homoeomerous stuffs, and τἀναντία, opposites], through supposing that the common belief of the physicists was true, that nothing comes to be from what is not. For it is for this reason that they say things like 'all [things] were together' and 'to come-to-be such and such is to be altered' (or, as some say, combination and dissolution).

Aristotle's main point here is that we may explain Anaxagoras's acceptance of an infinite number of elements (of the sort he posited) as a consequence of his acceptance of the principle that nothing comes to be from what is not. The principle seems rather too jejune to generate such consequences. Probably we should expand it to read: nothing comes to be from what is not, nor from anything which is not of the same kind as itself; or (more briefly): nothing comes to be from what *it* is not.[23] Anaxagoras (on Aristotle's interpretation) will have differed from monists and from pluralists such as Empedocles (who believed in four elements only) simply in thinking that there were an infinite number of irreducible kinds.

It is in order to support his diagnosis of Anaxagoras's view on elements that Aristotle refers to the original mixture thesis. I take it that by the words οὕτω λέγουσιν, ἦν ὁμοῦ πάντα he means to suggest not that anyone besides Anaxagoras actually used the phrase, but that all physicists posited something which preexisted any coming into being, and which was the origin from which things first came to be. He implies that this is clear evidence of their acceptance and use of the principle that nothing comes to be from what is not. Does he also imply that Anaxagoras and the other physicists explicitly formulated and argued from the principle (together no doubt with other premisses) to the existence of an original source of all coming into being? This seems unlikely, in view of the generality of his claim, which is presumably meant to cover primitive figures like Anaximander and indeed Thales. Aristotle surely means just that the principle represents the assumption which, whether explicitly or not, governed their hypothesis of a primordial origin of things. Even though it is plain enough that Anaxagoras did actually formulate the principle, it would be unwise to suppose that Aristotle wants to go so far as to maintain that he explicitly deduced his original mixture thesis from it. Admittedly, Fragment 17 reveals Anaxagoras (like Empedocles) explicitly invoking the principle in support of his stricture upon the ordinary use of γίγνεται, 'comes to be', and ἀπόλλυται, 'perishes': contrary to the implications of ordinary usage, 'things are *mixed together* and *dissolved* from existing things; so the right way to speak is to call coming into being "being mixed together", and perishing "being dissolved"' (ἀλλ' ἀπὸ ἐόντων χρημάτων συμμίσγεταί τε καὶ διακρίνεται καὶ οὕτως ἂν ὀρθῶς καλοῖεν τό τε γίνεσθαι συμμίσγεσθαι καὶ τὸ ἀπόλλυσθαι διακρίνεσθαι). Admittedly, Aristotle probably has Fragment 17 confusedly in mind in the last clause of our text (καὶ τὸ γίγνεσθαι...διάκρισιν).[24] But he is prone to mix report and interpretation in a single breath.

I turn now to the longer and more interesting text, *Phys.* III 4, 203a23-33, where again it is not altogether clear whether Aristotle is reporting or merely interpreting Anaxagoras:

καὶ ὁ μὲν ὁτιοῦν τῶν μορίων εἶναι μίγμα ὁμοίως τῷ
παντὶ διὰ τὸ ὁρᾶν ὁτιοῦν ἐξ ὁτουοῦν γιγνόμενον· ἐντεῦθεν γὰρ
ἔοικε καὶ ὁμοῦ ποτὲ πάντα χρήματα φάναι εἶναι, οἷον ἥδε   25
ἡ σὰρξ καὶ τόδε τὸ ὀστοῦν, καὶ οὕτως ὁτιοῦν· καὶ πάντα ἄρα·
καὶ ἅμα τοίνυν· ἀρχὴ γὰρ οὐ μόνον ἐν ἑκάστῳ ἔστι τῆς διακρίσεως, ἀλλὰ καὶ πάντων. ἐπεὶ γὰρ τὸ γιγνόμενον ἐκ τοῦ
τοιούτου γίγνεται σώματος, πάντων δ' ἔστι γένεσις πλὴν οὐχ
ἅμα, καί τινα ἀρχὴν δεῖ εἶναι τῆς γενέσεως, αὕτη δ' ἐστὶν   30
μία, οἷον ἐκεῖνος καλεῖ νοῦν, ὁ δὲ νοῦς ἀπ' ἀρχῆς τινος ἐργάζεται νοήσας· ὥστε ἀνάγκη ὁμοῦ ποτε πάντα εἶναι καὶ ἄρξασθαί ποτε κινούμενα.

And Anaxagoras held (i) that any part is a mixture in the same way as the All, through seeing anything come to be from anything. (ii) For it is apparently for this reason that he says also that all things were once together. (iii) E.g. this flesh and this bone; and by the same token anything; and so all things; and in consequence at the same time. (iv) For there is a beginning of separation not only in each thing but of all things. (v) For since what comes to be comes to be from that sort of body [sc. one which is a mixture], and there is a coming-to-be of all things (although not at the same time), it follows that there must also be an origin of the coming-to-be. (vi) And this is a single origin, viz. what he calls mind. (vii) And mind having taken thought begins its work from some starting-point. (viii) So necessarily all things were once together and once they began to be moved.

Aristotle's exegesis is laconic, complicated, and in parts obscure.[25]

Our first task must be to set the passage in its context.

Aristotle has been maintaining that all the physicists make the infinite some sort of ἀρχή, 'principle'.[26] But, he says, whereas Plato and the Pythagoreans treat it as a substance in its own right,[27] the physicists properly so called introduce it as an attribute of some other, elemental substance.[28] The examples he gives of such substances – water, air, something intermediate between them – make one think of figures like the Milesians or Diogenes of Apollonia. Aristotle next (and rather too quickly for comfort) qualifies these generalizations, to take account of thinkers who posited more than one element. He makes those who proposed a limited number of elements (we think of Empedocles) an exception to the rule that *all* the physicists introduce the infinite into their systems: such philosophers do not make their elements infinite (sc. in extent).[29] Then he turns to those who believed in an infinite number of elements. He instances as examples Anaxagoras and Democritus.[30] Unlike Empedocles, they do believe (according to Aristotle) that the universe as a whole is infinite in extent: '[They] say that the infinite [sc. universe] is continuous by contact – compounded of the homoeomerous stuffs according to the one [sc. Anaxagoras], of the seed-mass of the shapes according to the other [sc. Democritus]' (203a21-3, Oxford Translation adapted). But, of course, this is not yet to show that these pluralists come anywhere near holding that the infinite is a *principle* of being. In the lines which follow, therefore, Aristotle seems to be trying to show that, despite appearances, their systems do in fact bear strong resemblances to the old Milesian conception of a universe consisting of a *single elemental* infinite substance. He makes his intention clearer in the case of Democritus than of Anaxagoras. He explicitly interprets Democritus's elements (sc. the atoms) as constituting a single common body, whose bits merely vary in size and shape; and this body is said to be the principle of all things (203a33-b2). His point with respect to Anaxagoras is apparently that, since every part of his universe, like the whole,[31] is a mixture of all substances, the Anaxagorean infinite can fairly be interpreted as consisting of a single, homogeneous stuff, which is the principle of all things (203a23-4).

This assimilation of pluralist doctrines to those of the Milesians is a good deal more plausible for Anaxagoras than for

Democritus, at any rate so far as concerns the topic of the infinite. For Democritus's characteristic doctrine of void is ignored in the attempt to father upon him the idea of a universe continuous by contact. It is not surprising, therefore that Aristotle devotes 10 of the 13 lines in which he discusses the two thinkers to Anaxagoras.

They are mostly taken up with a proof, attributed by Aristotle with some hesitancy (ἔοικε, 203a25) to Anaxagoras, of the thesis that all things were once together. And it is this proof which is our immediate concern. But if I have interpreted Aristotle's intentions correctly, it is not *his* main concern. He is more intent upon stating and then explaining Anaxagoras's idea that homoeomerous stuffs - the 'parts' or elements of Anaxagoras's physical system, according to Aristotle - are mixtures, i.e. mixtures which are in essence each identical with the universe as a whole and with each other in composition. For then, as I have suggested, Aristotle will have shown, even if he does not explicitly remark, how closely Anaxagoras's system approximates to the Milesian view of the world.

There are two main reasons for thinking that sentence (i) of the translation expresses Aristotle's main point in the passage, apart from the obvious consideration that it fits the passage intelligibly into its context. First, when he comes to consider Democritus at 203a33-b2, he begins by admitting that Democritus denied (sc. contrary to Anaxagoras) that any element could come to be from any other. But he continues: 'But nonetheless for him the body common to them is the principle of all things, differing from part [i.e. element] to part in size and in shape.' Plainly Aristotle here wants to insist that on a fundamental point - *the* fundamental point for his present purposes - Democritus agreed with Anaxagoras. That point is not concerned with the original state of things, but with the basic identity of nature shared by the elements within the system of each thinker. Secondly, the whole train of argument concerning the original state of things at 203a24-33 is introduced by γάρ. This suggests that an important part of Aristotle's purpose in developing that argument is to support what he says in sentence (i).

Sentence (i), then, expresses the main thing Aristotle wants to say in the passage. Our next concern must be to understand the force of the γάρ with which he links sentence (ii) to sentence (i).

Unfortunately Aristotle himself does not make it clear enough just what supporting job he wants it to do. But the interpretation which most readily recommends itself is something on the following lines. Aristotle begins by maintaining that Anaxagoras believed that each bit of homoeomerous stuff is a mixture because he saw anything whatever coming to be from anything whatever (sentence (i)). In making this claim he very likely relies upon evidence (a τεκμήριον or σημεῖον) offered by Anaxagoras himself, as we shall see in Chapter 4: from bread and water there come to be flesh, bone, hair, etc. We now understand an ellipse: the importance Anaxagoras attached to the 'anything from anything' principle can be gauged from the fact that he seems to have exploited it in advancing another, related doctrine. For (we return to the text) it is apparently for this reason that he says also that all things were once together (sentence (ii)). In short: ἐντεῦθεν refers to διὰ τὸ ὁρᾶν κτλ.; and γάρ effectively says: 'And he attached great importance to this principle, for...' Thus the focus of the two sentences (and consequently of the whole passage) is on the 'anything from anything' principle and its relation to the idea of mixture; and it is presumably for this reason that when he turns to Democritus, Aristotle begins by pointing out that the atomist *denied* that any of his elements could come to be from any other. No doubt he had an independent motive for introducing the primordial mixture thesis in (ii) in this context. For by making the point in (i) that Anaxagoras holds that the infinite universe is made of a single homogeneous stuff, Aristotle could claim - as we have seen - to have shown that he uses an infinite ἀρχή, i.e. ultimate material substratum. It may then have occurred to him that Anaxagoras's homogeneous mixture was an ἀρχή also in the further sense of ultimate material *origin* of all things (ii).

The rest of the passage is taken up with an explanation of how the reasoning which, according to Aristotle, led Anaxagoras from the 'anything from anything' principle to the primordial mixture thesis is to be reconstructed. In sentence (iii) Aristotle presents a brief preliminary sketch of the reasoning. His idea is that Anaxagoras inferred (or is best represented as inferring) that, just as my flesh and my bone were once mixed together (in all sorts of apparently quite different substances, such as bread or water, or again, sperm), so *all* things were at one time mixed together with each other. In sentence (iv) Aristotle begins to show that he recognizes that this conclusion cannot be derived from the 'anything from anything' principle alone. Sentence (iv) in effect states a lemma from which the conclusion *can* be properly deduced. Sentences (v) and (vi) then each supply premisses from which in sentence (vii) the lemma itself is proved in turn. Included among them is the premiss: 'What comes to be comes to be from a mixture', which despite appearances is a way of referring to the 'anything from anything' principle. Finally sentence (viii) draws the desired conclusion from the lemma.

So in sentences (iii) to (viii) we can discern three arguments: the initial argument (I) from the 'anything from anything' principle to the original mixture thesis; the subsidiary argument (II) for the lemma; the final argument (III) for the original mixture thesis from the lemma. We shall consider each in turn.

Argument I
This is given in sentence (iii), which reads: 'E.g. this flesh and this bone; and by the same token anything; and so all things; and in consequence at the same time.' Its drastically telegrammatic sequence of clauses conceals, I suggest, the following argument:

(A) Individual bits of flesh and bone (e.g. those in my body) were once mixed together (e.g. in bread, water, or sperm).
(B) So [generalizing] any bit of homoeomerous stuff was once mixed [sc. with other bits of homoeomerous stuff].
(C) So [further generalization] all bits of homoeomerous stuff were once mixed.
(D) So all bits of homoeomerous stuff were mixed [with all of each other] at one and the same time.

This argument is plainly invalid, because it viciously exploits the vagueness of (C), an inadequately but multiply quantified sentence. If (C) is to follow from (B), it can be nothing but a restatement of it in trivially different language; it can say no more than that, of each bit of homoeomerous stuff, it is true that at some time it was mixed with some other bit or bits of homoeomerous stuff. But if (D) is to follow from (C), (C) must be taken as saying that there was once a time when each bit of homoeomerous stuff was mixed with each other bit of homoeomerous stuff.

It is less immediately plain what the 'anything from anything' principle has to do with the argument. But I take it that we are to understand (following sentence (i)) that from it Anaxagoras derives his premisses (A) and - more generally - (B). Both here and in sentence (i) Aristotle takes 'from' in the principle in a strong sense. If anything (e.g. flesh or bone) can come from anything (e.g. bread or water), then it follows that each thing (e.g. bread or water) is a mixture of things of every kind only if what is extracted *from* it must already have been actually (not just potentially) *in* it. Alternatively, one might say that the principle is tacitly conjoined with another, which we might call the 'like from like' principle,[32] and which Aristotle in *Phys*. I 4 seemed to recognize as the 'nothing from nothing' principle. It is the axiom attributed to Anaxagoras by the scholiast on Gregory, when he represents him as asking the famous question: 'How could hair come to be from not hair, or flesh from not flesh?'[33] However we put the point, its consequence is that any coming to be which satisfies the 'anything from anything' principle will be or involve the *separation* of homoeomerous stuff from some *mixture*. And that is why the statement in sentence (v) that 'what comes to be comes to be from a mixture' is to be read as a reminiscence of the principle.

Aristotle evidently sees the implausibility of Argument I as it stands. For immediately he sets about shoring up its holes.

Argument II

Sentence (iv) enunciates a lemma which is to be used in the final proof of the primordial mixture thesis; sentences (v) to (vii) argue for the lemma.

In sentence (iv) Aristotle's Anaxagoras says that:

(T) There is a beginning of the separation of all things [into distinct bodies] as well as a beginning of separation in each thing.

In sentences (v) to (vii) he argues as follows:

(P) What comes to be comes to be from a mixture.[34]

(Q) Of all things there is a coming-to-be (although not at the same time).

So (R) there is an origin of the coming-to-be [sc. which is

mentioned in (Q)].

   (S) This origin is a single origin, viz. mind.

   So (T^1) there was a beginning of its activity [a reformulation of (T), omitting specific reference to the separation of all things, and including reference to mind].

This argument is obscure and ambiguous in a number of respects. My comments are designed only to show what I take to be the nerve of the reasoning, and to emphasize the chief ideas which Aristotle is introducing by way of supplement to the 'anything from anything' principle.

That principle is recalled in (P), where 'mixture' means 'mixture of things of every sort'. (P) is not actually required for the deduction of (T^1), but is needed to justify the claim in (T), the fuller version, that there is a beginning of the *separation* of all things, with its implication that coming-to-be is coming-to-be from a mixture.

Why should it be supposed that (R) follows from (Q)? The simplest explanation is that it is so derived by an application of (Q) to itself. I.e. coming-to-be is itself treated as one of the 'things' of which (Q) is true: there is a coming-to-be of the process of coming-into-being, which means that coming-into-being must have a first moment or phase, a beginning.[35] But however the reasoning goes exactly, it is evidently supposed to turn on a principle of universal coming to be or separation.

The other main issue of interest is the relation of (S) to (R). First, a minor problem: how can the *beginning* of coming to be asserted in (R) be identified with a *cause* in (S)? The identification is certainly infelicitous. But such is the ambiguity of ἀρχή, 'origin', that it is intelligible enough why the identification is made, especially since the causal origin here envisaged operates at the temporal beginning of all coming into being. Aristotle immediately retrieves the situation by reintroducing the notion of a temporal origin in (T^1), which is clearly to be understood as an inference from the conjunction of (R) and (S). More importantly - indeed, this is the principal question any interpreter of Argument II will ask - why does Aristotle's Anaxagoras assert (S) in the first place? Perhaps it is an illicit inference from (R): from the premiss that any coming into being must have a beginning we are perhaps spirited to the conclusion that there is one and the same starting-point of all coming into being.³⁶ We may then blame an equivocation on τῆς γενέσεως, 'the coming to be' (in (R)) - all it can legitimately mean in (R) is 'any coming into being', but what (S) requires it to mean is 'the coming into being (of all things collectively)'. To my mind, however, Aristotle in this context shows himself sufficiently aware of relevant differences in the scope of existential and universal quantifiers for it to be unlikely that he commits the fallacy thus imputed to him.³⁷ I prefer to suppose that (S) is offered as a thesis independent of (R). Anaxagoras will then be interpreted as saying that, *as a matter of fact*, every individual process of coming to be could be traced back along a causal chain to the same single act, namely the separating act of mind: that one act is the beginning of each process of coming into being which occurs ever after. In any event, whatever the truth about the status of (S) in Aristotle's argument, it is clear that he is in effect introducing another new principle on Anaxagoras's behalf, viz. the thesis that there was a cosmogonic act which is the ultimate cause of every process of coming into being that occurs thereafter.

Argument III
In sentence (viii) Aristotle's Anaxagoras concludes simply that 'all things were once together and once they began to be moved'. In effect, he affirms the conjunction of (D) and (T), although he means really to infer (D) from (T), as the γάρ at 203a27 indicated.

So at the end of the day Aristotle takes Anaxagoras's primordial mixture thesis to follow, not from the 'anything from anything' principle alone, but from that principle together with a principle of 'universal separation' or 'extraction' (Q) and a cosmogonical hypothesis of an ultimate cause of change (S). These principles he sums up in (T).

REFLECTIONS ON ARISTOTLE'S INTERPRETATION
Does Aristotle mean to claim that Anaxagoras's own explicit reasoning is contained in the argumentation of *Phys.* 203a25-33 (i.e. sentences (iii) to (viii))? Probably not. He introduces that argumentation with the words: ἐντεῦθεν γὰρ ἔοικε καὶ ὁμοῦ ποτὲ πάντα χρήματα φάναι εἶναι (203a24-5) - 'For it is *apparently* for this

reason that he says also that all things were once together.' That ἔοικε looks like an apology for a piece of interpretation which goes beyond anything Aristotle could find in black and white in the text. One might even suspect that, when Aristotle began writing the passage, he really thought that he could construct a plausible argument which derived Anaxagoras's primordial mixture thesis from his 'anything from anything' principle alone - viz. Argument I. Reflection on the shortcomings of that argument, together with a recognition of the importance of the ideas of cosmogony and of incessant and universal change in Anaxagoras's thought, will perhaps have led him to add Argument II and to incorporate its essential point in the final Argument III.

Whether or not Argument I represents Aristotle's first thought, and Arguments II and III his second, there is no denying that the beginning of the passage suggests a rather different picture of the motivation of Anaxagoras's thesis of primordial mixture from the one that we come away with by the end of the passage. Aristotle begins by saying that 'Anaxagoras held that any part is a mixture...through *seeing* anything come to be from anything. For it is apparently for this reason that he says also that all things were once together.' This, together with the examples of flesh and bone which he goes on to give, suggests an Anaxagoras led to posit an original mixture chiefly by appreciation of empirical phenomena. At the basis of the Anaxagorean system stands the 'anything from anything' principle; and that principle in turn rests upon observation.

But it could hardly be a matter of *pure* observation. And Aristotle's expression '*seeing* anything come to be out of anything' must be reckoned a considerable exaggeration. Let us concede the plausibility of the idea that Anaxagoras was deeply impressed by the thought that anything can come out of anything. Let us not allow that the principle was a summary of empirical observations. It is rather a bold metaphysical thesis which must have shaped Anaxagoras's perception of the phenomena that had struck his attention no less than it explains them. For common sense might well see no similarity between the emergence of flesh from food and that of water from clouds. Indeed, common sense might not think that flesh originated from food at all (nor for that matter - and to take the examples which in my view exercised more influence on Anaxagoras's general thinking about mixture and change - earth from water or stones from earth). To persuade himself that he saw all this Anaxagoras must have been guided by metaphysical intuition. I say 'metaphysical' partly because of the similarity of the 'anything from anything' principle to other indubitably metaphysical theses which Aristotle ascribes to Anaxagoras in our passage; partly also because there is no sign in the fragments or in the doxographical reports that Anaxagoras envisaged any possible falsification of such a principle or any method of attempting to test it. It may present the appearance of a scientific hypothesis to an incautious modern eye, but for Anaxagoras there was surely nothing hypothetical about it. For him it would simply have expressed a universal truth about how things are - or rather come to be.

If in stressing the empirical basis of the 'anything from anything' principle Aristotle leaves its metaphysical aspect unremarked, his final version of the train of thought which must have led Anaxagoras to the original mixture thesis implies a very different story. Our examination of sentences (iv) to (viii) of the passage has shown Aristotle implicitly or explicitly attributing to him several highly metaphysical assumptions. It will be easier to discuss this more metaphysical version of Anaxagoras's reasoning if I abstract from the complexities and obscurities of the text and offer a reconstruction of Aristotle's interpretation.[38] We need at least four premises:

(1) For any pair of stuffs S S^1 and object x: if x is S, then from x there is extractable a distinct bit of S^1.

This is the 'anything from anything' principle. The version of it given in (1) states that any distinct bit of stuff (Aristotle is thinking of homoeomerous stuffs)[39] can come from any object which is (i.e. is made up of) any other stuff. Notice that it does not require that such an object should itself be a distinct bit of homoeomerous stuff. Obviously in most cases of extraction from an object the object *will* be a distinct bit of stuff - a piece of cheese, a cupful of coffee, etc. But in order to derive the original mixture thesis, in Aristotelian fashion, from - *inter alia* - (1), if for no other reason, it will be important to allow for the possibility of reckoning as objects items which consist of some homoeomerous stuff but are not distinct bits of it.

(2) For any stuffs S S^1 and object x: if x is S, then if a distinct bit of S^1 is extractable from x, x contains S^1 but not a distinct bit of S^1.

This expresses the tacit premiss which Aristotle assumes in interpreting Anaxagoras both at *Phys.* I 4 and in our text, viz. what I have called the 'like from like' principle. Notice that (2) does not state that in any object which is made of homoeomerous stuff there is contained a *distinct bit* of every other stuff extractable from it; indeed, it holds that there are no such distinct bits in it. Thus in coffee there is water, but not distinct bits or particles of water. I take it that (2) is highly plausible at any rate so long as we read 'distinct' as 'distinguishable by the naked eye'.

(3) For any stuff S^1 and time t_n there is a time t_{n-m} and an object x and another stuff S such that: x is S, and if a distinct bit of S^1 exists at t_n, then it did not exist but was being extracted from x at t_{n-m}.

This we might call the 'universal extraction' principle. It is meant to correspond very roughly with *Phys.* 203a29-30. It says that any distinct bit of homoeomerous stuff must have been in the process of being extracted from some other stuff before it existed as a distinct bit of stuff.[40]

(4) There is a mind M and a time t_1 such that for any stuff S or S^1: if a distinct bit of S or S^1 exists, then at t_1 it did not exist but began to be extracted by M.

A formulation of Anaxagoras's cosmogonical hypothesis, corresponding to *Phys.* 203a30-2. It assumes (as does Aristotle's text) that there is a sense in which *every* process of coming to be can be traced back to the start of the cosmogony.

We are now ready to infer some further Anaxagorean theses from these premisses. From (1) and (2) we elicit a version of the doctrine that in everything there is a portion of everything:

(5) For any stuffs S S^1 and object x: if x is S, then x contains S^1.

On this formulation of the doctrine 'portion of stuff S^1' cannot be taken as 'distinct bit of S^1'. All that is required for there to be a portion of S^1 in something is that there be some S^1 in it in some form other than that of a distinct bit.

Our next step is to derive from (3) and (4) the consequence

that of any distinct bit of stuff which ever exists it is true that at the moment of cosmogony it did not exist but began to be extracted from some object (not necessarily the same object for each bit):

(6) There is a time t_1 such that for any stuff S^1 there is an object x and another stuff S such that: x is S, and if a distinct bit of S^1 exists, then it did not exist but began to be extracted from x at t_1.

(6) implies that, besides any intermediate things from which a particular bit of stuff is extracted, there is one which is its original source.

It remains to show that it is not merely the case that - as (6) says - for each distinct bit of stuff there is an object from which it was extracted at the moment of cosmogony, but also that such objects as then existed constituted a mixture in which nothing was distinct. Now it is a trivial inference from (6) that

(7) There is a time t_1 such that for any stuff S or S^1: no distinct bit of S or S^1 exists at t_1.

But from (5) and (7) we can deduce:

(8) There is a time t_1 such that for any stuffs S S^1 and object x: if at t_1 x is S, then at t_1 x is not a distinct bit of S and x contains S^1.

(8) is effectively a version of the original mixture thesis. For if we assume (as Aristotle supposed Anaxagoras did) that homoeomerous stuffs are the basic constituents of all matter, then (8) implies that such objects as existed in the primordial state of things, at the moment of cosmogony, were not distinguishable bits of whatever stuffs they were made of (i.e. not distinguishable by the naked eye); and that they each contained portions of everything. It suggests a picture very like that of Fragment 1 of Anaxagoras, which envisages a world where the eye could make no discriminations between different things, whether or not there were any to be made.[41]

I propose to regard (8) as a sufficient statement of this version of the original mixture thesis. Admittedly it is hypothetical when Anaxagoras is not ('all things *were* together'). But *Phys.* 203a23-33 suggests no answer to the question: what objects are there in the original mixture? It is presumably the case either that they are microscopically (or at any rate non-casually) distinguishable bits of stuff or that they are purely arbitrary segments of the mixture. From other passages[42] it is clear that Aristotle accepted the former option. But if one took the latter option, one might be very tempted to assume a principle of identity of indiscernibles and reformulate (8) as:

(9) There is a time t_1 and a unique object x such that for any stuffs S S^1: at t_1 x is S and x is not a distinct bit of S and x contains S^1.

Or in other words: at the origin of cosmogony there existed an object which uniquely was everything and in which uniquely everything was contained.

So much, then, by way of articulating more precisely the reasoning which Aristotle attributes to Anaxagoras. It remains to examine the logical character of its premisses.

We need say nothing further about (1): the 'anything from anything' principle, as we saw, has a metaphysical aspect even if, as Aristotle claims, it rests in part upon an empirical basis. The other three premisses – (2), (3) and (4) – are all yet more emphatically metaphysical principles.

Consider first (2) (the 'like from like' principle):
For any stuffs S S^1 and object x: if x is S, then if a distinct bit of S^1 is extractable from x, x contains S^1 but not a distinct bit of S^1.

Or: hair cannot come from not-hair. Barnes[43] raises the question whether this principle is 'borrowed from Elea' or is 'an empirical observation' or is, 'in intention at least, a truism'. He opts for the third diagnosis: Anaxagoras, according to Barnes, was stating what appeared to him to be a self-evident conceptual truth about extraction:

'If I take an egg out of the egg-box, the egg was in the box; if I draw milk from a cow, the cow contained the milk; and in general, if Y comes *out* of X, then Y was *in* X.'

Barnes dismisses the first two explanations of the principle:
'When the iron-master extracts metal from ore, he does not need Parmenides to tell him that the metal does not spring into being: he knows that it was there all along. When the milkmaid extracts butter from her milk, she has not previously *observed* the butter in the unchurned milk.'

I agree that (2) must be taken as a purported conceptual truth

about extraction. It is unlikely, however, that any proponent of
(2) would have regarded it as 'a truism'. Anaxagoras surely knew
that it was paradoxical to say 'hair cannot come from not-hair'; he
must have had some other ground for thinking it nonetheless a true
thing to say (always supposing that he *did* say it or something like
it). In the first place, (2), like (1), has some basis in observation, inasmuch as it fits perfectly some paradigm cases of extraction (e.g. Barnes's eggs and milk). But other cases (e.g. Barnes's
butter example) seem to make (2) incredible: not only did the milkmaid not observe butter in her unchurned milk, but she knows very
well that there was none there until she did her churning. So
Anaxagoras needs some additional support for (2) besides examples
like Barnes's eggs, or some reason for limiting the scope of (2) to
exclude its application to items such as butter, or both. Such considerations would presumably have to be metaphysical in character.
Aristotle's suggestion elsewhere (*Phys.* I 4, 187a26-31) that Anaxagoras relied on the axiom that nothing comes to be from what is not
is hard to resist; and in view of other evidence for his responsive-
ness to Parmenides's philosophizing it is equally hard to reject the
idea that the Parmenidean defence of the axiom may have helped to
commend it to Anaxagoras.[44] Any restrictions he may have tacitly
accepted on the range of (2)'s application will no doubt have been
dictated by his conception of elements: opposites and homoeomerous
stuffs, according to Aristotle's account.

Our discussion of the metaphysical character or premisses (3)
and (4) can be briefer. (3) states:

> For any stuff S^1 and time t_n there is a time t_{n-m} and an object
> x and another stuff S such that: x is S, and if a distinct bit
> of S^1 exists at t_n, then it did not exist but was being extrac-
> ted from x at t_{n-m}.

We called (3) the principle of 'universal extraction'. It comes
from the same stable as: 'Every event has a cause.' Like that principle, it generalizes from what we might call observed cases of extraction to an unfalsifiable and unverifiable law (if we cannot
actually find anything from which some distinct bit of homoeomerous
stuff underwent a process of extraction, we posit that there must
nonetheless have been one). (4) was the cosmogonical hypothesis:

> There is a mind M and a time t_1 such that for any stuff S or

S^1: if a distinct bit of S or S^1 exists, then at t_1 it did not exist but began to be extracted by M.

What could be more quintessentially metaphysical than to posit a First Cause transcending all possible experience and explaining at one blow the fact of all coming into being?

A PROBLEM FOR ARISTOTLE'S INTERPRETATION

Let the argument from (1), (2), (3) and (4) to (8) stand as representing Aristotle's reconstruction of the line of thought which must have led Anaxagoras to assert his original mixture thesis. How plausible a reconstruction is it?

A difficulty emerges if we consider proposition (4), the cosmogonical hypothesis. In our account of Aristotle's reconstruction of Anaxagoras, (4) is unargued (although we noted in our discussion of the text that Aristotle *may* have meant to derive it - fallaciously - from a version of the 'universal extraction' principle, formulated above as (3)). The problem arises when we enquire into Anaxagoras's motive for postulating a First Cause.

Evidently Anaxagoras felt that the phenomena in the world about him, and indeed the very fact of the existence of that world, needed an overarching explanation, simpler and more comprehensive than any specific explanations which common sense or observation or imagination might suggest for particular processes, whether of nutrition or sense perception or meteorology or whatever. We can identify more precisely what Anaxagoras wanted of such an explanation. For what job is mind, the First Cause, called upon to do? Mind accounts above all for the general structure and dynamism of change in the world - for the very existence of a κόσμος - as Fragment 12 makes clear.[45] These two functions of mind can be called διακόσμησις, ordering, and περιχώρησις, rotation. Rotation, in its turn, accounts for a good deal else: principally, as we shall see in Chapter 4, for the separation of heavy matter so that it collects at the centre of the universe, and for the dispersal of light matter to the periphery.

Why should Anaxagoras suppose that the hypothesis of an initial act of mind supplies an adequate and acceptable explanation of cosmic order and rotatory separation? No doubt the question deserves a complex answer. But it must surely include two central components:

(i) mind has certain characteristics and powers which make it uniquely capable of initiating a cosmogony; (ii) matter is in itself naturally more or less homogeneous and unorganized. Only if one found (i) compelling would one consider Anaxagoras's hypothesis a sufficient explanation; only if one were prepared to believe (ii) would one think it acceptable, the sort of explanation that is needed.

This brings us to the crux of the difficulty. For to believe that matter is in itself naturally homogeneous and unorganized is already to accept most of what is essential in Anaxagoras's primordial mixture thesis. And this is very damaging to the credibility of Aristotle's reconstruction of the thinking which must have led Anaxagoras to maintain that thesis. It turns out that one would be likely to accept one of the crucial premisses of that reconstructed argument, viz. (4), the cosmogonical hypothesis, only if one were already committed to most of what is contained in the conclusion which is supposed to be derived from it.

What is missing from (ii), but asserted by the primordial mixture thesis, is, of course, just the claim that matter was *originally* homogeneous and unorganized. But it is questionable whether even this claim should be seen as a consequence of the cosmogonical hypothesis. It seems no less likely that Anaxagoras was led to posit an initial act of mind because he had already decided that matter originally constituted a confused mixture. After all, it is with matter in such a condition that his book began. And the slide from 'in itself naturally' to 'originally' is one to which philosophers, like everyone else, have proved themselves very susceptible over the centuries. It is the stock in trade of proponents of a social contract, to cite but one example.

It may be objected on Aristotle's behalf that there could hardly be a more ultimate idea than the conception of a creative cosmogonical agent, whose decisive act explains everything. We may acknowledge, in reply to the objection, that the God of the Judaeo-Christian tradition does indeed explain the existence of *everything*. The first verse of the first chapter of Genesis seems to answer the question: 'Why should there be anything at all?' Whether because that question was one which did not worry the Greeks, or whether because Parmenides had convinced him that *creatio ex nihilo* was an impossibility, Anaxagoras's νοῦς supplies an answer to less all-embracing questions. *Something* is taken for granted, as it usually was by Greek thinkers: homogeneous, unorganized matter in Anaxagoras's case; disorderly, confused, agitated matter in Plato's *Timaeus*. Anaxagoras's νοῦς is, in fact, much more akin to Plato's Demiurge than to the Judaeo-Christian God.[46] For both Anaxagoras and Plato κόσμος, order, and determinate differentiations between things are what pose the fundamental question, not the very fact that there are things. And this is the question answered by positing mind or the Demiurge.

AN ALTERNATIVE INTERPRETATION

In the previous section we have seen reason to doubt Aristotle's suggestion in *Phys.* III 4 that Anaxagoras must have been led to hold his original mixture thesis by a set of considerations which included the idea of the cosmogonical act of mind. It seems at least as likely that it was the primordial mixture thesis which partly inspired that idea. But we have as yet no ground for questioning Aristotle's initial suggestion in the passage, that Anaxagoras accepted the thesis partly 'through seeing anything coming to be from anything'; nor for denying that the principles formulated above as propositions (1), (2) and (3) may all have been factors which inclined him to the thesis. There remains an obvious plausibility in the idea that (1) and (2) are at any rate intimately connected with it, not least because their consequence (5) - the principle that in everything there is a portion of everything - is plainly very close to it in logical structure, and is of course associated with it by Anaxagoras himself in the words: 'But as in the beginning, so too now all things are together' (Fragment 6: ἀλλ' ὅπωσπερ ἀρχὴν εἶναι καὶ νῦν πάντα ὁμοῦ). Again, it is hard to resist the thought that (3), the proposition that everything is extracted or separated from something, must be very closely linked in Anaxagoras's thinking with the primordial mixture thesis.

But was the thesis derived from these principles, or were they inspired by the thesis? Consider (1), the 'anything from anything' principle. We agreed with Aristotle that this principle had an empirical basis; yet we also noticed the metaphysical character of its generalization. Perhaps the metaphysical intuition Anaxagoras here relied upon was nothing but the idea that all matter is naturally homogeneous. Perhaps the 'anything from anything' principle was the progeny of a marriage between that idea and empirical observation of the variety of the separations involved in change. Consider (3), the principle of universal extraction. Observation tells us that countless objects in the world about us came into being by some process or other which Anaxagoras would regard as separation or extraction. But there are other objects of whose origins, if any, observation by the naked eye can tell us nothing: the heavenly bodies, seas, mountains, and so on. Why was Anaxagoras prepared to say that they and any other distinct objects in the world must be the products of separation? Perhaps because he trusted a metaphysical intuition that all matter is naturally unorganized: no distinct object could therefore be in its original state.

Anaxagoras's book told a cosmogonical story. The structure of the story was presumably meant to indicate an explanatory scheme, in which the earlier state of things (earlier both chronologically and in the narrative) was supposed both to be immediately plausible in itself and to account for later developments. This suggests that the primordial mixture thesis was a fundamental assumption of Anaxagoras's system, not derived from nor explicable in terms of any of the other central theses of the system that are known to us. It is a suggestion which our examination of premiss (4), the cosmogonical hypothesis, does something to confirm; and our reflections on (1) and (3) in the last paragraph support its plausibility.

That, then, is the case for regarding primordial mixture as an axiom of Anaxagoras's system. What should we suppose to have been his grounds for holding it? The obvious answer is: the principle of sufficient reason; the idea that there is no reason why matter should exhibit one form of determination or organization rather than any other, so long as it is left in its own natural state.

Attribution of an implicit reliance on the principle of sufficient reason in this form to Anaxagoras must, of course, remain a hazardous piece of speculation. But the speculation has something to be said for it.

In the first place, reasoning from a principle of sufficient reason is, as Professor Owen remarks, 'a very Greek pattern of argument'.[47] He reminds us that:[48] 'Anaximander, asked why the earth stayed still in the middle of his universe, is credited with the reply that since the earth was symmetrically related to all the extremities of the universe there was no reason for it to move in any direction (*De Caelo* 295b10-16).' Secondly, it is commonly believed that Anaxagoras set out to construct a physical theory which would escape the charges of incoherence that Parmenides had levelled at all belief in the existence of a world of plurality and change. In particular, his introduction into philosophy of a first cause quite distinct from the matter of the universe is often construed as a deliberate answer to the taunt Parmenides had cast in the face of believers in cosmogony or indeed in any form of coming into being: 'And what *need* could have stirred it up later or earlier, if it *did* begin from nothing, to grow?' (B8, 9-10). Anaxagoras has no truck with an initial 'nothing', but the question has equal force upon his own supposition of an original homogeneous, unorganized mass. According to the interpretation I am reporting, he tacitly recognizes that some sufficient reason for cosmogony must be supplied. It will readily be seen how close this interpretation is to the speculation I have advanced: if we grant that Anaxagoras is in effect thinking of cosmogony in terms of the complementary pair mind and matter, then any account of his thought which makes him introduce mind as sufficient cause of cosmogony can hardly avoid supposing that he could see no sufficient reason why matter should naturally take on one form of determination or organization rather than another.

It is worth adding that there is a special reason for conjecturing Parmenidean influence on the doctrine of primordial mixture. There are, of course, probable signs of it elsewhere in the fragments: thus Anaxagoras probably banned γίγνεται ('comes to be') and ἀπόλλυται ('perishes') from philosophical vocabulary (Fragment 17) because he was persuaded by Parmenides's arguments on the subject (B8, 5-21);[49] and in denying that the hot and the cold are chopped apart in the single κόσμος (Fragment 8), he was very likely echoing Parmenides's insistence that mind 'will not cut off what is from holding to what is' (B4, 2), but deliberately rejecting his claim that in a κόσμος there can be no true unity, only opposite forms set apart from each other (B8, 56: χωρὶς ἀπ' ἀλλήλων).[50] In Fragment 1, however, disagreement with Parmenides is as explicit as it could be short of mentioning his name. Professor Owen writes:[51]

> '[Anaxagoras] began his book with a sentence that is plainly framed as a flat contradiction of Parmenides on some major issues. Postulating a beginning of the physical world, he wrote: "All things were together, limitless both in number and in smallness." Parmenides had written "Nor was it ever nor will it be, since it is now, all of it together, single, continuous." 'All of it together, single' is discarded for 'All things together, limitless in number'. 'Continuous', which Parmenides understands (to Aristotle's indignation) as excluding divisibility into parts, is replaced by 'limitless in smallness' which is shortly afterwards explained by the continuous divisibility of things. Even 'together' takes on another sense; for part of Parmenides' argument was to deny not only temporal but spatial distinctions in the last analysis – to the mind, he says, distant things are present (B4); whereas Anaxagoras' collection of seeds takes up limitless space. And now all that is left in Anaxagoras' sentence is the verb in the past tense, 'was'; and all that is left to be contradicted in the counterpart sentence in Parmenides is the phrase 'nor was it ever nor will it be'. Anaxagoras, I submit, must have read this phrase as disallowing the use of tenses other than the present.'

The closeness with which Anaxagoras sticks to Parmenides's words at B8, 5-6, indicates not only how important he thought it to contradict the Eleatic but also how greatly he was indebted to him. In specifying where he disagrees with Parmenides Anaxagoras cannot help simultaneously marking out an area of agreement with him. He agrees on 'all together'. Why did Parmenides assert 'together'? It is not altogether clear. But perhaps Anaxagoras was struck by his argument at B8, 22: 'Nor is it divisible, since it all exists alike.' And that argument is plausibly construed as an appeal to a principle of sufficient reason.

CONCLUSION

When Anaxagoras wrote: 'All things were [originally] together [mixed indistinguishably]', he was probably expressing something fundamental and irreducible in his thought about the world, not inferred or extrapolated from any more basic elements. This conclusion is what we might have expected to be able to draw from the appearance of those words at the very beginning of a largely dogmatic account of the nature of things. It is a conclusion we have found to be supported by a variety of considerations. First, a search through the fragments failed to discover any argument for the thesis of a primordial state, even though it showed that Anaxagoras was ready to argue from other propositions in his system to certain characteristics of the original state: that it included all the things (or kinds of thing) distinguishable in our present world (Fragments 4c, 5); that they were so present as to be unlimited in smallness (Fragment 1); that they were dominated by air and aither (Fragment 1). Second, we examined Aristotle's claim in *Phys.* III 4 that the thesis depended mainly on the observation that anything comes to be out of anything. We saw that, in order to defend this claim, Aristotle was forced to attribute to Anaxagoras a line of reasoning which relied on a number of further highly metaphysical assumptions. We showed that at least one of these assumptions, the cosmogonical hypothesis, actually presupposes the core idea of the primordial mixture thesis: it is plausible only if it is already plausible that matter is in itself naturally homogeneous and unorganized (the very thought that there was an original act of separation may have arisen because Anaxagoras assumed that if matter is *in itself naturally* homogeneous and unorganized, then it was so *originally*). And we suggested that some of the other assumptions, including the 'anything from anything' principle itself, may have owed some of the attractiveness they held for Anaxagoras because of a prior commitment on his part to that same core idea. Finally, we were able to advance an explanation alternative to Aristotle's of why Anaxagoras should have been thus committed to the notion that matter is naturally homogeneous and unorganized: he may have been persuaded of it by reflection upon a Parmenidean principle of sufficient reason.

Nonetheless, Aristotle was surely quite right to suppose that it was reflection upon how our present world is which led Anaxagoras to posit a primordial *mixture*. Without evidence of irreducible plurality and of the key role of separation in change, Anaxagoras would have had no reason to make his primordial condition differ from Parmenidean being. Such evidence was to be found only in the

world about him. Moreover, Fragments 4c and 5 lend credence to
Aristotle's specific suggestion that Anaxagoras came to hold the
original mixture thesis 'through seeing anything come to be from
anything'. Fragment 4c should probably be interpreted as showing
that Anaxagoras *argued* that the total mass of matter in its primordial state contained all the things (or all the kinds of thing)
which exist in our present world. And Fragment 5 suggests that he
may well have appealed to the phenomenon of the extraction or separation of distinct substances from bodies in which they were not
distinct in the course of that argument.

It is tempting to go on and paint the following picture.
Anaxagoras's thesis 'All things were together' contains a core idea
which seems to be fundamental and irreducible: that matter is in
itself homogeneous and unorganized. But it also contains an idea,
that of original *mixture*, which needs to be supported with other
principles, including the 'anything from anything' principle. At
the same time the 'anything from anything' principle presumably
claims Anaxagoras's allegiance partly on the strength of some irreducible facts of observation, but partly because he was willing to
venture a metaphysical generalization which is perhaps facilitated
by his commitment to the core idea of the primordial mixture thesis.
On this interpretation, the thesis and the principle interlock, each
supporting and being supported by each other.

It is also tempting to regard such interlocking as by no means
an isolated phenomenon in Anaxagoras's system. I have been keen to
stress the difficulty of supposing that the primordial mixture
thesis was derived by Anaxagoras from a set of premises including
the cosmogonical hypothesis: we noticed that a disposition to accept
that hypothesis presupposes a disposition to think that matter is in
itself naturally homogeneous and unorganized. But it would be hazardous to claim that either belief in an *original* homogeneous mass
or belief in a cosmogony is prior: each idea may have prompted Anaxagoras to accept the other. Consider also the relation between
Anaxagoras's proposition that in everything there is a portion of
everything and his proposition that of the small there is no least.
As we shall see in Chapter 3, he offers the latter proposition in
support of the former (Fragment 6); yet we shall find also that the
former proposition entails the latter - since from any substance you

must be able to extract any other and yet leave behind portions of all.

If this picture of what I can only think of as Anaxagoras's metaphysics is broadly correct, then perhaps we can understand a little better the relative absence and unimportance of arguments in his work. For purposes of exposition and analysis we may and should break his thought down into its elements. But the final impression left by the fragments is of a dogmatic, unitary system, whose elements are appropriately regarded as organic parts, each distinct but none properly intelligible until its relations to the others are understood. There is a certain appropriateness in the reemergence of the central tenet of Anaxagoras's philosophy in Neoplatonism: 'all things in all, but in each according to its own nature' (πάντα μὲν ἐν πᾶσιν, ἀλλ' οἰκείως τῇ ἑκάστου οὐσίᾳ: Porphyry, Sent. 10).[52]

Chapter 3
UNLIMITED SMALLNESS

THE CONSTITUENTS OF THE PRIMORDIAL MIXTURE
The dogmatism of Anaxagoras's opening sentence provoked the question which detained us throughout Chapter 2. In the present chapter we shall be exercised by the ambiguity and indeterminacy of the account of the primordial mixture which he goes on to develop in the rest of Fragment 1. The problems on which we shall focus can be best approached by considering a deliberate and conscious ambiguity in the expression πάντα ὁμοῦ ('all things together').

In Fragment 6 Anaxagoras declares that 'as in the beginning, so now all things must be together' (ὅπωσπερ ἀρχὴν εἶναι καὶ νῦν πάντα ὁμοῦ). Our discussion in the previous chapter of the logical relation between the primordial mixture thesis and the doctrine that in everything there is a portion of everything suffices to show that they cannot both be summarized by the single formula πάντα ὁμοῦ except by a sort of pun. When he states that all things are now together, Anaxagoras means that in every substance of a given kind there are portions of substances of every other kind; he assumes the existence of instances, discriminable one from another, of substances of different kinds, and indeed of the same kind. But when he says that all things were together, he means to exclude the existence of a plurality of discriminable instances of any substance or substances. What exactly he intends to be affirming is less clear (here we meet an unintended ambiguity). Is he trying to indicate (a) that the total quantity of each kind of substance was so mixed with the total quantity of every other kind of substance that together they constituted a single undifferentiated thing?[1] Or is his idea rather (b) that there were different instances of different substances (and presumably of the same substance), but that these were too small or too indistinct to be discriminable by a human or animal eye, and thus constituted a single mixture so far as we are able to discern.[2]

This unclarity in Anaxagoras's meaning is related to an

unclarity in his use of the concept of smallness in Fragment 1.
Again we may conveniently introduce the difficulty by a comparison
with Fragment 6. In Fragment 6 Anaxagoras argues to his doctrine
that in everything there is a portion of everything from the premiss
that there is no least (ὅτε τοὐλάχιστον μὴ ἔστιν εἶναι), i.e. that
there is no limit on how small a small thing can be. As we shall
see later, this premiss does not so much supply an independent positive reason for holding the thesis as remove an obstacle to its
acceptance: if there were minimum particles, might that not be
because they were simples, i.e. instances of substances of whatever
kind or kinds which do not contain portions of substances of any
other kind? Anaxagoras's point in referring to the notion of unlimited smallness is to insist that complexity of composition is no
function of size. In Fragment 1 he gives similar prominence to a
conception of unlimited smallness: 'All things were together, unlimited both in multitude and in smallness; for the small, too, was
unlimited' (ὁμοῦ χρήματα πάντα ἦν, ἄπειρα καὶ πλῆθος καὶ σμικρότητα·
καὶ γὰρ τὸ σμικρὸν ἄπειρον ἦν). Is this the same conception as we
met in Fragment 6 - is it the conception that there is no limit on
how small a small thing can be? And if it is the same, is its relation to the ὁμοῦ πάντα thesis of Fragment 1 the same as the relation
between the conception of unlimited smallness and the ὁμοῦ πάντα
thesis which we diagnosed in Fragment 6? A proponent of option (a)
above would probably be inclined to think that in Fragment 1 we find
the same conception in at least a very similar role. Unlimited
smallness is stressed here, he might explain, because Anaxagoras
wants to emphasize the complete and radical nature of the primordial
mixture: what is implied (even if not quite said) is that however
many and however small the bits into which you might notionally divide the mixture, it will remain no less thorough a mixture. A def-
ender of option (b), on the other hand, might rather argue that,
whatever the exact meaning of the phrase: καὶ γὰρ τὸ σμικρὸν ἄπειρον
ἦν, its role in Fragment 1 does not much resemble the role of the
premiss: ὅτε τοὐλάχιστον μὴ ἔστιν εἶναι in Fragment 6. For (he
might say) the phrase is designed to support or explicate or emphasize the claim that in the beginning things were unlimited in multitude and smallness; and on option (b) that claim would very likely
be construed as an assertion that there was originally an unlimited

number of small discrete things. On this reading the smallness of
things to which Fragment 1 refers makes a crucial difference: the
difference between a state in which distinct things can be discerned
and the original state in which they cannot; whereas in Fragment 6
the point remains that smallness makes *no* difference - although here
the difference in question is difference in complexity of composition.

Before we examine these opposite interpretations of Fragment 1,
we need to have its full text in front of us:

ὁμοῦ χρήματα πάντα ἦν,[3] ἄπειρα καὶ πλῆθος καὶ σμικρότητα· καὶ
γὰρ τὸ σμικρὸν ἄπειρον ἦν. καὶ πάντων ὁμοῦ ἐόντων οὐδὲν
ἔνδηλον ἦν ὑπὸ σμικρότητος· πάντα γὰρ ἀήρ τε καὶ αἰθήρ κατεῖχεν, ἀμφότερα ἄπειρα ἐόντα· ταῦτα γὰρ μέγιστα ἔνεστιν ἐν τοῖς
σύμπασι καὶ πλήθει καὶ μεγέθει.

(i) All things were together, unlimited both in multitude and
in smallness; (ii) for the small, too, was unlimited. (iii)
And all being together nothing was manifest on account of
smallness; (iv) for air and aither enveloped/dominated[4] all
things, both being unlimited; (v) for these are the largest in
the sum of things, both in multitude and in magnitude.

It will immediately be apparent that the unclarities we have noticed
so far by no means make the full tally of difficulties in the passage.
On any overall interpretation of Anaxagoras's train of thought
it is hard to untangle his network of subordinate clauses (how is
the remark about the unlimited nature of air and aither related to
the claim that they are the largest in the sum of things?); nor is
it easy to conceive what difference, if any, is intended by the separate
specifications 'both in multitude and in magnitude'.[5] And
there are further obscurities connected with those relating to πάντα
ὁμοῦ and to the notion of unlimited smallness: when Anaxagoras
offers the explanation 'on account of smallness', we ask in puzzlement
'the smallness of what?'; and the uncertainty signalled above
in the translation of κατεῖχεν is one which arises from wavering
between the two opposed interpretations of what sort of mixture he
envisages.

We shall consider first the strengths and weaknesses of the
interpretation which I have hitherto labelled option (b) but will
henceforth call, at the cost of some inaccuracy, the particulate

interpretation. It is the interpretation to which a reader of Fragment 1 just on its own might more readily incline, the interpretation which first impressions might suggest.

According to the particulate interpretation, then, what Anaxagoras means by 'all things were together' is that in the beginning all things - i.e. all discrete individuals or bits of matter and all stretches of stuffs (such as air and aither) which do not form discrete objects - were mixed together. Not much is said about the specific modes of mixture involved: no doubt Anaxagoras felt he had inadequate grounds for making such specifications. But he indicates the consequence of the mixture, viz. that things formed what would have appeared to the eye as a single indistinct mass: 'And all being together nothing was manifest.' And he explains what brought this consequence about: '(iii) nothing was manifest on account of smallness; (iv) for air and aither enveloped all things, both being unlimited; (v) for these are the largest in the sum of things'. The particulate interpretation takes it that Anaxagoras here specifies two conditions responsible for the indistinctness of the primordial mass. First in (iii) he indicates that most of the things in the mixture were very small particles (small, that is, relative to our powers of perception). It is hard, but not impossible, to perceive very small particles and to distinguish their features. Anaxagoras accordingly goes on in (iv) to add a further condition which made it impossible to have done so in the original state of things: the particles were enveloped in a mixture of 'air', presumably conceived of in traditional Ionian fashion as wet, murky, cold, dense mist, and of 'aither', presumably taken to be air (in our sense) endowed primarily with the opposite qualities.[6] By adding the phrase 'both being unlimited' Anaxagoras perhaps means to imply that there was no ontological basis for firmly individuating one stretch of this mixture of air and aither as distinct from another. It is at least a natural way of making the point that neither of these stuffs has of itself determinate internal or external boundaries. In (v) Anaxagoras infers the degree and extent of their dominance in the original state from the fact (as he construes it) that even in our discernibly differentiated and organized world air and aither (as the lower and upper atmosphere) are the predominant substances throughout greater areas of the universe than are predominantly occupied by any other substance, and perhaps by all other substances together. He evidently thought it reasonable to suppose that in the original state the dominant stuff in *any* area of the universe visible to the eye would have been a mixture of air and aither. For in the beginning, before the separation caused by the cosmogonic rotation, there was no reason for air and aither to collect in one particular part of the universe rather than another.

Why should Anaxagoras have believed that in the beginning most things were very small particles? According to the particulate interpretation we should look for light on this question in sentences (i) and (ii), not least because sentence (iii), when it says: 'And *all being together* nothing was manifest on account of *smallness*', appears to recapitulate the salient points of sentences (i) and (ii). Sentences (i) and (ii), we recall, hold that: '(i) All things were together, unlimited both in multitude and in smallness; (ii) for the small, too, was unlimited.' The anti-Parmenidean cast of (i) suggests a reason for thinking that there was originally an unlimited plurality of things, i.e. of discrete objects and of somewhat object-like stretches of stuff. For believing as he did in the reality of a present world of many such things, Anaxagoras may have thought that his acceptance (in Fragment 17) of the Parmenidean interdict on the possibility of coming to be and perishing committed him to an original plurality of discrete objects and stretches: if you do not include an actual plurality in the original state of things, you will never be able to conjure one up at a subsequent stage.[7] And once admit - *contra* Parmenides - an actual plurality, and you have no sufficient reason to make it a finite plurality: why stop here rather than there? Here, then, are grounds for 'things... unlimited...in multitude'. The particulate interpretation takes Anaxagoras to have different reasons for saying what he does about the smallness of things. This is what sentence (ii) would lead one to expect, for in claiming that 'the small, too, was unlimited' it suggests that the thesis about smallness in sentence (i) has a basis distinct from that which supports the thesis about multitude. The basis in question is none other than the metaphysical doctrine that there is no limit on how small a small object may be. From this it is very plausible to infer that, given an actual infinite plurality of actual things, they were 'unlimited in smallness', in the sense

that there was none of them so small that you could not have found
another smaller than it. It does not follow, nor is it stated by
Anaxagoras (except by implication in (iii): 'on account of smallness'), that *most* members of this actual infinite plurality *were*
small. But this is presumably the *point* he has in view when he says
that things were originally unlimited in smallness (why else should
he have introduced this claim about unlimited smallness?). And it
is not hard to reconstruct a line of reasoning to this further conclusion. For, as we have already seen, the principle of sufficient
reason requires that the original state be as homogeneous as possible. The way to meet this requirement while requiring also that
there be an actual infinite plurality of actual things is to stip-
ulate - assuming that most kinds of thing naturally take the form of
discrete objects - that the great majority of actual things be small
particles. In this manner those sorts of substance which constitute
a significantly great proportion of the total volume of matter in
the universe could be distributed as evenly as possible throughout
it. What Anaxagoras chooses to emphasize, however, is that there
was no more limit on the smallness of actual things than on their
number.

So runs the particulate interpretation. Its merits may be left
to speak for themselves; they will come more clearly into focus when
we consider the rival proportionate interpretation, which was earlier designated option (a). But its principal weaknesses deserve
notice now.

Chief among them is the embarrassing circumstance that, although the interpretation reads Anaxagoras as holding that most of
the things in the primordial mixture were small particles, there is
no explicit statement of this thesis in Fragment 1. It is true that
the interpretation has an explanation available of why this should
be so. For it can say that Anaxagoras is more intent in the opening
sentence of his book on impressing upon the reader the crucial
importance of the concept of the unlimited (which recurs so frequently in the fragments), and on introducing at the first available
opportunity his bold idea of unlimited smallness. In order to
achieve these ends he may have been content to postpone the definite
implication that most things were small until the phrase 'on account
of smallness' in sentence (iii). It is true, too, that a proponent

of the interpretation can plausibly appeal to Fragment 4b for confirmation that Anaxagoras intended the implication. There it is stated that in the original mixture there was 'much earth and seeds unlimited in multitude, in no way like each other' (γῆς πολλῆς ἐνεούσης καὶ σπερμάτων ἀπείρων πλῆθος οὐδὲν ἐοικότων ἀλλήλοις). It is at least very natural to associate this claim about seeds with the doctrine of Fragment 1 that 'all things were together, unlimited both in multitude and in smallness', and to suppose that since it is plausible, if not obligatory, to take these seeds to be small particles, small particles are presumably what Anaxagoras is chiefly thinking of in Fragment 1. Nonetheless, an explicit statement of that thought would have enhanced the credibility of the particulate interpretation - indeed, it would have clinched it.

Another unwelcome feature of the interpretation is that it proliferates speculative hypotheses about the reasons Anaxagoras may have had for maintaining the various theses it attributes to him. It diagnoses one rationale for 'unlimited...in multitude' and another for 'unlimited...in smallness' (admittedly claiming textual support in καὶ γὰρ τὸ σμικρόν); another still is postulated for the implicit doctrine of innumerable small particles. Again, the interpretation supplies two separate lines of thought to support the considerations Anaxagoras himself offers in connexion with his claim that 'nothing was manifest' (viz. 'on account of smallness' and 'air and aither enveloped all things'). The previous two chapters have shown how Anaxagoras's dogmatism makes interpretative speculation at this rate inevitable. It is none the more palatable for that.

Finally, the interpretation threatens to commit Anaxagoras to an exceedingly complicated theory of matter. Anaxagoras would presumably have maintained that the principle: 'in everything there is a portion of everything' held good in the original state of things as it does now. That principle already expresses a complex account of the constitution of matter. But recent scholarship, and particularly the work of Colin Strang, has shown that its complexity may be kept within bounds if we take the principle to say that in every *object* (or object-like stretch of stuff) of a given kind there is an *ingredient* of every other kind of object or stuff, and if we suppose that ingredients are not themselves objects or object-like stretches of stuff. For then the principle will not apply to ingredients, nor *a fortiori* to their ingredients; and so a regress *ad infinitum* will be avoided.[8] The particulate interpretation of Fragment 1, however, appears to invite a regressive application of the principle. For it would be natural to suppose that if air and aither contained, in the beginning as now, portions of everything else, those portions were constituted by the things which they enveloped, i.e. mostly small particles or seeds, according to the interpretation. But particles are themselves objects, and it must therefore have been true of them, too, that they contained portions of everything else, including air and aither. And if it was reasonable to believe that the portions in air and aither were constituted by objects or object-like stretches of stuff, it is presumably the reasonable thing to believe that the portions in the particles were similarly constituted by objects or object-like stretches. Thus an infinite regress looms ahead. Of course, it might be expected that Anaxagoras would be happy enough to accept that prospect, in the light of his insistence that 'the small was unlimited', and given that the regress is not (as Strang held it was) a vicious one.[9] But it remains the case that the degree of complexity which the regress imports into the theory of matter is greater than Anaxagoras anywhere explicitly shows himself ready to allow.

The proportionate interpretation (option (a) above) of Fragment 1 opts for the simpler reading of the principle of everything in everything to which reference has just been made. According to this view, the ingredient portions of every sort of thing which are contained in each object or stretch of stuff of a given kind need not themselves take the form of parts individuated in the same general fashion as objects or stretches, nor need they be distributed among such parts. Their very name μοῖραι indicates that they are to be thought of simply as proportions. The proponent of the proportionate interpretation approaches Fragment 1 with the expectation that the same sort of notion of mixture will be operative in Anaxagoras's account of the original state as is involved in the principle of everything in everything, understood in this simpler manner. Thus he trusts not first impressions of the meaning of the fragment but the overall conception of Anaxagoras's philosophy which he derives from the whole body of fragments.

Like the adherent of the particulate interpretation, he finds

the most instructive clues to the theory expressed in the text in
sentences (iii) to (v):

> '(iii) And all being together nothing was manifest on account
> of smallness; (iv) for air and aither dominated all things,
> both being unlimited; (v) for these are the largest in the sum
> of things.'

On reading (iv) and (v) he is put in mind not only of the principle
of everything in everything but of the connected principle of predominance, formulated at the end of Fragment 12: 'What things it
contains most of, these each single thing is and was most manifestly' (ὅτων πλεῖστα ἔνι, ταῦτα ἐνδηλότατα ἓν ἑκαστόν ἐστι καὶ ἦν).
He interprets Anaxagoras as explaining the indistinctness of the
primordial mixture (iii) as due to the predominance within it of the
featureless and indeterminately bounded stuffs air and aither (iv),
since the total amount of these substances in the universe is
greater than that of any other (v). It follows from this that the
proportion of any other substance in the universal mixture was too
small for its features to be manifest: which is what Anaxagoras
means when he says that 'nothing was manifest on account of smallness'. As Barnes puts the point:[10] 'The "smallness" of, say, gold,
consists not in its being divided into minute particles but rather
in the simple fact that there is very little gold in the world.' A
further inference is now possible for the interpreter. For if when
Anaxagoras says 'all being together nothing was manifest' he means
by 'nothing' 'no kind of substance', he must mean by 'all' something
like 'all kinds of substance'. The first clause of the book can
accordingly be taken as claiming that all the kinds of substance
that there are were together - or more precisely, perhaps, that the
total amounts of all kinds of substance that there are were together, constituting a single mass.

So far the proportionate interpretation proceeds very smoothly.
We have already noticed that it commits Anaxagoras to a less complicated theory of matter than the particulate interpretation. It is
more economical in other respects, too: eschewing particles, it
avoids the embarrassments attendant on the hypothesis that Anaxagoras meant to assert their existence in the primordial mixture for
a good reason, but omitted to make the assertion or supply the
reason; and it postulates a single rationale, not a double one, for

the train of thought in (iii) to (v), since it supposes that 'on account of smallness' and 'for air and aither etc.' articulate a single cause for the indistinctness of the mixture. Its success in explaining 'unlimited both in multitude and in smallness', however, is more doubtful.

On the particulate interpretation there was no difficulty in seeing how to connect 'unlimited' with 'all things' in (i): Anaxagoras was naturally taken to be asserting that things constituted an unlimited plurality, such that no member of the plurality was the smallest member. It is much less clear what he is asserting on the proportionate interpretation. Perhaps the most plausible guess is the one I assumed in presenting the view at the beginning of this chapter: according to that conjecture, Anaxagoras treats 'all things' as a collective designation of the primordial mixture, and thus asserts that there was no limit on the number or the smallness of the arbitrary slices it was possible to make in the mixture – for the single reason that (ii) there was no limit on how small a small slice might be.[11] But other possibilities have found support. Conceivably Anaxagoras is asserting that there was an infinite number of kinds of substance,[12] each theoretically divisible into portions as small as you like; or perhaps he is saying merely that each kind was theoretically divisible into portions as small (and consequently as many) as you like.[13] The very proliferation of alternatives weakens conviction in the correctness of any one of them. Furthermore, it was a merit of the particulate interpretation that it was able to relate the reference to 'smallness' in (iii) ('on account of smallness') to the use of the same word in (i): in both instances the concept was to be taken as applying to the size of things – indeed, to particles. But on the proportionate interpretation 'on account of smallness' means something like 'on account of the small *proportion of most substances* relative to the proportions of air and aither in the total mixture', whereas 'unlimited in smallness' means something like 'without limit on *how small they may be divided up*'. In short, the reference to smallness in (iii) has despite appearances nothing whatever in common with the reference in (i). Appearances, of course, are apt to be misleading; but they should be saved if possible.

The gravest qualm one might feel about the proportionate

interpretation, however, concerns a more fundamental issue. We have noticed, in this as in the previous chapter, the anti-Parmenidean attitude which Anaxagoras strikes in the first sentence of his book. Crucial to his disagreement with Parmenides is his espousal of pluralism. Yet it might well be doubted whether the primordial state envisaged by the proportionate interpretation is pluralistic enough. The interpretation affirms, of course, a plurality of kinds, existing as proportions of the total mixture. But is that existence more than potential - a promise that once the cosmogonic revolution begins, different objects and stretches of stuff of different sorts *will* be separated out? Probably the interpretation should stress here the 'unlimited' which Anaxagoras sets against Parmenides's 'one'. Its best tactic is to argue that the infinite divisibility of the mixture entails the existence of an infinite number of part stretches of stuff - since the mixture itself is a vast stretch of stuff. Their existence is still potential in comparison with the robust actuality of the particles of the rival interpretation. Yet infinite divisibility was an infinity good enough for Zeno.

The proportionate interpretation has a clear edge over its rival in elegance and economy; and its weaknesses are less certainly real weaknesses. It is not clear that we should therefore subscribe to it. When Anaxagoras wrote: 'All things were together' he did not specify the scope of the concept of thing or the criteria of identity of things which he had in mind. Nor does the sequel contain any decisive indication of the intended specification. Conceivably he never settled in his own mind on any determinate interpretation of 'thing' in this context. Such an indeterminacy in Anaxagoras's thought would not surprise us after our examination of his concept of mind in Chapter 1, particularly when we reflect that in Fragment 1 (as in other fragments, too) he was intent primarily on introducing metaphysical principles and concepts of the highest generality. It is plain that he was preoccupied with the general ideas of the mixture of all things and of unlimited smallness and of the predominance of air and aither. It is not at all evident that he was much interested in articulating, whether for himself or for his reader, the fine structure of a theory designed to formulate in precise and determinate terms an account of matter in its primordial condition which embodies those ideas. In this respect his predilections stand in extreme contrast to the professional tastes of contemporary Anglo-American philosophical scholarship and to the poetical imagination of a Lucretius, by whom the doctrine that soul atoms are distributed rarely thoughout the body - to take one example among a countless number - is supported by an exuberant list of finely observed examples (III 374-95):

> nam neque pulveris interdum sentimus adhaesum
> corpore nec membris incussam sidere cretam,
> nec nebulam noctu neque aranei tenuia fila
> obvia sentimus, quando obretimur euntes.
>
> For neither on occasion do we feel the clinging of dust on our body, nor chalk shaken on us settling on our limbs, nor mist at night, nor do we feel the fine threads of the spider in our path when we are entangled in them as we go.

THE IRRELEVANCE OF SIZE

The reader of Fragment 1 is left in no doubt of the importance Anaxagoras attaches to the principle of unlimited smallness. It is put to work in sentence (i) and enunciated with deliberation in sentence (ii). But as we have seen, it is less clear why Anaxagoras thinks it pertinent to assign to the principle the prominent place he gives it on the first page of his book. According to the particulate interpretation, it is because he wishes to stress the smallness of the majority of the discrete things in the original mixture; while the proportionate interpretation can say either that the principle is what carries the weight of the pluralism which Anaxagoras so designedly opposes to Parmenides's monism in his first sentence, or that he hopes thereby to emphasize the complete and radical nature of the primordial mixture (for complexity of composition is not to be thought a function of size), or both. We might hope for further light on this question from an examination of the other fragments in which the principle is mentioned. For this reason (and of course because of the great interest, both intrinsic and historical, of Anaxagoras's assertion of the principle) we shall turn now to a study of Fragment 3, where he appears to present an argument for infinite divisibility (or rather, as I shall in the main continue to put the point, unlimited smallness), and of Fragment 6, where he argues from unlimited smallness to the central thesis of his physical system, the principle that in everything there is a portion of everything. First, however, I shall venture a few words on the intractable question of the relation between the thoughts of Anaxagoras and Zeno on the subject of infinite divisibility.[14]

(a) Anaxagoras and Zeno
Fragment 3 begins: 'For of the small there is no least but always a lesser (for what is cannot not be)' (οὔτε γὰρ τοῦ σμικροῦ ἐστι τό γε ἐλάχιστον, ἀλλ' ἔλασσον ἀεί (τὸ γὰρ ἐὸν οὐκ ἔστι [τὸ] μὴ οὐκ εἶναι)).[15] This sentence has not unnaturally reminded readers of Zeno's conclusion (B1) that if there are many things, then they must be both large *and* small: *so small as to have no size*, and so large as to be infinite.

Some have thought that Anaxagoras was contradicting and indeed replying to Zeno's dilemma.[16] The words I have quoted from Fragment 3 certainly contain some materials for a denial that there could be anything which is both small and of no size. But Zeno knew his conclusion was paradoxical: the mere statement of its contradictory would hardly constitute a reply to the reasoning which led him to that conclusion. And it is hard to see disagreement with Zeno's reasoning in Fragment 3. Professor Guthrie takes Anaxagoras's polemical point to be that things 'can go on becoming smaller to infinity without thereby becoming mere points without magnitude'.[17] A strange polemic, for Zeno himself makes substantially the same claim in the reasoning of B1:

'If it exists, each must necessarily have some magnitude and bulk; and one part of it must be distinct from another part. And the same story holds good for the outstanding part - it too will have magnitude and part of it will stand out. Indeed to say this once is to say it always, since no such part of it will be last or not related as one part to another part.'

This reasoning is in fact offered in support of the second horn of the dilemma enunciated at the end of B1 - that things are so large as to be infinite. Zeno's argument for the other horn - that things are so small as to have no size - is unfortunately lost, but from Simplicius's report seems to have had nothing to do with infinite division.[18] We do know of an ancient argument about division to which Anaxagoras's reasoning in Fragment 3 would be a more apposite rebuttal, but it is associated by Aristotle with Democritus, not with Zeno. This is the argument that if (contrary to atomism) bodies are held to be divisible *everywhere* (πάντῃ, i.e. at every point), then a complete division of a body will establish that the body is composed of non-magnitudes – either points or (what is relevant for us) nothing at all.[19] But there is nothing other than the enigmatic truism: 'what is cannot not be' to suggest that Anaxagoras had an argument like Democritus's in mind in Fragment 3; and in any case he would have done much better to mount a frontal attack on its pivotal idea of a division at every point.

Other scholars have been so impressed by the similarity we have noted between Anaxagoras's reasoning at the beginning of Fragment 3 and Zeno's in B1 that they have diagnosed borrowing on Anaxagoras's part.[20] Certainly both philosophers envisage the infinite divisibility of what is; i.e. a division of what is into parts of finite size such that at any stage in it there are always more and smaller parts of finite size which it could produce. Both make argumentative use of the hypothesis that what is thus divided is what is, τὸ ἐόν, and not nothing.[21] But now we face another difficulty: we do not know whether Zeno wrote before Anaxagoras did or vice versa; whether Zeno heard Anaxagoras first or Anaxagoras Zeno. Apparent echoes of Zeno in Anaxagoras may be echoes of Anaxagoras in Zeno – or (although this is unlikely) sheer coincidences.[22]

Other scholars again have been struck by the very different philosophical attitudes to infinite divisibility taken by Anaxagoras and Zeno. Anaxagoras betrays no sign in Fragment 3 or elsewhere of finding the notion at all problematical, either in theory or in his handling of it in practice. For Zeno it is notoriously riddled with paradox. He apparently inferred from the reasoning of B1 that if something which has size is infinitely divisible, it must have an infinite number of parts each having size, and so be infinitely large. Elsewhere – as in the Achilles – he implies that an infinite division both must and cannot be completed. These differences in attitude have inspired an argument for the proposition that Anaxagoras wrote before Zeno, or at any rate was unacquainted with his work.[23] How could he have taken over the idea of infinite divisibility from Zeno (it is asked), yet done nothing to divest it of paradox? To suppose him capable of this, says Professor Furley, is to embrace the implausible and unattractive proposition that 'he either stupidly misunderstood or shamelessly ignored Zeno's point'.[24] Furley's alternatives are not, however, exhaustive. It is by no means impossible or unflattering to conceive that Anaxagoras took the notion of infinite divisibility from Zeno, but found his attempts to prove it paradoxical too unconvincing to require rebuttal (they are, of course, fallacious; and Anaxagoras seems to keep a clear head when talking of the infinitely small). After all, he both borrows from and signifies disagreement with Parmenides,[25] but does not feel obliged to refute his monism or his argument against the possibility of change. In general, Anaxagoras's book appears to have contained a largely dogmatic exposition of his system, in which the views of predecessors and contemporaries were silently adopted or opposed, not given the honour of counter-argument, still less that of mention of their authors. His manner was no doubt as arrogant as it was arresting: was it therefore shameless?

(b) Fragment 3

We shall not, then, get much light on Anaxagoras's conception of unlimited smallness from the comparison with Zeno. Understanding must be sought - as Furley has forcefully argued - from its role in Anaxagoras's own theory. The natural place to begin is Fragment 3, which appears to contain, among other things, an argument for the principle, given in sentence (ii) below:

οὔτε γὰρ τοῦ σμικροῦ ἔστι τό γε ἐλάχιστον, ἀλλ' ἔλασσον ἀεί (τὸ γὰρ ἐὸν οὐκ ἔστι [τὸ] μὴ οὐκ εἶναι) - ἀλλὰ καὶ τοῦ μεγάλου ἀεί ἔστι μεῖζον. καὶ ἴσον ἐστὶ τῷ σμικρῷ πλῆθος, πρὸς ἑαυτὸ δὲ ἕκαστόν ἐστι καὶ μέγα καὶ σμικρόν.

(i) For of the small there is no least but always a lesser ((ii) for what is cannot not be) - (iii) but also there is always a larger than the large. (iv) And it is equal in number to the small. (v) But with respect to itself each thing is both large and small.

Apart from its assertion in sentence (i) of the thesis that there is no least, Fragment 3 is pretty obscure. The initial γάρ indicates that it represents the argument for some further

proposition; but we have lost the context which would have told us
what that proposition was. Nor is the detail and structure of the
fragment very clear. It is hard to see what support sentence (ii)
gives to sentence (i), or whether it is meant to furnish that same
support to sentence (iii). The meaning both of sentence (iv) and of
sentence (v) is in doubt, as is their connexion with each other and
what precedes. We have no alternative but to try out an overall
interpretation of the fragment, for in no other way is it likely
that we can arrive at any definite proposal about the meaning and
relation of its parts.

Notice first that the fragment falls into three units: sentences (i) to (iii); sentence (iv); sentence (v). These are linked by
the coordinating particles καί ('and') and δέ ('but'). Notice next
that each unit explicitly or implicitly compares the large with the
small, and explicitly or implicitly concludes that there is no difference between them. Thus sentences (i) and (iii) hold that just as
there is always a lesser than the small, so there is always a larger
than the large. Sentence (iv) holds that the large is equal in number to the small. Sentence (v) affirms that with respect to itself
each thing is large no less than it is small.

It is not unnatural to infer that Anaxagoras means to *list*
three ways in which the large and the small are alike; and that he
is not interested in bringing out any logical relations which may
subsist between the three ways. It is a short further step to suggest that the proposition which Fragment 3 was written to support was
something like: the small is no different from the large (e.g. ἀλλὰ
χρὴ γινώσκειν ὅτι τὸ σμικρὸν ὁμοίως ἔχει τῷ μεγάλῳ). Anaxagoras
writes as though he hopes to persuade us of some such thesis as this
by assembling reminders of points more fully explained or exploited
elsewhere.

The first item on the list forms a partial exception to this
rule, since sentence (i) is both perspicuous and supported by argument. But sentence (iii) has more of that enigmatic brevity. As I
shall argue later, it is probably not meant to rest upon the argument of sentence (ii). Probably,[26] Anaxagoras has in mind the point
that since the universe is infinite in size,[27] you will always be
able to find something larger than any given large thing – just by
adding to it in thought some further bit of the universe. If so,

he will be relying on an idea presented elsewhere in his treatise, viz. that the sum of things is infinite in size. I suspect that one reason for the relative curtness of his presentation of this point (when compared with the fuller treatment of the small) is that the concept of largeness without limit is not thematic in his thought in the way that the notion of unlimited smallness is, but is introduced here simply to make a neat parallel with the case of the small.

In the second item (sentence (iv)) Anaxagoras says that the large is equal in number or quantity to the small. This dictum is so general and so ambiguous as to be almost meaningless unless it is given a sense from other passages in his book. Fortunately an appropriate parallel survives in Fragment 6, where Anaxagoras declares that 'in all things there are many...equal in number in both the larger and the smaller' (ἐν πᾶσι...πολλὰ ἔνεστι...ἴσα πλῆθος ἐν τοῖς μείζοσί τε καὶ ἐλάσσοσι) and (what comes to the same thing) 'there are portions equal in number of both the large and the small' (ἴσαι μοῖραί εἰσι τοῦ τε μεγάλου καὶ τοῦ σμικροῦ πλῆθος). So probably he means in sentence (iv) to remind us that the small is exactly as complex (contains exactly as many sorts of stuff) as the large, the doctrine expressed (as I shall argue) in those clauses of Fragment 6.

Other interpretations are theoretically possible. One in particular might deserve support as a candidate if we could be surer that the thesis of sentence (iv) was envisaged by Anaxagoras as a consequence of the thesis of sentences (i) to (iii). For then we might construe (iv) according to a partitive version of the protasis of the first sentence of Fragment 6; i.e. as saying that there is an equal number of portions of largeness and smallness, and meaning that (because there is always something smaller than any given small thing, and always something larger than any given large thing) there is an infinite number of both large and small things.[28] Happily the general intention of (iv) remains the same whether this or any other specific interpretation corresponds to what Anaxagoras meant: the large and the small are *alike* in respect of quantity or number.

For the final item on Anaxagoras's list (sentence (v)) we have no comparative material. Perhaps we have lost the bit of Anaxagoras which would have illumined this text; perhaps there never was such a bit. At all events the detail of his meaning here is irrecoverable.

The principal blame attaches to the ambiguity of πρὸς ἑαυτό. Some[29] have supposed that Anaxagoras means: if you *compare* each thing *to itself*, it will be found to be both large and small - large because it contains portions of every substance, or because it can be divided into an infinite number of bits; small because portions are smaller than the thing whose portions they are, or because there is no limit on how small the bits of a thing may be. Against this one might object that it makes things large relative not to themselves but to their parts, and makes not them but their parts small. Others[30] suppose Anaxagoras to mean: if you consider each thing not in relation to others, but *just in itself*, you will find it indifferently large *and* small, no more large than small (these predicates only make real sense, or only have real application, in comparisons between two things). But would not Anaxagoras have expressed this point more naturally and perspicuously by writing '*neither* large *nor* small'? I myself am attracted by the reading: if you take each thing as its own *standard*, it will turn out to be both large and small - larger than whatever is smaller than itself, smaller than whatever is larger than itself. I suppose it might be objected against this interpretation that the supplement it requires for 'large' and 'small' is contrary to the expectations aroused by 'with respect to itself'.

But if the precise sense of sentence (v) eludes us, the general intention of the remark is clearer, at any rate in the light of my general account of the fragment. In the first two items of his list, Anaxagoras has been treating the large and the small as opposed classes of object, as though it was in general determinate to which of them any given object belonged (e.g. large: mountains, trees, men, dogs; small: leaves, petals, ants). The third item constitutes a departure from this practice (δέ, 'but'). It concerns objects on their own, i.e. considered not in terms of the comparisons presupposed in the establishment of opposed classes of object called 'the large' and 'the small'. Its point is to confirm the moral of the first two items by suggesting that it is too modest: not only are the large and the small similar in the important ways indicated there, but the very contrast between the large and the small evaporates if one considers objects on their own - for so considered they turn out to be both large and small.

So far we have been concerned with the general purport of Fragment 3 and of the contribution made to its overall object by the individual parts of the fragment. But the chief interest of Fragment 3 lies in the fact that it contains an argument for the proposition that there is no least. We must now turn to examine the relation between sentences (i) and (ii).

Anaxagoras argues: '(i) For of the small there is no least but always a lesser ((ii) for what is cannot not be).' The interpreter's chief problem is to supply the argument, as plausibly and uncontroversially as he can, with some bite. As it stands, sentence (ii) contains nothing but a tepid tautology, to which any atomist could agree.

One popular solution is that of Strang:[31]

'The sort of reason required is: repeated bisection cannot yield a part of zero size (cannot therefore yield a smallest part, i.e. the last part bisected), for *no bisection of something can yield nothing*; it must therefore yield something, which can be further bisected. This is simply a variant of Zeno's dichotomy argument. The crucial step is given by the sentence in italics, which is a direct translation of the τομῇ version [sc. of sentence (ii)], and the rest hardly needs stating.'

There are two main drawbacks to this solution. First, it is improbable that Anaxagoras wrote τομῇ in sentence (ii);[32] and if he did not, there is no clear appearance of the idea of bisection in the text. Secondly, an atomist might in any case feel unmoved by the argument Strang spells out, because he might wish to claim just that a least part of something *cannot* itself be bisected.

If we read the version of (ii) given above, then we must surely declare unpromising any approach which, like Strang's, attempts to find the main weight of argument for the proposition that there is always a lesser in sentence (ii). Truisms have their place in informal argumentation ('Business is business'), but only in counterpoint to more interesting and ambitious lines of thought. It seems more likely that Anaxagoras has in mind some more positive reason for asserting that there is always a lesser, which the truism 'what is cannot not be' is meant to call to mind in the face of the contradictory suggestion: 'there is a least'.

Such a reason has been found by some scholars, following Simplicius's comment on Fragment 3,[33] in Anaxagoras's theory that in everything there is a portion of everything. Professor Furley, for example, interprets the thesis of sentence (i) as a simple deduction from that theory:[34]

> 'What Anaxagoras says can be wholly explained as part of his defence of his principles of latency and predominance. A change from A to B is possible, in his view, only if B is latent in A. So if A is so small that it contains nothing latent in it, it cannot change. Since he apparently wanted to set no limits to change, he had to maintain that there is nothing so small that it can contain nothing latent in it - that is, "there is no least, but always a lesser".'

With such a deduction up his sleeve, Anaxagoras could adduce the truism of sentence (ii) as 'a reminder that a *reductio* argument is readily constructed'[35] against anyone who might be rash enough to try to hold both that in everything there is a portion of everything and that there is a least. For if a least exists it cannot not exist; but if in anything, however small, there is a portion of everything else, then a least does not exist.

Unfortunately the idea that Anaxagoras would have been prepared to defend the thesis that there is no least, but always a lesser, only by deducing it from his mixture theory, is pure speculation.[36] Worse than that, it would involve him in a circularity of reasoning which we ought not without positive grounds to impute to him. For in Fragment 6 Anaxagoras explicitly argues *from* the proposition that there is no least *to* his theory that in everything there is a portion of everything. But what point or plausibility would there be in offering the proposition that there is no least as additional support for his theory, when his reason for holding that proposition is nothing but his acceptance of the theory?

Pace Furley, then, we must suppose Anaxagoras's reason for maintaining that there is no least, but always a lesser, to have been independent of his commitment to the mixture theory. I can suggest only that Anaxagoras took the idea of infinite divisibility or (better) of unlimited smallness to express a deep metaphysical fact about the continuity of the world. And I imagine the reasoning which underlies sentences (i) and (ii) to be something like this:

Suppose someone held that there is a least bit of matter. We can surely conceive of that bit as having parts - some to one side, some to another. But these parts evidently exist no less than the suppositious least bit. Yet that very supposition of a least bit implies their non-existence. That supposition must therefore be mistaken. For what is cannot not be.

My rather Zenonian interpretation is vulnerable, like Furley's, to the objection that it makes sentence (ii) otiose. For on both accounts, the basic reason Anaxagoras has (and wants his reader to share) for holding the proposition advanced in sentence (i) is not that supplied by sentence (ii). On my view, the essential reason is just the self-evident metaphysical appeal of the principle of unlimited smallness; on Furley's it is the mixture theory, or (more precisely) the 'principles of latency and predominance'.[37] Against this objection it has simply to be said that since truisms *are* logically redundant, no more can reasonably be demanded of an interpretation of Fragment 3 than that it give sentence (ii) a plausible *rhetorical* point - as emerged in our discussion of Strang's interpretation.

It should by now be clear to the reader why earlier I settled for an account of sentence (iii) which took its contention that there is always a larger than any given large thing to be supported not by sentence (ii) but by considerations extraneous to Fragment 3. Anaxagoras's positive reason for that contention could not be the bare truism: what is cannot not be. And since the syntax of the fragment does not require it, it seems pointless to try to reconstruct some rhetorical connexion between sentences (ii) and (iii).

To conclude: Fragment 3 remains a frustrating text - at least if one looks in it for something more than the mere assertion (which is perhaps reward enough) that there is no least, but always a lesser. Reconstruction of its overall purport and of the precise meaning of some of its component sentences is necessarily a matter of more or less sanguine conjecture. Most tantalizing of all is the promise of a justification of the principle of unlimited smallness which the bracketed clause: 'for what is cannot not be' seems to hold out only to disappoint. Disappointment, of course, is a function of one's expectations. Fragment 3 serves to remind us of the moral we have derived from Fragments 1 and 12: Anaxagoras is a

more dogmatic, pregnant and rhetorical writer than a philosopher of
a more literate age like Aristotle. His use of γάρ can be more
elliptical and less syllogistic than modern commentators, schooled
in a basically Aristotelian conception of what a philosophical text
should be like, almost automatically assume.

(c) Fragment 6
It is natural next to turn to Fragment 6, which has been invoked
explicitly more than once in the course of our conjectural interpretation of Fragment 3, and tacitly in our suggestion that the proposition which Fragment 3 was written to support said that the small
is no different from the large. In some respects the claims which
Anaxagoras makes in Fragment 6 about infinite divisibility are as
obscure as what he has to say about it in Fragments 1 and 3, but at
least it shows us the nature of one use to which he uncontrovertibly
(if opaquely) puts the idea:

καὶ ὅτε δὲ ἴσαι μοῖραί εἰσι τοῦ τε μεγάλου καὶ τοῦ σμικροῦ
πλῆθος, καὶ οὕτως ἂν εἴη ἐν παντὶ πάντα· οὐδὲ χωρὶς ἔστιν
εἶναι, ἀλλὰ πάντα παντὸς μοῖραν μετέχει. ὅτε τοὐλάχιστον μὴ
ἔστιν εἶναι, οὐκ ἂν δύναιτο χωρισθῆναι, οὐδ' ἂν ἐφ' ἑαυτοῦ
γενέσθαι, ἀλλ' ὅπωσπερ ἀρχὴν εἶναι καὶ νῦν πάντα ὁμοῦ. ἐν πᾶσι
δὲ πολλὰ ἔνεστι καὶ τῶν ἀποκρινομένων ἴσα πλῆθος ἐν τοῖς
μείζοσί τε καὶ ἐλάσσοσι.

(i) And since, too, there are portions equal in number of both
the large and the small, in this way too all things will be in
everything; nor can they exist separately, but all share in a
portion of everything. (ii) Since the least cannot be, none of
them could be separated, nor come to be on its own; but as in
the beginning so too now all things must be together. (iii)
And in all things there are many even of the things that are
separating off, equal in number in both the larger and the
smaller.

Two things emerge plainly from this text. First, Anaxagoras
uses the assumption of the infinite divisibility of matter to argue
his central contention: in everything there is a portion of everything (see sentence (ii) in particular). Second, the expression
'infinite divisibility', natural enough in the comparison with Zeno,
does not capture the focus of Anaxagoras's thought here (nor,

indeed, in Fragment 3). Anaxagoras is concerned with *the small*. His main message is not one about the consequences of infinite divisibility but about the irrelevance of size to complexity of composition.[38]

Sentences (i) and (ii) seem to draw roughly the same inference. Each concludes that there can be no separation and that everything contains a portion of everything else (or, more loosely, that all things are together). Each infers this from a premiss which conjures with the notion of smallness. Let us examine their premisses more closely.

Sentence (i) says (as I suppose; the Greek is ambiguous):

(1) The small is as complex as the large.

In other words, small things contain exactly the same number of component stuffs as do large. In sentence (ii) the premiss is:

(2) There is no least.

In other words, there is no limit on how small a small thing can be.

Anaxagoras does not indicate what logical relationship he supposes there to obtain between (1) and (2). The two propositions are enunciated again, cheek by jowl, in Fragment 3; but there they are linked uninterestingly by καί, 'and'. Thus: after stating (2) at the beginning of Fragment 3, Anaxagoras continues: - ἀλλὰ καὶ τοῦ μεγάλου ἀεί ἐστι μεῖζον. καὶ ἴσον ἐστὶ τῷ σμικρῷ πλῆθος (' - but also there is always a larger than the large. And it is equal in number to the small'). καὶ ἴσον κτλ. (so at least I have suggested) express (1).

If Anaxagoras leaves the logical relationship of (1) and (2) unspecified, he gives us to understand that (1) is for him a more important idea than (2) in the context of his argument for the doctrine of everything in everything.[39] His main message in Fragment 6, as I have said, is that because complexity of composition is not a function of size, we have a reason (further, apparently, to one already given) for holding that in everything there is a portion of everything. The greater importance of (1) emerges in two ways. First, Anaxagoras first announces this additional proof of his central doctrine as an argument from (1) (sentence (i)). Second, he takes care to round it off with a reference to (1) in sentence (iii), when he writes: 'In all things there are many...equal in number in both the larger and the smaller.'

What sort of support does Anaxagoras think (1) gives to his
doctrine of everything in everything? Presumably (1) does not so
much supply an independent positive reason for holding the doctrine
as remove an obstacle to its acceptance.[40] Someone might agree with
Anaxagoras that phenomena such as those of reproduction and nutrition (which he allegedly adduced) suggest that macroscopic, phenomenal things are mixtures, but doubt whether the same is true of
microscopic entities: could not a complex bit of phenomenal stuff be
made up of unmixed microscopic building blocks? If it were, then
mixture would not be a radical fact about the world, as Anaxagoras
believed it to be; and in consequence the κόσμος could one day disintegrate into pure elements, as Anaxagoras was committed to denying. (1) is designed to rule out these possibilities.

That this is its function is confirmed by the argument from (2)
in sentence (ii). In the clause: 'Since the least cannot be, none
of them could be separated nor come to be on its own', Anaxagoras
anticipates an argument for the possibility of the separation of
pure substances along the lines I have just sketched, and denies
what he takes to be presupposed by its conception of the separation
of unmixed microscopic entities - viz. the existence of minima. As
sentence (i) affirms that the microscopic and the macroscopic are
equally complex, so sentence (ii) denies that a necessary condition
of the isolation of microscopic purity is satisfied.[41]

Comparison of the inferences in sentences (i) and (ii) has put
us in a position to consider the logical relationship which Anaxagoras may be presumed to have taken to subsist between their premisses, (1) and (2). One might on this basis be tempted to guess
that he conceived the relationship as a formal one: perhaps

(2) There is no least

is supposed to deny a necessary condition for the possibility of

(Not-1) The small is not as complex as the large.

Anaxagoras's line of thought will then have been that only if there
is a least could a microscopic pure stuff be isolated, and only if a
microscopic pure stuff is isolated will the small differ from the
large in complexity.

Against this interpretation we may object simply that (Not-2)
is not in fact a necessary condition of (Not-1), even supposing we
accept the argument of sentence (ii) that the isolation of a

microscopic pure stuff is contingent on the existence of minima. For microscopic entities *might* conceivably be considerably less complex than phenomenal objects without being altogether pure. It will not do to reply that Anaxagoras himself, in both sentences (i) and (ii), treats the notions that there is a portion of everything in everything (large and small alike) and that pure substances can be separated out as exhaustive alternatives. The fact that he does so shows not that he regarded them formally as the only logical possibilities, but that he conceived them to be the only reasonable options.

This last observation suggests a better account of the relationship which Anaxagoras assumes between (1) and (2). According to this account his idea will have been that if (2) is true, then we have no *reason* not to accept (1). For (by the argument of sentence (ii)) if there is no least, then no pure stuff can be isolated; but if no pure stuff can be isolated, what reason could there be for thinking that the microscopic is not just as complex as the phenomenal? Consider what Anaxagoras could say in support of the claim that to maintain (Not-1) while accepting (2) is unreasonable. He could make a persuasive case for holding that if the microscopic is complex but less complex than the phenomenal, then an implausible instability is introduced into physical theory. For why should the microscopic have this lesser degree of complexity? The only plausible physical reason seems to be that there is some tendency for matter to assume less complex forms than those exhibited by phenomenal objects. But if there were such a tendency, and if it were realized particularly at the microscopic level, what ground could we have for holding that it would not lead to the creation of yet less complex microscopic entities and so eventually to the isolation of pure substances? Suppose that we could find some such reason - suppose, for instance, that the tendency is only superficially described as a tendency to the less complex, but more fundamentally as the disposition of stuffs to coagulate at the microscopic level into distinct groups which - unlike phenomenal objects - do not have all their members in common. Then, contrary to the hypothesis, phenomenal objects would surely tend to acquire the lesser degree of complexity exhibited by their microscopic counterparts.

In such terms Anaxagoras might defend the position that there

are only two reasonable conceptions of the microscopic: either
phenomenal objects are composed of pure minima or they consist of
matter exactly as complex as themselves; any intermediate conception
threatens to collapse into one or other of the extremes. What
matters here is not the particular manoeuvering I hypothetically
attribute to Anaxagoras, but the fact that an argument can be made
for holding the two alternatives which he envisages to be the only
reasonable ones, given certain physical or metaphysical assumptions.
Constructing such argument is, of course, a precarious business: in
order to make Anaxagoras's position reasonable *we* have to *make* it
reasonable.

It is time to sum up these remarks about the argument of Fragment 6
and to set them in a larger context. According to my account, the
supplementary proof which Fragment 6 offers of the thesis that in
everything there is a portion of everything advances no positive
reason for holding it. It rather removes an obstacle to its acceptance. The obstacle in question is the idea that microscopic entities may be pure substances or stuffs, even if macroscopic, phenomenal things are – as Anaxagoras maintains – mixtures. In sentence
(i) Anaxagoras accordingly infers his mixture thesis from a premiss
designed to counter this idea, viz.:

    (1) The small is as complex as the large.

But why should we accept (1)? Anaxagoras indicates his answer in
sentence (ii), where he now derives the impossibility of separation
and the necessity of the mixture of all in all from:

    (2) There is no least.

Only if there is a least, he implies, could a microscopic pure stuff
be isolated; and that condition is not satisfied. Now sentence (ii)
is not advanced explicitly as an explanation or defence of (1). And
this might mislead one into supposing that its purpose is simply to
argue the mixture thesis from infinite divisibility. But then the
relationship between sentences (i) and (ii) would be left unexplained, when Anaxagoras evidently takes them to be making roughly
the same point – and a point more importantly expressed by sentence
(i). We avoid this difficulty if we suppose Anaxagoras's thought to
be that if (2) is true, then there is no reason not to accept (1):
if there is no least, then no microscopic pure stuff can be

isolated; but if no microscopic pure stuff can be isolated, what reason is there for thinking (contrary to (1)) that the microscopic is not just as complex as the phenomenal? To put the matter differently: Anaxagoras conceives that there are only two reasonable alternative theories of mixture. Either pure substances can be separated out or mixture is as thorough at the microscopic as at the phenomenal level. Sentence (i) asserts the latter alternative, taking (1) as its premiss, and concentrating on the positive thesis that all things are in everything. Sentence (ii) says what is needed to make the assertion of (1), and consequently the argument of sentence (i), convincing. It denies the former alternative, concentrating on the negative contention that nothing can be separated out.

We originally embarked on our study of Fragments 3 and 6 in the hope that light would be shed on Anaxagoras's reason for stating the principle that there is no least and applying it to the things in his original mixture at the outset of Fragment 1. Examination of Fragment 3 paid small dividends. But from the way Anaxagoras employs the principle in Fragment 6, we should expect him to have introduced it in Fragment 1 (as was remarked at the beginning of this chapter) in order to emphasize the thoroughness of the primordial mixture, by indicating that however small be the bits into which it may notionally be divisible, each of these would have been a mixture of all things no less than the whole. Our analysis of Fragment 6 has therefore elicited evidence which supports the proportionate interpretation of Fragment 1. The scales tilt a bit further in favour of that interpretation than they seemed to do at the end of the previous section of the chapter.

CONCLUSION

Some Greek philosophical texts, and above all the writings of Aristotle, invite and richly repay exact scrutiny of the kind practised by scholars working in the tradition of contemporary Anglo-American philosophical analysis. Certain Presocratic writers, notably Parmenides and Zeno, surrender at least some of their secrets to probes from the same critical laboratory. It might have been expected that Anaxagoras could be rewardingly anatomized in this same fashion, given his affinities with Zeno in Fragments 3 and 6 and given the presence of some highly abstract *inferences* both in Fragments 3 and 6 and in Fragment 1. We duly prepared a list of questions with which to bombard the texts: e.g. (i) Why, in Fragment 6, does Anaxagoras suppose that the impossibility of separating a pure substance follows from the fact that the large and the small have equal portions? (ii) Why does he go on immediately to derive the same conclusion from the premiss that there is no least? (iii) Why, in Fragment 3, is that premiss itself supported by the truism that what is cannot not be? (iv) What logical connexions does Anaxagoras recognize between these and the various further propositions in Fragment 3, and what are his grounds for asserting the latter? (v) Why, in Fragment 1, does he say that all things in the beginning were unlimited in smallness? (vi) What has this claim to do with the assertion that they were imperceptible on account of smallness? The object of such questions was to clarify the logical structure of Anaxagoras's views about the small. Where he indicates that one proposition supplies a reason for holding another, our aim was to articulate the reasoning more exactly and more explicitly (as in (i), (ii), (iii) and (vi)); where he remains silent on the logical relationship between propositions which he may seem to assume to be connected, our aim was to specify that relationship (as in (ii) again) or to correct the impression (as in (iv)); and where he leaves an important claim undefended, we tried to supply a premiss to which it seems likely that he would have assented, and from which the thesis in question can very plausibly be derived (as in (iv) again and (v)).

But the exercise has achieved no more than limited success. It is not that we could not think of persuasive answers to our questions: we could - indeed we sometimes had difficulty in choosing between eligible rivals (as above all in (iv), (v) and (vi)). It is not that our answers individually made Anaxagoras an illogical or otherwise weak reasoner, or that collectively they attributed to him a circular or confused system of ideas: we found a way to explain how he could support the principle of infinite divisibility appropriately enough by a truism (iii), and to make reasonable his belief that the principle constitutes in its turn a reason for holding the inseparability of pure stuffs (ii); and our account of these two matters saved him from the charge of circularity which must be levelled at other accounts of them. What spoils these successes is, first, the way they have been achieved. They have been secured not by deeper insight into the text of Anaxagoras, but by little more than controlled speculation (a necessary *ingredient*, of course, in any interpretation of any text) about it. Thus in (iii) we took it for granted that no reasonable man would ground a substantial doctrine like the principle of infinite divisibility on a truism, and concluded that Anaxagoras's appeal to his tautology could be only in essence a rhetorical device. Using the *argumentum ex silentio* we then proposed that the principle probably represented simply a metaphysical intuition. In (i) we interpreted Anaxagoras's 'since' (ὅτε) in what we took to be the sense which would make his inference most compelling. And we answered question (ii) on the same principle. A second and related cause for disappointment is the indeterminateness of many of our answers. We often thought we grasped the gist of Anaxagoras's meaning, without knowing exactly what he had in mind. For example, in (iv) it was plausible to suppose that Anaxagoras wanted mainly to reinforce his proposal that the large and the small are in important respects very similar when he said at the end of Fragment 3: 'but with respect to itself each thing is both large and small'. But what exactly he meant by that we shall never know. Nor, more embarrassingly, were we able confidently to settle in (v) what motivated his claim that things were originally unlimited in smallness. Indeed, we were not even sure quite what he meant by 'things' (χρήματα).

Our difficulties are, of course, partly due to the fragmentary character of the evidence. It is only too easy to conceive that our view of Fragment 3, and particularly of question (iv), might be materially, even radically, altered if we were to discover the context in which it was embedded, and if we were to find more of Anaxagoras's original words on any of the points it covers. But this is surely not the whole story. It is hard to believe that we would be much better placed to solve the problems we have been considering in Fragments 1 and 6 (and above all (i), (ii), (v) and (vi)) if we had more of the neighbouring parts of Anaxagoras's book. Fragment 6 looks pretty self-contained; and the sequel to Fragment 1 might have made it clearer what exactly Anaxagoras took to be the denotation of 'all things' (χρήματα πάντα) in his very first sentence, but the evidence of the fragments in general suggests rather that he remained content to write at a level of high generality throughout.

The chief obstacle to analysis is simply Anaxagoras's dogmatic style. Two features of the style are particularly important in this regard. First, despite the inferential particles and the explanatory preposition ὑπὸ ('on account of smallness'), Anaxagoras is not arguing with his reader in the manner of a Plato or an Aristotle, save perhaps when he appeals to the truism in Fragment 3. He is just explaining the way things are. Secondly, he communicates his meaning very broadly, as a teacher often will; and where the thought is particularly difficult (as in Fragment 6), repetitively. It is significant that in each of the three fragments we have examined we found it easier to be sure of the general message being taught than of the meaning and connexions and grounds of their individual parts (contrast, again, what is sometimes true of Aristotle). Thus in Fragment 6 it was clear *that* Anaxagoras was insistently affirming that the principle of a portion of everything in everything was assured by the irrelevance of size to complexity of composition; in Fragment 3 his theme seemed fairly evidently to be the essential similarity of the large and the small; and Fragment 1 communicated forcefully enough his commitment to some very general theses about the nature of the primordial mixture. But we could at best infer a fine structure of rationality beneath the broad sweep of the exposition.

It would be wrong to conclude that we should never have applied the analytical method to the fragments of Anaxagoras in the first place. Our argument has suggested that, while his thinking about smallness may be represented by us as a consistent system (more or less complicated, according to the type of interpretation adopted) of rational beliefs, his own presentation of it comes some way short of fully exhibiting such rationality and consistency: his text is gross-textured and imprecise, although no doubt pregnant. This in itself is an interesting and substantial conclusion, and one which lends no support to any idea that Anaxagoras's thought is marked by a special sort of archaic rationality which is in principle inaccessible to the analytic method. What we do need to bring to our reading of Anaxagoras, besides a quite universal notion of consistency and rationality, is a conception of the rhetorical and didactic devices of style which might naturally be employed by an archaic sage who wished to appeal to a wider circle than that constituted by his own disciples and those of rival sages.

Consider in this light Fragment 6. It would be dangerous to suppose that Anaxagoras penned its argument with oral performance before a general audience principally in mind. But it seems reasonable to suppose that we see here writing still governed by habits associated with oral teaching. Judged by the standards of blackboard formalization or of more purely literary exposition the argument of Fragment 6 is open to harsh criticism. Its logic, as we have seen, is opaque and not fully explicit. It is wordy and repetitious: its second sentence (ii) infers the same conclusion as its first (i) - as (i) concludes that things cannot exist separately (οὐδὲ χωρὶς ἔστιν εἶναι), so does (ii) (οὐκ ἂν δύναιτο χωρισθῆναι οὐδ' ἂν ἐφ' ἑαυτοῦ γενέσθαι), and as (i) couples that conclusion with the positive claim that everything contains a portion of everything (ἂν εἴη ἐν παντὶ πάντα, πάντα παντὸς μοῖραν μετέχει), so too does (ii) in a variant form (καὶ νῦν πάντα ὁμοῦ). Sentence (iii)[42] no longer argues but asserts the positive limb of this same conclusion in yet another variant form (ἐν πᾶσι πολλὰ ἔνεστι); and it incorporates in the fashion of 'ring composition' a reference to the premiss of sentence (i), that the small is as complex as the large (καὶ ὅτε δὲ ἴσαι μοῖραί εἰσι τοῦ τε μεγάλου καὶ τοῦ σμικροῦ πλήθους), naturally in a slightly different form (ἴσα πλῆθος ἐν τοῖς μείζοσί τε καὶ ἐλάσσοσι). But judge these sentences as an informal attempt to present a line of thought as it were to a general *audience*, and they are evidently more successful. Wordiness and repetition turn into an advantage: it is of the essence of oral exposition to repeat oneself, making the same point in slightly different ways and contexts, and introducing qualifications or clarifications or elaborations in the process. The points on which Anaxagoras wishes to lay stress get more time to register themselves, and if there is an ambiguity in one place (should the genitives in the premiss of sentence (i) be taken as possessive or partitive?), it may get ironed out at another (sentence (iii) - ἴσα πλῆθος ἐν τοῖς μείζοσί τε καὶ ἐλάσσοσι - shows that the possessive reading was intended).[43] Nor does one have any difficulty in perceiving what the main message is - that since complexity is no function of size, we need let no scruples about the very small trouble our conviction that all things are in everything. Opacity and inexplicitness of logic, too, are excused by the need to concentrate on the main ideas to be brought into connexion. Anaxagoras's reasoning in the fragment is in fact, as our analysis shows, quite complicated. To have exhibited all that complexity would have been to run the risk of confusing the audience – or rather, readers not yet practised in the art of reading, and any way envisaged by Anaxagoras in the image of an audience.

Le style c'est l'homme; or at any rate we are obliged to suppose so in the case of a thinker, like Anaxagoras, whose manner of thought is accessible to us only through his written words. Analysis of Fragments 1, 3 and 6 accordingly suggests a philosopher whose thinking has not attained analytical precision and clarity, even though sympathetic interpretation may find in it subtlety and a certain architectonic complexity. Should we attribute this lack of analytical quality to a concern on Anaxagoras's part to make himself intelligible to hearers and to readers thought of as having the same needs and expectation as hearers? Or should we rather say that, if Anaxagoras had been fired by a more analytical passion, he would have forged an intelligible analytical style? Probably we should do both: no doubt Anaxagoras's manner of writing and thinking reflects the fact that he was a man of his time; but he might have been a different sort of man of that time, or less of one.

Chapter 4

SEEDS, PORTIONS AND OPPOSITES

ANAXAGORAS'S DEFENCE OF HIS CENTRAL DOCTRINE

From Aristotle on, interpreters of Anaxagoras have been in no doubt that his central doctrine was the thesis that in everything there is a portion of everything. Many of the more interesting contemporary essays on his thought are largely or entirely devoted to the elucidation of that thesis.[1] In this book examination of the thesis has been reserved for the final chapter: partly in recognition of its supreme importance in Anaxagoras's system of ideas - it would be anticlimactic to conclude in any other way; but partly for reasons of evidence. The first of these is that, despite the cardinal role of the doctrine of everything in everything in his philosophy, the fragments which have survived indicate that in his exposition Anaxagoras assigned at least as prominent a place to his account of primordial mixture and to his description of mind and its cosmogonic activity. His book began with the primordial mixture; and his treatment of mind was designed as a magnificent *pièce de résistance*. But we do not know in what manner he introduced the doctrine of everything in everything. There was therefore an obvious advantage to be gained in beginning our enquiry with an examination of what we know to be passages (and so doctrines) of his book on which Anaxagoras laid special weight. A second reason is furnished by the results of our examination of those passages - Fragments 1, 3, 6 and 12. We saw that in them Anaxagoras writes in a didactic (indeed dogmatic) style at a very high level of generality. If one attempts to press a greater degree of specificity and precision on his text, one is constantly frustrated by the multiplicity of possibilities which its ambiguity and indeterminacy leave open. The experience of trying to elicit precise, specific sense from continuous stretches of actual fragments is surely a necessary preparation for the daunting task of interpreting the doctrine of everything in everything, couched as it is in terms of the most extreme generality to which the surviving fragments supply no continuous commentary and

few exegetical clues. The experience of failing or of doubtfully
succeeding is likewise the appropriate check to any sanguine expectation that any single, consistent, determinate, sophisticated
interpretation of the doctrine can be properly fathered upon Anaxagoras himself.

This gloomy reflection is mitigated by evidence that Anaxagoras
supported the doctrine of everything in everything - alone of his
principal doctrines, so far as we can tell - by explicit arguments.
The news is welcome both in itself and because, as we have observed
in previous chapters, explicit arguments supply the guidelines we
need for confident interpretation. Unfortunately, the evidence in
this case is hard to evaluate. I consider first that of the
fragments.

Fragment 6 begins with the words: 'And since, too, there are portions equal in number of both the large and the small, in this way
too all things will be in everything' (καὶ ὅτε δὲ ἴσαι μοῖραί εἰσι
τοῦ τε μεγάλου καὶ τοῦ σμικροῦ πλῆθος, καὶ οὕτως ἂν εἴη ἐν παντὶ
πάντα). Anaxagoras's use of particles here is very naturally taken
as indicating an *additional argument* for his main thesis; and our
analysis of Fragment 6 showed that it could only be a *supplementary*
argument. What, then, was Anaxagoras's principal argument for the
thesis?

Among the Anaxagorean texts preserved by Simplicius there is
only one other that looks as though it might contain an argument for
the thesis that in everything there is a portion of everything.
This is Fragment 4a:

τούτων δὲ οὕτως ἐχόντων χρὴ δοκεῖν ἐνεῖναι πολλά τε καὶ
παντοῖα ἐν πᾶσι τοῖς συγκρινομένοις καὶ σπέρματα πάντων χρημάτων καὶ ἰδέας παντοίας ἔχοντα καὶ χροιὰς καὶ ἡδονάς. καὶ
ἀνθρώπους τε συμπαγῆναι καὶ τὰ ἄλλα ζῷα ὅσα ψυχὴν ἔχει. καὶ
τοῖς γε ἀνθρώποισιν εἶναι καὶ πόλεις συνῳκημένας καὶ ἔργα κατεσκευασμένα, ὥσπερ παρ' ἡμῖν, καὶ ἡέλιόν τε αὐτοῖσιν εἶναι καὶ
σελήνην καὶ τὰ ἄλλα, ὥσπερ παρ' ἡμῖν, καὶ τὴν γῆν αὐτοῖσι φύειν
πολλά τε καὶ παντοῖα, ὧν ἐκεῖνοι τὰ ὀνῆστα συνενεγκάμενοι εἰς
τὴν οἴκησιν χρῶνται. ταῦτα μὲν οὖν μοι λέλεκται περὶ τῆς ἀποκρίσιος, ὅτι οὐκ ἂν παρ' ἡμῖν μόνον ἀποκριθείη, ἀλλὰ καὶ ἄλλῃ.

These things being so, it is right to think that there were, in

all the things that were being put together, many things, of
all kinds, and seeds of all things - [seeds] having forms and
colours and savours of every kind. And [sc. these things being
so, it is right to think that] men were compounded and the
other living creatures that have soul; and that by the men
cities were settled, and farms established, as is the case with
us, and that they have a sun and moon and the rest, as is the
case with us, and that the earth grows much of every variety
for them, of which they collect what is useful into their
dwelling and make use of it. This, then, is my doctrine about
the separation: that the separation would take place not only
with us, but elsewhere too. (Furley's translation,[2] slightly
modified)

This fascinating and tantalizing fragment has been variously understood; and there is no sign of an incipient scholarly consensus about the crucial question: does Anaxagoras here - and particularly in the last sentence - commit himself to an *actual* plurality of worlds (or of civilizations in the one world)?[3] I myself favour the negative answer of Fränkel and Vlastos,[4] according to which we should construe that last sentence as a true potential, entertaining no more than a hypothesis: 'The separation [sc. just such a separation as in fact produced our world] would take place not only [as it has done] with us, but elsewhere too [if mind were to act upon some part of our world's infinite surrounding envelope - τὸ περιέχον - which is not yet drawn into the cosmic rotation, but still exists in the condition of primordial mixture].' We then have to read the preceding part of the fragment as premissed on the assumption (presumably enunciated in the lost passage summarized by: 'These things being so'): let us suppose that mind *did* so act on some other part of the primordial mixture. And we take it as a description of the origin and full development of that hypothetical world - a description whose categorical verbs (above all χρῶνται,[5] 'make use of') indicate only that Anaxagoras preferred, no doubt for stylistic and rhetorical reasons, to paint his hypothetical cosmogony as actually coming about, stage by stage, rather than to sustain a less vivid sequence of potential infinitives.

Fortunately Anaxagoras's chief message in Fragment 4a remains the same on either construction of his attitude here to plurality of

worlds. His point is that, if mind were to set in train another
separation, then that separation would *not* produce an alternative
set of effects, a different sort of κόσμος: it would result in a
world exactly the same as ours, right down to the specific institutions of farming and city life. For this point it does not matter
whether mind has caused or will cause another cosmogony, or whether
the speculation is merely hypothetical - except, of course, insofar
as we are concerned with issues of verification and falsification
which do not seem to have troubled Anaxagoras. Anaxagoras is content merely to declare that this is how things must be or would be.
As Vlastos has suggested, Fragment 4a seems to constitute in essence
nothing but an arresting way of asserting, and not of proving, that
'the cosmic antecedents named in his theory [viz. Mind at work on
a primordial mixture of the correct, Anaxagorean, specification]
were the necessary and sufficient conditions of all that came thereafter, from sun to horticulture'.[6]

Our present interest in Fragment 4a is confined to its first
sentence, which asserts a version of the doctrine of everything in
everything when it says: 'it is right to think that there were, in
all the things which were being put together, many things, of all
kinds, and seeds of all things'. It asserts it, of course, about
some supposed second world besides our own; but that does not
matter, since (as we have seen) the point is that such a world must
be just like ours. It asserts it, too, in the past tense - at any
rate according to my interpretation of the indeterminate infinitive
of Anaxagoras's *oratio obliqua* (I assume that it is reasonable to
posit a tense analogous to the aorist συμπαγῆναι in the next sentence, particularly since seeds are chronologically prior to men).
But this, again, does not matter, because Anaxagoras is committed to
the view that at *any* time subsequent to the beginning of the cosmogony it remains true that in everything there is a portion of everything. So the tense could as well be the present in which the
thesis is usually stated. The sentence says: 'it is right to think
that...'. Why so? Because 'these things [are] so' (τούτων δὲ οὕτως
ἐχόντων): i.e., according to our general account of the fragment,
because mind (hypothetically or actually) got to work on some part
of the primordial mixture other than that exploited in the making of
our world. If we again discount Anaxagoras's concern here with a

duplicate world, we can extract the general claim that, *given* the action of mind on the primordial mixture, there results a world in which it is true that there is in everything a portion of everything.

It might perhaps appear that Anaxagoras at the beginning of Fragment 4a therefore indicates a reason for holding his central doctrine, viz. that if there was once a primordial mixture of the sort he describes, and if that mixture was subject to the sort of cosmic rotation which he says was started by mind, then we should accept that all things will in an important sense always remain mixed - in everything a portion of everything. It is because such an interpretation might suggest itself to the reader that I have included discussion of Fragment 4a at this point: perhaps we have here Anaxagoras's main ground for asserting the doctrine of everything in everything. But the suggestion is not very plausible. In Fragment 4a Anaxagoras is not (as conceivably he is in Fragment 6) presenting reasons why some thesis or theses of his system should be accepted in the first place. He is rather asserting a property of the system as already developed and expounded, namely, that from its original state (primordial mixture) and its initial separating device (the rotation caused by mind), everything else follows.

We should not go on to infer that the words καὶ οὕτως of Fragment 6 ('in this way too'), if they imply a preceding argument for the doctrine of everything in everything, could not be looking back to Fragment 4a. For Anaxagoras could in Fragment 6 be adding support *either* to a demonstration altogether internal to his system (as Fragment 4a is) *or* to what one might call dialectical persuasion - i.e. to an argument which appeals to evidence or common sense or metaphysical intuition. Yet a connexion with Fragment 4a is unlikely. For καὶ οὕτως leads us to expect a preceding text concerned principally with mixture and the presence of all things in all. But Fragment 4a is, on the contrary, a passage which defends Anaxagoras's general view of separation - its reference to the mixture thesis is subordinated to that general theme.

It is in any case doubtful that καὶ οὕτως *does* imply an immediately preceding *argument* for the doctrine of everything in everything, more important than the one contained in Fragment 6 itself. An alternative possibility can best be indicated and given plausibility by considering the idea that what preceded Fragment 6 in Anaxagoras's book was Fragment 8, so that the text ran:

> οὐ κεχώρισται ἀλλήλων τὰ ἐν τῷ ἑνὶ κόσμῳ οὐδὲ ἀποκέκοπται πελέκει οὔτε τὸ θερμὸν ἀπὸ τοῦ ψυχροῦ οὔτε τὸ ψυχρὸν ἀπὸ τοῦ θερμοῦ. καὶ ὅτε δὲ ἴσαι μοῖραί εἰσι τοῦ τε μεγάλου καὶ τοῦ σμικροῦ πλῆθος, καὶ οὕτως ἂν εἴη ἐν παντὶ πάντα· οὐδὲ χωρὶς ἔστιν εἶναι, ἀλλὰ πάντα παντὸς μοῖραν μετέχει.
>
> The things in the one world-order have not been separated apart from each other, nor yet chopped apart with an axe, neither the hot from the cold nor the cold from the hot. And since, too, there are portions equal in number of both the large and the small, in this way too all things will be in everything; nor yet can they exist separately, but all share in a portion of everything.

The two fragments fit easily together. Both are concerned to deny radical separation; Fragment 8 states what is true of hot and cold, one pair of opposites, Fragment 6 appeals to what is true of another, large and small. The only difficulty is that, if we were looking for a principal *argument* for the doctrine of everything in everything, Fragment 8 must disappoint us. It is flatly an *assertion* about the inseparability of things, although no doubt Anaxagoras hopes that consultation of our experience will help us to assent to what he says about hot and cold. But must the καὶ οὕτως of Fragment 6 ('in this way too') imply a prior argument? Surely it is enough that Anaxagoras should have affirmed simply *that* the doctrine of everything in everything applies to entities such as the hot and the cold which on any reckoning are *fundamental* in his scheme of things (see, for example, their role in cosmic and meteorological separation: Fragments 12, 15, 16). With 'in this way too' in Fragment 6 he may then be read as claiming *that* the doctrine applies *in another way too*, viz. at the level of the very small indicated by his speaking of 'portions...of both the large *and the small*'. This mode of application can be taken as less fundamental inasmuch as there would be no question of discussing the *level* at which the doctrine applied, large or small, if it was not first established that it did actually apply to things – in the manner indicated in Fragment 8.

So much for evidence in the fragments of arguments for the doctrine of everything in everything. The secondary sources give pride of place to another line of argument. As we saw in Chapter 2, Aristotle ascribes to Anaxagoras the view that everything is mixed in everything because anything can come to be from anything.[7] And he and the doxographical tradition (with which I associate the scholium on Gregory of Nazianzus, rashly printed by Diels in his B section, as supposedly containing an actual fragment of Anaxagoras)[8] give the impression that it was particularly (although not exclusively) the biological phenomena of reproduction and nutrition which led Anaxagoras to hold this view. According to the tradition, Anaxagoras observed that from the bread we eat and the water we drink comes the nourishment which sustains the many diverse parts of our bodies and makes them grow - hair, flesh, bones, nails, veins and so on. But, as the scholiast's Anaxagoras asks: 'How could hair come to be from not-hair, or flesh from not-flesh?' There must, then, be hair, flesh, bones and the rest already in bread and water, and in the very sperm which originated our existence; and if the constituents of bread and water can be shown by such simple reflection to be so varied, is it safe to deny of *any* basic sort of stuff that it is a constituent of them and indeed of everything else?

This Aristotelian and doxographical evidence is often accepted by scholars without question as reliable testimony of Anaxagoras's main argument for his central doctrine. But its reliability needs testing, both because of its secondary status and because of the notorious fallibility of Aristotle and the doxographers as reporters and interpreters of Plato and the Presocratics. We should be particularly cautious before we endorse secondary evidence which commits us to attributing a major argument to Anaxagoras, whom we have seen to be so sparing in his provision of arguments. Moreover, examination of the fragments preserved in Simplicius might lead one to doubt the credibility of witnesses who would make consideration of biological phenomena so important for Anaxagoras's physical theory. Simplicius recorded his extracts from Anaxagoras's book specifically for the purpose of illustrating Aristotle's account of him (principally in the *Physics*) and its weaknesses. It is therefore particularly interesting and significant that the Simplician fragments contain little which suggests an especially biological orientation in the physical theory, and that they supply no direct, unequivocal evidence that Anaxagoras put living tissues among the elements (i.e. basic components) of the physical world - although Simplicius fails to remark upon this himself.[9] The chief impression which the fragments do communicate is rather of a cosmogony and meteorology along traditional Ionian lines, but rethought in terms of a subtle and complex theory of mixture, and of a rigorously physical notion of separation, conceived as the effect of causal (albeit psychological) agency.

In the next section of the chapter I propose to work out an interpretation of the doctrine of everything in everything which exploits only the fragments themselves and such secondary evidence as fills out, without introducing radically new features, the picture of Anaxagoras's position one might naturally derive from the fragments. We shall find reasons for supposing that the 'things' to which the doctrine applies were envisaged primarily as opposites, and not in the first instance as including ὁμοιομερῆ, 'homoeomerous stuffs' (the genus of which tissues like flesh, bone, etc., are members) as such. This interpretation will obviously, therefore, discount or at least play down the Aristotelian and doxographical evidence which we have been noticing. I shall then go on to ask whether there is anything in the fragments pertinent to the doctrine which is left unexplained or inadequately explained by the interpretation, and whether our confidence in it is high enough to warrant setting such small store by what Aristotle and the doxographers tell us.

PORTIONS AND OPPOSITES

'All things were together', says Anaxagoras of the original state of the world (Fragment 1, ὁμοῦ χρήματα πάντα ἦν). He conceives that all matter was mixed together to form a more or less homogeneous, indistinct mass. Mind intervened to set this mass in rotation. The ensuing revolution caused one sort of matter to separate off from the other: the dense from the rare, the hot from the cold, the clear from the murky, the dry from the wet (Fragment 12). The dense, wet, cold, murky matter gathered here, at the centre of the revolution, where the earth now is (for, of course, the predominant dense, wet, cold, murky stuff in the universe *is* earth); and the rare, hot, dry matter receded to the further region of the aither (or upper air) (Fragment 15). But the separation of the opposites is never complete (Fragments 8, 12). And this is doubtless the general reason why there remain in the heavens bodies such as the sun, moon, and stars, which revolve no less than the air and aither that are the main participants in the continuing rotation (Fragment 12). It is probably also the general factor responsible for the constancy of meteorological phenomena. For example, it is only because the air retains a certain density that it can be further rarified by the heat of the sun to form winds (A1 (9); A42 (11)); and clouds cannot be wholly wet, or else they would actually be the rain which is separated off from them (Fragment 16).[10]

In a sense, then, it is true for Anaxagoras that 'as it was in the beginning, so also now all things are together' (Fragment 6, ὅπωσπερ ἀρχὴν εἶναι καὶ νῦν πάντα ὁμοῦ). In a sense it is not true, since in the beginning the mixture was so homogeneous that nothing could be distinguished by the eye (Fragment 1, καὶ πάντων ὁμοῦ ἐόντων οὐδὲν ἔνδηλον ἦν ὑπὸ σμικρότητος), whereas now things are separated out (Fragments 12 and 13). Anaxagoras gives expression to both viewpoints in his theory of mixture, which is his own original contribution to the Ionian philosophical account of the natural world. At the heart of the theory stands the mysterious metaphysical thesis, often repeated, that 'in everything there is a portion of everything' (Fragments 6, 11, 12: ἐν παντὶ παντὸς μοῖρα): Thesis 1. But it is qualified by the claim that the predominant ingredients in a substance are responsible for its manifest features (Fragment 12 *ad fin.*: 'Each thing is most manifestly those of which there are the most in it'; ἀλλ' ὅτων πλεῖστα ἔνι, ταῦτα ἐνδηλότατα ἓν ἕκαστόν ἐστι): Thesis 2. Thesis 2 explains how, though Thesis 1 be true, one thing in our present world can be manifestly different from another: the portions which predominate in it are different from those which predominate in the other thing.

Theses 1 and 2 suggest an ontology of *substances* and *ingredients*.[11] *Substances* are individual, directly individuatable bits of matter, which possess *ingredients* of every sort (Thesis 1), but manifest only those which predominate in them (Thesis 2). *Ingredients* are more obscure: they are what *substances* are made of; and whether simple or complex, presumably (on pain of a regress) they differ from *substances* in not themselves possessing *ingredients* (i.e. Theses 1 and 2 are not true of them).[12] Such an ontology leaves open the possibility of an account of the physical status of *ingredients* compatible with modern concepts of matter. It is consistent with (for example) our belief that the water in the tap is composed largely of elementary microscopic particles whose molecular structure is that conventionally symbolized as H_2O. (We do not also believe that it contains also microscopic particles of every other stuff; but that is beside the present point.) There is, however, a third proposition maintained by Anaxagoras which excludes this possibility that, in his ontology, *ingredients* could be elementary particles. In Fragment 6 he asserts that the small contains exactly as many portions as the large (ἴσαι μοῖραί εἰσι τοῦ τε μεγάλου καὶ τοῦ σμικροῦ πλῆθος; ἐν πᾶσι δὲ πολλὰ ἔνεστι...ἴσα πλῆθος ἐν τοῖς μείζοσί τε καὶ ἐλάσσοσι); or as we could put it, following a formulation of Colin Strang,[13] 'structural complexity is not a function of size': Thesis 3. Thesis 3, conjoined with Theses 1 and 2, entails that however small you divide matter up, you will always, even if you employ a microscope, find *substances* - i.e. entities of which Theses 1 and 2 are true. *Ingredients*, therefore, cannot be elementary particles or elementary microscopic pieces of matter.

Even though the status of *ingredients* remains so far mysterious, it is already possible to see that Anaxagoras's ontological scheme can readily be interpreted in such a way as to capture well our prescientific thoughts about the composition of many of the stuffs with which we are most familiar. Consider, for example, a cup of sweet, black coffee.[14] Pre-scientific common sense agrees with Anaxagoras that this stuff contains *ingredients* - in fact, portions of coffee-bean extract and water and sugar. Common sense similarly agrees with him that, however minute the quantities into which the liquid is divided, there is no prospect of reaching pure particles of water or sugar or coffee-bean extract - they will remain quantities of sweet black coffee, or some of them (perhaps) wet, half-dissolved, coffee-stained sugar. And if common sense could be got to concede the likelihood of there being all sorts of impurities in the materials of which the cup of coffee was made, then no doubt it would agree likewise that the liquid contains a large number of other *ingredients* besides those we have named, and that its

manifest characteristics are due to its predominant *ingredients*.
(The ancient Greeks had no coffee, but they did dilute their wine
with water.)

Anaxagoras supposes that Theses 1, 2 and 3 hold throughout all
time. Although the cosmic revolution gains ever greater sway and
causes more and more separation, and although (as Strang points
out[15]) 'Anaxagoras's favourite term for substances is τὰ ἀποκρινόμενα ("the things that are separated off")', the process of
separation which makes different *ingredients* predominate in different areas of the universe is never complete: παντάπασι δὲ οὐδὲν
ἀποκρίνεται ('nothing is altogether separated off', Fragment 12; cf.
Fragment 8).[16] Anaxagoras offers an argument for this contention in
Fragment 6. He undertakes in effect to show that if at any time the
world is made up of *substances* (i.e. individual bits of matter of
which Theses 1 and 2 are true) which satisfy Thesis 3, then complete
separation of the *ingredients* of these *substances* will never at any
later time be possible. His proof is obscure, but in Chapter 3 I
have suggested that he thinks that no separating process could get a
purchase on matter in such a way as to separate *ingredients* off from
a *substance* in pure form, unless the *substance* already contained
within it minima consisting each of a single pure ingredient – a
hypothesis excluded by Thesis 3.

Anaxagoras's second individual contribution to Ionian physical
speculation consists in his reduction of all forms of change to the
physical processes of combination and separation,[17] and in his making all combination and separation directly or indirectly contingent
on locomotion. There would have been no combination and separation
without the rotatory motion set in train by the cosmogonical act of
mind; and that rotation was directly responsible for the original
separation of opposite sorts of stuff:

ἡ δὲ περιχώρησις αὐτὴ ἐποίησεν ἀποκρίνεσθαι. καὶ ἀποκρίνεται
ἀπό τε τοῦ ἀραιοῦ τὸ πυκνὸν καὶ ἀπὸ τοῦ ψυχροῦ τὸ θερμὸν καὶ
ἀπὸ τοῦ ζοφεροῦ τὸ λαμπρὸν καὶ ἀπὸ τοῦ διεροῦ τὸ ξηρόν.
(Fragment 12)
The rotation itself caused separation. And the dense is separated off from the rare, and the hot from the cold and the clear
from the murky, and the dry from the wet.

Birth and death are nothing but combination and separation; and no doubt the same goes for less radical forms of alteration:

> τὸ δὲ γίνεσθαι καὶ ἀπόλλυσθαι οὐκ ὀρθῶς νομίζουσιν οἱ "Ελληνες·
> οὐδὲν γὰρ χρῆμα γίνεται οὐδὲ ἀπόλλυται, ἀλλ' ἀπὸ ἐόντων χρημάτων συμμίσγεταί τε καὶ διακρίνεται. καὶ οὕτως ἂν ὀρθῶς καλοῖεν
> τό τε γίνεσθαι συμμίσγεσθαι καὶ τὸ ἀπόλλυσθαι διακρίνεσθαι.
> (Fragment 17)
> The Greeks have an incorrect belief in coming to be and perishing; for nothing comes to be or perishes, but it is mingled together from things that are and separated [into them]. Thus it would be correct of them to call coming to be 'mingling together' and perishing 'being separated'.

This simple theory of change is tailored exactly and economically to the ontology of *substances* and *ingredients*. What we wish to explain is why *substances* come to be, change, and perish. The general form of the answer is simply that the ratios of the *ingredients* in *substances* get altered through the redistribution caused by separation and combination of those *ingredients*. *Ingredients* take on extra work: they help to explain not only why *substances* have the distinctive characteristics which they do (Thesis 2), but also why they come to be and change and perish. Anaxagoras hints at this in the sentence where he states Thesis 2, which reads in full: 'Each thing is *and was* most manifestly those of which there are [*and were*] most in it' (Fragment 12 ad fin.; ἀλλ' ὅτων πλεῖστα ἔνι, ταῦτα ἐνδηλότατα ἓν ἕκαστόν ἐστι κ α ὶ ἦ ν). What can be the point of 'and was' but to indicate that *change* of manifest characteristics is simply change in predominant *ingredients*? What suggestion could be less unexpected at the end of a passage about separation whose beginning we have already quoted ('The rotation itself caused separation...'), and which continued:

> μοῖραι δὲ πολλαὶ πολλῶν εἰσι. παντάπασι δὲ οὐδὲν ἀποκρίνεται οὐδὲ διακρίνεται ἕτερον ἀπὸ τοῦ ἑτέρου πλὴν νοῦ.
> But there are many portions of many things. And nothing is completely separated off nor distinguished[18] the one from the other, except mind.

This last text, read in context, promises to throw light on the identity of Anaxagoras's *ingredients*, a topic which we have so far avoided. It is natural to take him to be checking an inference which might be drawn from his immediately preceding assertion that the rotation makes the dense separate off from the rare, the hot from the cold, etc. Those words might suggest that in the world produced by the rotation there are some areas occupied entirely by the hot, others entirely by the cold, others again wholly by the dense, others yet again by just the rare. This is the suggestion Anaxagoras appears to be blocking in the text quoted above: in anything or in any area of the universe there are always *many ingredients* - rare things will always have many characteristics other than their rare texture, e.g. heat, warmth, dryness; and nowhere is any ingredient entirely separated off from its opposite - so the rare will always be mixed with at least a little of the dense, the hot with at any rate some cold. The reading of 'But there are...except mind' we thus propose indicates in its turn a plausible interpretation of the last sentence of Fragment 12: 'Each thing is and was most manifestly those of which there are [and were] most in it.' Anaxagoras will have meant that each thing manifests most those *opposites* which predominate in it.[19]

Against the proposal that the portions envisaged in Fragment 12 are opposites it might be objected that when Anaxagoras says 'the dense is separated off from the rare' etc., he means that dense *substances* (collectively) are separated off from rare *substances* (collectively). But the proposal requires that 'the dense' and 'the rare' and so on denote not *substances* but *ingredients*. So it seems that we are confronted with the unfortunate choice of accepting the proposal, but admitting that it imputes to Anaxagoras an ambiguity or at least a silent and perhaps unconscious slide from one use of opposite terms to another;[20] or else of rejecting the proposal, at the cost of leaving the identity of the portions and of what is said never to be wholly separated off quite indeterminate, despite the reference to the separation of the dense from the rare, etc., immediately before.

The objection is easily resisted. To suppose that 'the dense' refers to dense *substances* (collectively) is too narrow and tendentious an interpretation. Anaxagoras simply means that dense matter is separated off from rare matter, hot from cold, etc. We can take 'matter' here as denoting *substance* stuff and *ingredient* stuff indeterminately: probably Anaxagoras did not intend one denotation rather than the other; and in any case - what matters for the

proposal - if dense *substances* separate off from rare, it follows
(by Thesis 2) that different areas of the universe become dominated
some by dense, others by rare *ingredients*. So when Anaxagoras continues by saying that 'there are many portions of many things', we
can cheerfully interpret this as meaning that in anything there are
many *ingredients* such as the dense (i.e. dense matter) and the cold
(i.e. cold matter), without fear of ambiguity, or at any rate of
significant ambiguity.[21]

This interpretation of Anaxagoras's portions gains support from
other texts among the fragments.[22] For example, other passages besides Fragment 12 *ad fin.* testify that the denial of separation (or
total separation) is closely tied to Thesis 1 and so is naturally
read as a rejection of the idea that *ingredients* can be completely
separated from one another: e.g. Fragment 6, 'Nor yet can they exist
separately, but all share in a portion of everything' (οὐδὲ χωρὶς
ἔστιν εἶναι, ἀλλὰ πάντα παντὸς μοῖραν μετέχει); Fragment 12 *ad init.*
'The others share in a portion of everything, but mind...is not
mixed with anything' (τὰ μὲν ἄλλα παντὸς μοῖραν μετέχει, νοῦς δέ...
μέμεικται οὐδενὶ χρήματι). But the most striking of all Anaxagoras's pronouncements against total separation concerns opposites:

οὐ κεχώρισται ἀλλήλων τὰ ἐν τῷ ἑνὶ κόσμῳ οὐδὲ ἀποκέκοπται
πελέκει οὔτε τὸ θερμὸν ἀπὸ τοῦ ψυχροῦ οὔτε τὸ ψυχρὸν ἀπὸ τοῦ
θερμοῦ. (Fragment 8)

The things in the one world-order have not been separated, nor
yet have they been chopped apart with an axe, neither the hot
from the cold nor the cold from the hot.

Probably, as in Fragments 4b, 12, 15, 'the hot' and 'the cold' refer
to hot matter and cold matter respectively; perhaps Anaxagoras is
again thinking indeterminately of *substance* stuff and *ingredient*
stuff. The claim of Fragment 8 must, however, be understood in the
light of the texts which we have quoted from Fragments 6 and 12; and
the theory upon which these texts all draw entails that it is in the
first instance *ingredients* or portions which are inseparable from
one another. Fragment 8, therefore, points to the opposites as
Anaxagoras's *ingredients*.

Consider, too, texts which testify to the general pattern of
change in cosmogony and meteorology. In Fragment 16 Anaxagoras
says:

ἀπὸ τουτέων ἀποκρινομένων συμπήγνυται γῆ· ἐκ μὲν γὰρ τῶν
νεφελῶν ὕδωρ ἀποκρίνεται, ἐκ δὲ τοῦ ὕδατος γῆ, ἐκ δὲ τῆς γῆς
λίθοι συμπήγνυνται ὑπὸ τοῦ ψυχροῦ, οὗτοι δὲ ἐκχωρέουσι μᾶλλον
τοῦ ὕδατος.

From these things being separated off earth is compacted; for
from the clouds water is separated off, and from the water
earth. And from earth stones are compacted by the cold (but
these move outwards [? to the outer part of the aither] more
than the water[23]).

Why does this process occur? Presumably because the pattern of
change first manifested in the cosmogony persists (notice the present tense of ἀποκρίνεται, 'is separated off', in Fragment 12: 'the
dense *is* separated off from the rare, etc.'; cf. Fragment 2). We
are told what that pattern was in Fragment 15:

τὸ μὲν πυκνὸν καὶ διερὸν καὶ ψυχρὸν καὶ τὸ ζοφερὸν ἐνθάδε·
συνεχώρησεν, ἔνθα νῦν ⟨ἡ⟩ γῆ, τὸ δὲ ἀραιὸν καὶ τὸ θερμὸν καὶ
τὸ ξηρὸν ἐξεχώρησεν εἰς τὸ πρόσω τοῦ αἰθέρος.

The dense and wet and cold and the murky collected here, where
the earth now is,[24] but the rare and the hot and the dry went
out into the further reach of the aither.

This pattern, applied to the changes specified in Fragment 16,
yields the following story: *substances* such as clouds, which are
away from the earth but manifestly more dense, wet, cold and murky
than not, will tend to change into *substances* which are closer to
the earth - such as falling rain - and still more obviously dense,
wet, cold and murky. Two consequences follow. First, insofar as
Fragment 15 suggests a general pattern of *change* - which is what we
require for interpretation of Fragment 16 - then 'the dense...and
murky' and 'the rare...and the dry' cannot be taken as collective
references to bodies or *substances*. For a statement about the
downwards or upwards *locomotion* of *substances* could not constitute
a description or explanation of the *changes* which substances
undergo - of the way in which clouds turn into rain, rain into
earth, and so on. We must take those expressions as specifying
ingredients, for change, according to Anaxagoras, is a matter of the
redistribution of *ingredients*. Anaxagoras's idea will be that in a
rotation, dense, wet, cold and murky *ingredient* stuffs cause whatever they dominate to adopt forms which manifest their presence in

ever greater concentrations, unless they are checked by other
forces. Secondly, insofar as Fragment 15 (and indeed the reference
to the separation of opposites in Fragments 8 and 12) suggests a
general and fundamental pattern of change, then *ingredients* which
are opposites, or are called by the names of opposites, must be
recognized as playing a more general and fundamental causal role in
Anaxagoras's physical theory than any other sorts of *ingredient* he
may have envisaged - e.g. (if we follow Aristotle) *ingredients* bearing the names of specific stuffs, such as 'gold' or 'flesh'. In
Fragment 16, for example, his very diagnosis of a single causal
pattern in the series of changes which he instances (water from
clouds, earth from water, stones from earth) requires that the
ingredients redistributed in the course of those changes be identified primarily in the same terms throughout - not as now cloud, now
water, now earth, etc., but as the dense, the rare, the cold, the
hot, etc.

We are presently concerned with the character of Anaxagoras's
philosophy as it emerges from the fragments alone, without assistance or interference from the doxographical evidence. But it is
only rational to point out[25] that there exists unimpeachable evidence that Anaxagoras invoked *ingredients* identified as opposites in
explaining sense perception (A92):

ἀλλὰ τῷ μὲν θερμῷ τὸ ψυχρόν, τῷ δ' ἁλμυρῷ τὸ ποτιμόν, τῷ
δ' ὀξεῖ τὸ γλυκὺ [γνωρίζειν] κατὰ τὴν ἔλλειψιν τὴν ἑκάστου·
πάντα γὰρ ἐνυπάρχειν φησὶν ἐν ἡμῖν.

We discern the cold by the hot, the drinkable by the brackish,
the sweet by the pungent, according as we are deficient in
each. For, he says, they are all present in us.

Admittedly the word 'portions' (μοῖραι) does not appear here, but
the verb 'be present in' (ἐνυπάρχειν) is the word Aristotle uses in
paraphrasing Anaxagoras's doctrine of portions (e.g. *Phys.* I 4,
187a32, 37).

It is often suggested that any acceptable interpretation of
Anaxagoras's Thesis 1 must satisfy the requirement that the expression 'everything' must (a) be understood absolutely generally,
(b) be allowed to take exactly the same range of values in each of
its occurrences ('in *everything* there is a portion of *everything*').
Could an interpretation of Anaxagoras which construed his portions

or *ingredients* as identified *solely* in terms of opposites meet this requirement? Yes,[26] it could. There is evidently no problem about its ability to meet condition (b). Applications of Thesis 1 will always have the form: 'In the hot there is a portion of the hot and of every other opposite', or more generally: 'In the F there is a portion of the F and of every other opposite', where 'F' stands for any given opposite. What of condition (a)? Obviously there is a sense in which the interpretation does not understand 'everything' in a perfectly general way. For to restrict the values it takes to opposite terms is to deny that other sorts of term, with a vast number of instances, are envisaged by Anaxagoras: e.g. sortals (such as 'man', 'tree') and mass terms (such as 'water', 'flesh'). But there is a ready defence available to the interpretation.[27] What it must do is argue that the sensible world can be described completely and adequately in terms solely of opposites; and that any other ways of describing the world - e.g. by using sortals and mass terms - are parasitic on the vocabulary of opposites, and are to be treated as introducing nothing but epiphenomena, or logical constructions out of opposites. Such a position lies close to the perennially attractive view that the external world presents itself directly and fundamentally only in the form of sensible qualities. It adds the idea that sensible qualities always fall within quality ranges which are specified in terms of opposites - the hot and the cold, the wet and the dry, and so on.

It would be idle to pretend that in the fragments Anaxagoras explicitly treats items such as men, trees, earth and water as logical constructions out of opposites. But our analysis of Fragment 16 suggests that some such account is presupposed by him at any rate for *substances* that change in accordance with the general pattern of separation (indicated in Fragments 12 and 15) caused by the cosmic rotation. The causal sequence he describes in Fragment 16 implies (if our analysis is correct) that water, for example, is in essence nothing but stuff in which the dense, the wet, the cold and the murky predominate - to a greater degree than they do in clouds, but less than in earth or stones.[28] According to the interpretation of Thesis 1 which we are considering, *every substance* called by a mass or a sortal term, or in general by any term not signifying an opposite, must be construed as a mixture of opposites in different ratios.

An interpretation which takes Anaxagorean portions or *ingredients* to be opposites has considerable epistemological and ontological advantages over one which, as the doxographical tradition did, identifies them primarily as the denotations of mass terms - or ὁμοιομερῆ. Consider, first, the following epistemological objection, canvassed (but not endorsed) by Barnes,[29] to *ingredients* conceived as ὁμοιομερῆ:

'It will not do to define earth by way of [Thesis 2], saying that *a* is earth if and only if *a* is a lump of stuff in which earth predominates. Such a definition is vainly circular. And if we evade the circle by putting subscripts to the term "earth" - "*a* is $earth_1$ if and only if *a* is a lump of stuff in which $earth_2$ predominates" - then "$earth_2$" remains unexplained. If $earth_2$ is elemental, it cannot be explained in terms of any components; and since $earth_2$ is never present in the world [sc. as a *substance*], we cannot learn the meaning of "$earth_2$" by "ostensive definition". In short, "earth", or "$earth_2$" if you prefer, is a bogus term: it has no use in science.'

This argument proceeds from an illicit assumption which, were it valid, would have devastating consequences. It assumes that we can explain the meaning of a term only if either we can analyse what it denotes into components or we can give an ostensive definition of it. Yet if this were so, the modern physicist or chemist would be in no position to explain the elements of modern physical science. The assumption is, of course, wrong: there are many ways of explaining the meanings of words besides the two envisaged in the objection; and a language which consisted solely of words which could be explained by those two methods alone would be so impoverished as to be useless for most practical and all scientific purposes. The question, then, is: could an Anaxagorean who construed *ingredients* as ὁμοιομερῆ avail himself of a mode of explanation alternative to the two envisaged in the objection?

The answer seems to be that he could do so only at the cost of renouncing his view that portions or *ingredients* are to be identified *primarily* as the denotations of mass terms. All things 'present in the world' (to use Barnes's expression) are for him *substances*; and *substances* are (by Theses 1 and 2) mixtures. His technique for identifying a predominant *ingredient* in a *substance* must therefore presumably resemble our familiar homespun methods for making clear to ourselves what it is about a mixture that makes us call it after one ingredient rather than another. Why do we call a cup of sweet black coffee 'coffee'? Not simply because coffee is its major ingredient besides the water which we take for granted, but because it has the distinctive savour and smell and colour of coffee-bean extract - i.e. because it has a certain set of predominant qualities. It is an appeal to a distinctive set of qualities which our Anaxagorean must make. He holds that coffee-bean extract is a mixture no less than the liquid made from it; and he will have to say that we call *it* 'coffee' because *it* has the distinctive savour and smell and colour and texture that it does. The difference in this case is that the distinctive set of predominant qualities referred to in the explanation can no longer be identified as the qualities characteristic of some further *substance*: there is nothing which stands to coffee-bean extract as coffee-bean extract stands to coffee in the cup.[30]

So it turns out that, if ὁμοιομερῆ were counted among Anaxagorean *ingredients*, they could not be the only nor the most fundamental *ingredients*. We would have to explain them in terms of the predominant qualities of *substances*. And the doxographical interpretation of Theses 1 and 2 would have to be construed as an immensely complex variant of the interpretation according to which 'everything' in Thesis 1 and 'most' in Thesis 2 take opposite terms as their values.[31]

The problem of making sense of the idea that manifestly hot *substances* are ones in which the hot predominates over the cold is much less severe. The very word 'manifestly' (ἐνδηλότατα) in Thesis 2 suggests that Anaxagoras considered sense experience to be the criterion normally used in deciding whether to call a substance 'hot' or not: when something makes you feel hot, you call it '(manifestly) hot'. So there is no difficulty in the idea of something being *manifestly* hot. What difficulty there is arises in the causal definition of the manifestly hot offered in Thesis 2, which we can write as:

Manifestly hot *substances* are those which contain a preponderance of stuff which causes *substances* to be hot.

On the interpretation, the *ingredient* hot is to be understood as a causal factor, viz. the factor which makes things hot. And a *substance* will only manifest the effect of that cause (will only be *manifestly* hot) when it predominates over the opposite *ingredient*, cold. Unfortunately, the definition contains a crucial unexplained term, namely 'hot' (in 'stuff which causes *substances* to be hot'). Experience is a guide only to manifest heat, not to whether something is hot (where this does not just mean – as it cannot in the definition – 'manifestly hot'), nor to what is then meant by calling it 'hot'.

This difficulty would not arise did Anaxagoras not wish to say (in consequence of Thesis 1) that every *substance* is hot, even if not manifestly hot. I take it to be clear that he did want to make that claim. For his talk (in Thesis 1) of a portion of everything in everything does not invite the reductionist interpretation that everything contains powers (e.g. the hot) which could have an effect on its actual character (e.g. make it actually or – on this view the distinction has no force – manifestly hot) if they were present in sufficient strength: the very denomination of portions as 'the hot', 'the cold', etc. suggests causes with fully actual effects on the constitution of things. And when in Thesis 2 he says that each thing is most manifestly those of which it contains most, he is naturally read as implying that there are many things which a given *substance* is although not (very) manifestly so, viz. things of which it contains comparatively little.

The obvious strategy for resolving the difficulty is to try to extrapolate a meaning for 'hot' from consideration of the well entrenched 'manifestly hot'. According to the criterion we found to be suggested by the language of Thesis 2, something is manifestly hot if and only if it causes feelings of heat. Such a criterion presupposes that such qualities as manifest heat exist independently of whether we are actually experiencing them. Can we exploit the objectivity of manifest qualities to introduce the notion of a quality *sans phrase*, and thence that of an imperceptible quality? Surely we can. The very fact that manifest qualities are independent of our experiences and are causally responsible for them entails that the fact of their being manifest is no part of their identity as qualities. And given that their identity is thus independent, there is no *a priori* reason why we should deny that they may sometimes be not only unperceived but imperceptible. Moreover, a particular, or rather, a fundamental feature of our experience of opposite qualities makes the idea that they may be imperceptibly present in things very persuasive. For our experience of hot and cold, wet and dry, clear and murky admits of degrees, as Anaxagoras must surely have recognized. This leads us to ascribe degrees of heat and cold, wetness and dryness, etc., to the things we believe to be responsible for the relevant feelings. But once we take the question of whether something is hot or cold to be a matter of degree, there is no obvious way of blocking the inference that there are degrees of heat and cold too low for us to feel: a conclusion which, of course, fits well with the common sense opinion that some persons are insensitive to degrees of heat and cold which do happen to affect the rest of us.

We argue, then, that if 'manifestly hot' is explained in terms of a causal theory of perception (such as we know Anaxagoras held),[32] then we can help ourselves to a use of 'hot' *sans phrase* applicable to things even when we have no reason to believe that they are making us feel hot or could make anybody do so. This use relies on a common sense notion of the objectivity of heat which remains obscure in many respects; but at least we know where we are with such a conception, unlike the idea of *ingredient* ὁμοιομερῆ.

Moreover, we can perhaps be a bit clearer about the ontological character of the *ingredients* conceived as opposites than we could about *ingredient* ὁμοιομερῆ. What would it be for there to be portions of all ὁμοιομερῆ in every *substance*? Consider a suppositious portion of gold in some flesh. There is little we could say about its mode of being other than that it is theoretically extractable from flesh and constitutes a certain percentage or proportion of all the matter in the flesh.[33] But it is fairly plain that Anaxagoras thinks of opposites as forces or active powers. In Fragment 16 he tells us that stones are compacted out of earth *by the cold* (ὑπὸ τοῦ ψυχροῦ): presumably the cold in the air acts on the earth, and comes to dominate it so much that it ceases to be earth and becomes stones. Again, why should cosmic rotation have the effect Anaxagoras ascribes to it, of separating the dense, wet, etc. to the centre and the rare, dry, etc. to the periphery? Presumably because

it creates the conditions in which the forces of heaviness and
lightness[34] no longer counteract each other (as they must have done
in the original mixture), but act in such a way as to maximize their
effects. Why does not the universe disintegrate altogether? Doubtless because even such dense, cold, murky *substances* as stones retain as *ingredients* portions of the rare and the hot and the bright;
i.e. the stuff of which they consist is subject to forces which
counteract the prevailing density, murkiness and cold at least inasmuch as they prevent it collapsing into a black hole.

Our long examination of the cosmological fragments preserved by
Simplicius has shown what little basis they provide for ascribing to
Anaxagoras a doctrine of elemental biological tissues, or for diag-
nosing an interest in the biological phenomena of nutrition and
growth as the chief impulse behind his complex theory of matter.[35]
Our reflections in the previous paragraph suggest an alternative motive. Perhaps Anaxagoras thought that the principle of a portion of
every opposite in everything would provide the ideal explanation of
two extremely general, but apparently conflicting facts: first, that
changes in the world are (as Aristotle and the doxographical tradition also emphasize) very diverse - all sorts of things come from
all sorts of things, as is particularly clear (here we diverge from
the doxographers and probably Aristotle, too) when one considers
large-scale physical changes, above all those we must infer for cosmogony and those manifested by meteorological phenomena (on which
Anaxagoras evidently had a great deal to say, to judge from the
doxographical reports) - and that there is an ever-increasing tendency to further change and greater differentiation; but second, that
the world nonetheless does *not* disintegrate, but remains a single
order of things, in which 'the hot has not been chopped off from the
cold with an axe' (Fragment 8). If urges are to be classified, this
is not the scientific urge of a biologist, but the metaphysical urge
of a cosmologist.

SEEDS

In elaborating this interpretation of Anaxagoras's physical theory,
and of its central doctrine of everything in everything, we have
obviously gone a good way beyond the letter of the text of the fragments. The citadel of the interpretation - its identification of

the opposites as Anaxagoras's 'portions' - is, I think, impregnable.
But some of its outworks may not be. There are two principal weaknesses which an opponent might probe. First, the interpretation
leaves us wondering why Aristotle and the doxographical tradition
should ever have come to believe that reflection upon biological
phenomena was of such general importance in Anaxagoras's scheme of
things. Second, it takes no account of the famous reference to
seeds (σπέρματα) in Fragments 4a and 4b.[36] The primary evidence
will once again command our attention first.

I quote the passages in question in Furley's translation
(slightly modified):[37]

> τούτων δὲ οὕτως ἐχόντων χρὴ δοκεῖν ἐνεῖναι πολλά τε καὶ παντοῖα
> ἐν πᾶσι τοῖς συγκρινομένοις καὶ σπέρματα πάντων χρημάτων καὶ
> ἰδέας παντοίας ἔχοντα καὶ χροιὰς καὶ ἡδονάς. καὶ ἀνθρώπους τε
> συμπαγῆναι καὶ τὰ ἄλλα ζῷα ὅσα ψυχὴν ἔχει. καὶ τοῖς γε
> ἀνθρώποισιν εἶναι καὶ πόλεις συνῳκημένας καὶ ἔργα κατεσκευασ-
> μένα, ὥσπερ παρ' ἡμῖν, καὶ ἡέλιόν τε αὐτοῖσιν εἶναι καὶ σελήνην
> καὶ τὰ ἄλλα, ὥσπερ παρ' ἡμῖν, καὶ τὴν γῆν αὐτοῖσι φύειν πολλά
> τε καὶ παντοῖα, ὧν ἐκεῖνοι τὰ ὀνήιστα συνενεγκάμενοι εἰς τὴν
> οἴκησιν χρῶνται. ταῦτα μὲν οὖν μοι λέλεκται περὶ τῆς ἀπο-
> κρίσιος, ὅτι οὐκ ἂν παρ' ἡμῖν μόνον ἀποκριθείη, ἀλλὰ καὶ ἄλλῃ.
> (Fragment 4a)
> πρὶν δὲ ἀποκριθῆναι ταῦτα πάντων ὁμοῦ ἐόντων οὐδὲ χροιὴ ἔνδηλος
> ἦν οὐδεμία· ἀπεκώλυε γὰρ ἡ σύμμιξις ἁπάντων χρημάτων, τοῦ τε
> διεροῦ καὶ τοῦ ξηροῦ καὶ τοῦ θερμοῦ καὶ τοῦ ψυχροῦ καὶ τοῦ
> λαμπροῦ καὶ τοῦ ζοφεροῦ, καὶ γῆς πολλῆς ἐνεούσης καὶ σπερμάτων
> ἀπείρων πλῆθος οὐδὲν ἐοικότων ἀλλήλοις. οὐδὲ γὰρ τῶν ἄλλων
> οὐδὲν ἔοικε τὸ ἕτερον τῷ ἑτέρῳ. (Fragment 4b)

These things being so, it is right to think that there were, in
all the things that were being put together, many things, of
all kinds, and seeds of all things - [seeds] having forms and
colours and savours of every kind. And [sc. these things being
so, it is right to think that] men were compounded and the
other living creatures that have soul; and that by the men
cities were settled, and farms established, as is the case with
us, and that they have a sun and moon and the rest, as is the
case with us, and that the earth grows much of every variety
for them, of which they collect what is useful into their
dwelling and make use of it. This, then, is my doctrine about

the separation: that the separation would take place not only
with us, but elsewhere too.

Before these things were separated off, when all things were
together, no colour was evident; for the mingling together of
all things prevented it - of the wet and the dry and the hot
and the cold and the bright and the dark, much earth being in
there also, and seeds infinite in number, in no way like each
other, for of the others no one is at all like the other.

There are few more contentious issues in the interpretation of
Anaxagoras than the identity of his 'seeds'. We shall find it convenient to explore the question by considering two opposed views of
what he meant:[38] the view (1) that he conceived a seed 'as an agglomerate of every kind of substance, but with a single kind predominating in it and giving it its character', and the view (2) that
he thought of it 'as like the seed of an animal or plant, a germ
which contains a variety of substances (flesh, hair, blood) each of
which gradually manifests itself as the organism develops'. Alternative (1) plainly treats seeds as *substances*; alternative (2)
leaves it open whether they are to be regarded as *substances* or
ingredients.

Professor Gregory Vlastos has defended alternative (1).[39] He
claims that in Fragments 4a and 4b

'we encounter the only new term that the surviving fragments of
Anaxagoras introduce into the technical vocabulary of Greek
cosmology. His other technical terms - mixture, segregation,
composition, and the rest - are strikingly traditional...But no
one before Anaxagoras had ever used "seed" as he did, while
after him the term became current in physical terminology.'[40]

Vlastos's view is that σπέρμα is a *technical* term: it is introduced
to signify entities which would not normally be called 'seeds', viz.
substantial bits of homoeomerous stuff, both of living tissue (e.g.
bone, flesh) and of inorganic matter (e.g. earth, gold). What would
normally be thought of as a seed (e.g. a plant or animal seed) is a
seed-aggregate, a mixture of every kind of 'seed' (in the technical
sense).

The first advantage of alternative (2) over alternative (1) is
that it allows Anaxagoras's word σπέρμα to carry its normal force.
Two occurrences of the word are precious little evidence for its
Anaxagorean meaning in any case; and we should surely need more or

more decisive instances before we accepted that so bold a redefinition as (1) requires is to be ascribed to Anaxagoras. No one reading Fragments 4a and 4b without theoretical preconceptions would very readily conclude that σπέρμα is a technical term. On the contrary, one might more readily infer that it is used in its normal way. Its context in Fragment 4a is firmly zoological and agricultural. The reference to seeds is immediately followed by an instruction from Anaxagoras to suppose that men and animals were compounded. And in Fragment 4b earth seems to be contrasted with seeds, not counted among them.[41]

Moreover, it is easy to conceive why Anaxagoras might have thought it necessary to include seeds of plants and animals in the primordial mixture. For perhaps the general disposition of the cosmic masses of earth, air, water and so on, together with associated meteorological phenomena, could be plausibly viewed as the product of conflicting forces acting in the conditions created by a cosmic rotation. But for two reasons this sort of explanation seems plainly inadequate to account for the generation of plants and animals: first, plants and animals are much too complicated and individual in structure and composition for it to be possible to rest content with a broad invocation of sets of opposites as an explanation of their origins and growth; second, there is a known mechanism whereby plants and animals are produced, viz. the propagation of seeds. The idea that the primordial mixture contained seeds of plants and animals takes account of both these points.

There is doxographical evidence which fits naturally with this interpretation of Anaxagorean seeds. The Theophrastan tradition, in reporting his views on the generation of animals, contrasts what he says about the original zoogony with what he says about reproduction. Thus Hippolytus says:[42]

ζῷα δὲ τὴν μὲν ἀρχὴν ἐν ὑγρῷ γενέσθαι, μετὰ ταῦτα δὲ ἐξ ἀλλήλων.

Animals originally came to be in the wet, but afterwards from each other.

The presumption that this is good Theophrastan material is borne out by the rather fuller parallel passage in Diogenes Laertius:[43]

ζῷα γίγνεσθαι ἐξ ὑγροῦ καὶ θερμοῦ καὶ γεώδους, ὕστερον δὲ ἐξ ἀλλήλων.

Animals came to be from the wet and hot and earthy, but later
from each other.
It is tempting to suppose that Anaxagoras saw as constant factors
both in the zoogony and in continued reproduction the presence of
animal seeds, which in each case begin to grow in the congenial
environment of damp, warm matter (whether that matter be the earth
or the flesh of the womb). This conjecture is strongly supported by
a testimony in Theophrastus about the parallel phenomenon of the
generation of plants:[44]

'Αναξαγόρας μὲν τὸν ἀέρα πάντων φάσκων ἔχειν σπέρματα καὶ ταῦτα
συγκαταφερόμενα τῷ ὕδατι γεννᾶν τὰ φυτά.

Anaxagoras says that the air contains seeds of all things and
that these, when carried down with water, generate plants.

Is it not very likely that Anaxagoras's zoogony was an extrapolation
from this view of how plants come to be? Just as the seeds of
plants can exist in the air independently of any parent body, and
begin to grow in the wet earth, so (he probably reasoned) the seeds
of animals existed in the air and aither which covered the primordial mixture, again independently of any parent body, and began to
grow once they had found a home in the warm, wet earth that became
concentrated at the centre of the cosmic rotation.[45] (Notice that
Theophrastus's botanic report leaves open the possibility that the
seeds to which he there refers *had* no parent bodies, were not repro-
duced - just as would have had to be the case with animal and plant
seeds alike in the original mixture. Such a possibility makes good
Anaxagorean sense, so long as we suppose that he recognized normal
plant reproduction, too. For if more air and aither are always
being separated off by the cosmic rotation (Fragments 2, 12), one
would expect seeds to be separated off with them.)

One advantage of exploiting these doxographical notices as we
have just done is that it enables us to make more precise sense of
the parallel Anaxagoras must have intended between animals emerging
from the earth in the zoogony (τὰ ζῷα ἐκ τῆς γῆς ἐξαγάγειν,
Aëtius)[46] and the earth's now producing plants (τὴν γῆν αὐτοῖσι
φύειν πολλά τε καὶ παντοῖα, Fragment 4a). Another is that it
suggests an explanation of why in Fragment 4b Anaxagoras singles out
from all the things he might have mentioned in the original mixture
'earth and seeds unlimited in number' (καὶ γῆς πολλῆς ἐνεούσης καὶ

σπερμάτων ἀπείρων πλῆθος). He will have specified just these because they constitute the crucial materials necessary for the emergence of plant and animal life: seeds the stuff and organizing principle of life, earth its essential nursery. Finally, whatever more ambitious constructions we build from them, these testimonia make it very probable that Anaxagoras used σπέρμα in its ordinary sense in some parts of his book even if we allow the instances in Fragments 4a and 4b to remain doubtful. For it is highly unlikely that, in the text which Theophrastus relied upon for his report about the way plant seeds are brought down with the rain, Anaxagoras used any other word than Theophrastus's σπέρμα. And Hippolytus continues his report about the generation of animals with a reference to animal σπέρμα which may very well be authentically Anaxagorean:[47]

καὶ ἄρρενας μὲν γίνεσθαι, ὅταν ἀπὸ τῶν δεξιῶν μερῶν ἀποκριθὲν τὸ σπέρμα τοῖς δεξιοῖς μέρεσι τῆς μήτρας κολληθῇ, τὰ δὲ θήλεα κατὰ τοὐναντίον.

And males are born, when the seed separated off from the right-hand parts [sc. of the father] is joined to the right-hand parts of the womb, but females when the opposite occurs.

(But if Anaxagoras used σπέρμα in the ordinary way in these contexts, then it is also probable that he did so in Fragments 4a and 4b, if my argument in this and the previous paragraph has been correct; for I have argued that these contexts and Fragments 4a and 4b all constitute fragments of a single picture of the origins and continuation of life.)

There is, then, a strong case for adopting alternative (2) as the right account of Anaxagoras's seeds.[48] Why has it been so resisted by scholars? I consider first some of the more unimpressive reasons that they have advanced.

Vlastos says of σπέρμα in Fragments 4a and 4b:[49] 'The context makes it perfectly clear that the term is employed with unrestricted generality. There are "seeds of *all things*" in all the products of the cosmogonic process; and wherever the expression "all things" occurs in the fragments it means just what it says; it would be forcing the texts to take it any other way.' But one might just as naturally take 'seeds of all things' to mean 'seeds of whatever can grow from a seed' (i.e. trees, horses, men; but not gold or earth). 'All things' (πάντα χρήματα) is intrinsically a vaguer expression than 'seeds' (σπέρματα); if one has to be accommodated to the sense of the other, it is πάντα χρήματα which would have to be bent to suit the meaning of σπέρματα, *ceteris paribus*. Compare, for example, what Anaxagoras says a little later in Fragment 4a: καὶ τὴν γῆν αὐτοῖσι φυεῖν πολλά τε καὶ παντοῖα, 'and the earth grows much of *every* variety for them': does this mean that it grows air and water? Vlastos actually restricts the sense of 'all things' here himself – to 'all homoeomerous stuffs'. In the strictly technical sense of σπέρμα which he takes Anaxagoras to be introducing, there are no σπέρματα of living species,[50] but only πανσπερμίαι, 'seed-aggregates'.[51]

Another reason Vlastos has for preferring alternative (1) is this:[52]

> 'There is no satisfactory explanation of the mention of earth in this connection [sc. in connexion with the 'seeds unlimited in multitude' mentioned in Fragment 4b], unless earth is one variety of seed. This interpretation is supported by the immediately following sentence: "For neither did any of the others (τῶν ἄλλων) in any way resemble one another." τῶν ἄλλων here must refer to σπερμάτων in the preceding sentence...The sense can only be "neither did any of the seeds other than the earth resemble one another", which would clinch my contention that the earth is here spoken of as a seed.'

Such dogmatism about the meaning of a writer so dense and suggestive as Anaxagoras is always unwise. And as I have argued above, it is surely much more natural to suppose that earth is *contrasted* with seeds – presumably because it is *not* itself a seed. We have seen that a perfectly reasonable explanation of the mention of earth and seeds can be given upon that interpretation. Vlastos's supporting argument unfortunately hinges on a mistranslation of the Greek. What Anaxagoras actually says is that none of the others *does* at all resemble any other (ἔοικε). I take it that he is here offering an argument from the nature of the world as it is now to justify the claim that the seeds were all different from one another. I imagine his idea is that if you look at all the plants and animals sustained by the earth (and 'other than the earth'), you will find none very similar to any other (if you look hard enough, presumably), whereas one bit of earth looks much like any other bit. So from differences in the effects you should infer differences in the causes - the seeds.⁵³

Still, even if Anaxagoras did not think of earth as a seed, and so did not posit seeds of absolutely *every* natural kind, there is a rather more potent reason for reading σπέρματα in Fragments 4a and 4b, in the spirit of alternative (1), as introducing tiny bits of living tissue as well as or rather than the animal and plant seeds recognized in alternative (2). The reason is that Aristotle probably took σπέρματα to include elemental living tissues, as two texts in particular suggest. Both contrast Anaxagoras's views with those of Empedocles, the first more sweepingly and less carefully than the second. It says that the followers of Anaxagoras took flesh and bone and those of the ὁμοιομερῆ of that sort to be simple and elemental, but earth and fire and water and air to be compounds - for they are a *seed*-conglomerate [consisting] of these ὁμοιομερῆ (*GC* I 1, 314a28-b1: οἱ δε ταῦτα [sc. σάρκα καὶ ὀστοῦν καὶ τὰ τοιαῦτα τῶν ὁμοιομερῶν] μὲν ἁπλᾶ καὶ στοιχεῖα, γῆν δὲ καὶ πῦρ καὶ ὕδωρ καὶ ἀέρα σύνθετα - πανσπερμίαν γὰρ εἶναι τούτων).⁵⁴ The second states more circumspectly that Anaxagoras took the homoeomerous stuffs (i.e. flesh, bone, and the like) to be elemental, but air and fire to be mixtures of them and all the other *seeds* (*Cael.* III 3, 302a31-b2 (= A43): τὰ γὰρ ὁμοιομερῆ στοιχεῖα (λέγω δ' οἷον σάρκα καὶ ὀστοῦν καὶ τῶν τοιούτων ἕκαστον), ἀέρα δὲ καὶ πῦρ μίγματα τούτων καὶ τῶν ἄλλων σπερμάτων πάντων). These texts are not without their problems and unclarities; and most scholars agree in finding mistaken Aristotle's belief that air and aither (and, in the more carefree version, earth and water) were in Anaxagoras's system nothing but a collection of all sorts of ὁμοιομερῆ.⁵⁵ But it seems reasonable to infer that: (i) Aristotle did not think that air, aither and earth were themselves viewed as seeds (or as consisting of air-seeds, aither-seeds, and earth-seeds) by Anaxagoras; (ii) he supposed that Anaxagoras's seeds included flesh-seeds, bone-seeds, and the like - presumably meaning by 'the like' living tissues in general. In the second passage Aristotle refers somewhat vaguely to 'all the other seeds'. Perhaps he assumes that Anaxagoras included seeds in the ordinary sense - seeds of animals and plants - among his σπέρματα; although then he would surely have been committed to regarding these, too, as elemental. Perhaps he imagines that there were seeds even of the inorganic stuffs which he recognizes elsewhere as ὁμοιομερῆ, such as ores, metals and stones.[56]

The proponent of alternative (2) has two lines of defence at his disposal. The more aggressive tactic is to suppose that Aristotle arrived at his view that Anaxagoras recognized seeds of bone, flesh, hair, etc. not on the basis of any explicit statement in his book, but as a result of an inference - an inference which may have been faulty. It is hard to resist the thought that behind Aristotle's preoccupation with flesh and bones whenever he thinks of Anaxagorean physics, there lay in Anaxagoras's treatise some such question as: 'How could hair come from not hair, or flesh from not flesh?' (Fragment 10), and some answer to the effect that 'flesh from food is added to flesh in the body' (*GA* I 18, 723a10-11). Aristotle may have inferred that when in Fragment 4a Anaxagoras says that we should suppose there to be 'many things, of all kinds, in all the things being put together, and seeds of all things', he means by 'seeds' to refer precisely to tissues like flesh and hair which were the subject of the question and answer. The inference is plausible: is it a necessary one? Surely not. Consider first the case not of nutrition but of generation - the case which the scholiast who attributes to Anaxagoras the famous question has in mind. The scholiast certainly supposes that in Anaxagoras's theory the flesh and blood in the growing embryo come from nothing but flesh and blood; and he also supposes that they arise from seed (although he uses the word γονή, not σπέρμα). But in his view it is not flesh-seeds or blood-seeds from which they originate, but the single seed of whatever species of animal it is that the embryo will mature into. Consider now the case of nutrition. Why should we not suppose that Anaxagoras simply extended his theory of generation to account for nutrition also, by postulating that as reproduction begins from animal seed which contains already flesh, blood, etc. in minute quantities, so growth continues with the absorption of countless more such seeds which lie latent in our food and drink? The likelihood of such an extension is supported by Anaxagoras's treatment of the analogous effects of plant seeds, whose importance for his thinking about seeds in general we have already stressed. For Theophrastus, at least, suggests that the plant seeds which according to Anaxagoras are brought down with the rain not only generate plants but supply them with nourishment while they are growing.[57] Moreover, if we allow (what is *ceteris paribus* the most obvious interpretation) that it was in order to launch zoogony that Anaxagoras chiefly wanted to have seeds in his original mixture, and that the obvious candidates for such a task are animal seeds, then we must similarly allow that he has no reason for not accepting that, in the continual absorption of the original mixture into the cosmic rotation, there are even now countless numbers of animal seeds, just as there are of plant seeds, dispersed everywhere - and therefore, presumably, in our food and drink.

The advocate of alternative (2) also has a more sophisticated tactic available to him, which may be substituted for the first or deployed in conjunction with it. This tactic takes its origin from a question about the ontological status of the seeds of which Anaxagoras speaks in Fragments 4a and 4b. Employing once more the terminology of *substances* and *ingredients*, we may put the question by asking whether seeds are to be construed as *substances* or *ingredients*. Jonathan Barnes replies: *ingredients*, as a quotation will show:[58]

> 'It is easy to imagine that "seeds" of S [where S is any given sort of homoeomerous stuff] are (minimal) particles of S: the original mass contains everything inasmuch as little seed-particles of every stuff are suspended in it like pollen in the summer air.
>
> 'That is a tempting interpretation, but not an obligatory one. *Sperma*, in Greek, is as much a biological as a botanical term: where the word "seed" suggests particles to us, the word *sperma* would not have done so to a Greek. The language of seeds does not imply a particulate theory of stuffs; and to say that X contains seeds of Y need mean no more than that Y may grow from X.'

Barnes's verdict receives strong confirmation from the contexts in Fragments 4a and 4b in which the word 'seeds' appears, at any rate given the general interpretation of 'portions' and of the doctrine of everything in everything which was advanced in the previous section. In both passages seeds are counted among the things which were *in* mixtures - whether the primordial mixture (Fragment 4b) or 'what was being put together' in separated worlds (Fragment 4a).

This already creates a presumption that *ingredients* are what Anaxagoras has in mind. The presumption is only reinforced by the observation that in Fragment 4a the reference to seeds seems to be intended as an elaboration of the basic doctrine of everything in everything: 'there were, in all the things that were being put together, many things, of all kinds, and *seeds of all things* - [seeds] having forms and colours and savours of every kind'. 'Many things, of all kinds' refers to *ingredients*; so too must 'seeds of all things, etc.'. Considerations of economy also favour Barnes's view. Consider the claim of Fragment 4b that in the original mixture there was 'much earth...and seeds infinite in number' (no doubt together with air and aither - mentioned in Fragment 1 - and a lot of other things, too). It is much more natural and economical to take it that by 'much earth' Anaxagoras means to refer to the *ingredient* earth, and not to stuff which is predominantly earth but contains all other things also, as he must be doing if he intends 'earth' to be construed here as a *substance* term. The same applies to 'air and aither' in Fragment 1 - and to 'seeds infinite in number'.[59]

If he arms himself with the *ingredient* interpretation of seeds in Fragments 4a and 4b, the proponent of alternative (2) has a ready defence against the complaint that Aristotle took Anaxagoras's seeds to include seeds of tissues like flesh and bone. He can simply admit that Anaxagoras may have extended the notion of seeds to apply to living tissue - but no further; and he can claim that the *ingredient* interpretation permits him to do so without embarrassment. For *ingredient* seeds are not nearly so firmly individuated as particle seeds. If something contains a particle seed of flesh, then it must contain a *substance* which is the sole occupant of a determinate location within it, and constitutes part of the stuff of which it is made as a building block goes to make up a house. But the criterion of something's containing an *ingredient* seed of flesh would simply be that *substance* flesh may (and in suitable conditions will) grow from it. Similarly, the criterion that something contains an *ingredient* seed of man would be that a *substance*, man, may grow from it. The seed of man and the seed of flesh are just two different natural potentialities within a thing - different but significantly interdependent potentialities: for if the *substance*, flesh, comes to be (i.e. if *ingredient* flesh comes to manifest its distinctive 'forms and colours and savours'), then either a man or a dog or some other animal comes to be; and if a man comes to be, flesh and hair and bone and other tissues come to be. Nor is there any purely ontological reason to think the one sort of seed clearly more fundamental than the other, as there is upon the particulate interpretation, which naturally takes flesh (and in general) tissue particles to be elemental constituents of animal and plant seeds. Indeed, Aristotle may have mistakenly concluded that only seeds of tissues, not also seeds of animals and plants, were envisaged in such general ontological contexts as Fragments 4a and 4b because of a no less mistaken commitment to the particulate interpretation of seeds.

Our reflection on the fragments in which Anaxagoras mentions seeds has led us to conclude that he counted among the *ingredients* of things not only opposites but also air, aither, earth (identified as such) and the seeds of animals and plants and (probably) their tissues. It is unclear how far we should extend the list: from Fragment 16 it would seem natural to add water; but should stones and clouds, also mentioned there, be included, too? In any event, it now appears that the doctrine of everything in everything makes a vastly more elaborate claim than what was suggested in our previous section: in every opposite a portion of every opposite. From sounding like a latter-day Milesian, Anaxagoras comes to resemble a harbinger of Leibniz:[60]

> 'Each portion of matter may be conceived as a garden full of plants, and as a pond full of fish. But every branch of each plant, every member of each animal, and every drop of their liquid parts is itself likewise a similar garden or pond.
>
> 'And although the earth and the air interspersed between the plants in the garden, or the water interspersed between the fish in the pond, are neither plant nor fish, yet they still contain them, though most usually of a subtlety which renders them imperceptible to us.'

Is it possible to accommodate the more elaborate version of the doctrine of everything in everything within the basic framework of an interpretation in terms of opposites? Or do the findings of the

present section compel us to abandon that framework? What we need
to reconcile the ideas of the present and the previous section is
the notion that the fundamental *ingredients* of things are to be
identified as opposite forces, from which further *ingredients* such
as air, earth, water and seeds may then be derived as logical constructions (not arbitrary constructions, but somehow selected by
nature). As I remarked earlier, Anaxagoras gives no sign of having
explicitly formulated this notion, which is certainly one that
requires considerable ingenuity to work out in detail. But he does
imply that, in contrast to the simplicity of those *ingredients* which
are opposites, other *ingredients* are complex, having or consisting
of a number of qualities: in most cases the implication is altogether tacit, but it comes near to explicitness when in Fragment 4a
he writes of 'seeds...having forms and colours and savours of every
kind'. And in Fragment 4b he writes as though the identification of
such *ingredients* as earth and seeds is somehow secondary to the
specification of the dense and the rare, the hot and the cold, and
so on.[61] Perhaps a part of the reason why it is so hard to make
out what is and what is not included in Anaxagoras's list of *ingredients* is that, taking non-opposite *ingredients* to be secondary,
he tended to mention only those of them which were of special rel-
evance to the explanation of some particular phenomenon - such as
the indistinctness of the primordial mixture (air and aither), or
the coming about of a zoogony (earth and seeds). Secondary *ingredients* did not need to be introduced into the basic story of the
forces active in cosmic separation.

THE SCHOLIAST'S QUESTION

Our argument in the preceding section has suggested that if and when
Anaxagoras introduced talk of seeds and tissues into general discussion of the composition of physical things, he did so - in part,
at least - because he thought the generation of plants and animals
too special and complex a phenomenon to be accounted for in the same
fashion as cosmogony: as the outcome of warring forces acting in the
conditions created by a cosmic rotation. He therefore felt obliged
to see in the seeds of plants and animals, and of their tissues,
irreducible natural tendencies of growth, whose physical basis he
may dimly have identified as logical constructions from the

fundamental *ingredients*, the opposites.

This rationale for Anaxagoras's recognition of flesh and hair and so on as *ingredients* is not the same as the reasoning which Aristotle and the doxographical tradition ascribe to him, when they say or imply (citing these examples) that he held everything to be a mixture of everything because he saw anything coming out of anything. Even so, it lies close enough to that reasoning for us to conclude that the references to seeds in Fragments 4a and 4b do quite a lot to support the reliability of this Aristotelian and doxographical evidence, at any rate insofar as it relates Anaxagoras's interest in the phenomenon of the growth of tissues to his central metaphysical concerns.

Of course, it is in any case difficult to conceive that Aristotle just invented this relationship on Anaxagoras's behalf. And there is other evidence of its Anaxagorean provenance. For example, it is possible that we have some evidence of Anaxagoras's presentation of his doctrine of everything in everything which strongly supports Aristotle's reliability but yet is independent of him. According to Diogenes Laertius,[62] Diogenes the Cynic held that 'according to right reason all things are in all and throughout all' (καὶ τῷ ὀρθῷ λόγῳ πάντ' ἐν πᾶσι καὶ διὰ πάντων εἶναι). His explanation of this view was apparently remarkably Anaxagorean:

> καὶ γὰρ ἐν τῷ ἄρτῳ κρέας εἶναι καὶ ἐν τῷ λαχάνῳ ἄρτον, καὶ τῶν σωμάτων τῶν λοιπῶν ἐν πᾶσι διά τινων ἀδήλων πόρων καὶ ὄγκων ἐισκρινομένων καὶ συνατμιζομένων, ὡς δῆλον ἐν τῷ Θυέστῃ ποιεῖ.
>
> For in bread there is meat and in vegetables bread; and all other bodies, too, by means of certain invisible passages and particles, find their way in and unite with all substances in the form of vapour - as he makes plain in the *Thyestes*.

The reference to meat suggests an explanation of the appearance of Anaxagorean doctrine in Diogenes's tragedy: when Thyestes discovered that he had eaten a meal consisting of his own children, he was perhaps offered the consolation that, because all things are in all, everyone eats human flesh every time he consumes a piece of bread. Diogenes need not himself have believed this, of course; he may simply have hoped to shock the reader with its shamelessness. But what matters for our purposes is that he must surely have borrowed the idea from Anaxagoras, and that his knowledge of Anaxagoras is not so likely to have derived from Aristotle.

Some scholars would find a further unequivocal argument for Aristotle's reliability in the famous repudiating question in a scholium on Gregory of Nazianzus[63] which Diels claimed as an actual fragment of Anaxagoras (Fragment 10).[64] The whole text runs as follows:

τὸ δὲ τὰ πάντα ἐν πᾶσι κεῖσθαι εἶπε μὲν καὶ Ἐμπεδοκλῆς, εἶπε δὲ καὶ Ἀναξαγόρας, πλὴν οὐ μετὰ τῆς αὐτῆς γνώμης ἀμφότεροι. ἀλλ' ὁ μὲν Ἐμπεδοκλῆς περὶ τῶν τεσσάρων εἶπε στοιχείων, ὅτι οὐ μόνον διωρισμένα εἰσὶ καὶ καθ' ἑαυτά, ἀλλὰ καὶ ἀλλήλοις μέμικται. καὶ δῆλον ἐντεῦθεν· πᾶν γὰρ ζῷον τοῖς τέσσαρσι στοιχείοις ζῳογονεῖται. ὁ δὲ Ἀναξαγόρας παλαιὸν εὑρὼν δόγμα, ὅτι οὐδὲν ἐκ τοῦ μηδαμῇ (μηδαμῶς ὄντος)[65] γίνεται, γένεσιν μὲν ἀνῄρει, διάκρισιν δὲ εἰσῆγεν ἀντὶ γενέσεως. ἐλήρει γὰρ ἀλλήλοις μὲν μεμῖχθαι πάντα, διακρίνεσθαι δὲ αὐξανόμενα. καὶ γὰρ ἐν τῇ αὐτῇ γονῇ καὶ τρίχας εἶναι καὶ ὄνυχας καὶ φλέβας καὶ ἀρτηρίας καὶ νεῦρα καὶ ὀστᾶ καὶ τυγχάνειν μὲν ἀφανῆ διὰ μικρομέρειαν, αὐξανόμενα δὲ κατὰ μικρὸν διακρίνεσθαι. πῶς γὰρ ἄν, φησίν, ἐκ μὴ τριχὸς γένοιτο θρὶξ καὶ σὰρξ ἐκ μὴ σαρκός; οὐ μόνον δὲ τῶν σωμάτων ἀλλὰ καὶ τῶν χρωμάτων ταῦτα κατηγόρει. καὶ γὰρ ἐνεῖναι τῷ λευκῷ τὸ μέλαν καὶ τὸ λευκὸν τῷ μέλανι. τὸ αὐτὸ δὲ ἐπὶ τῶν ῥοπῶν ἐτίθει, τῷ βαρεῖ τὸ κοῦφον σύμμικτον εἶναι δοξάζων καὶ τοῦτο αὖθις ἐκείνῳ. ἄτινα πάντα ψευδῆ ἐστι. πῶς γὰρ τὰ ἐναντία τοῖς ἐναντίοις συνέσονται;

The doctrine that all things lie in all was affirmed both by Empedocles and by Anaxagoras, although not by both in the same sense. Empedocles affirmed it with respect to the four elements, saying that they are not only distinct and on their own but mixed with one another. His view is clear from the following consideration: every animal is produced [? according to his theory] by means of the four elements. Anaxagoras, for his part, discovered the ancient doctrine that nothing comes to be out of what has no being at all, and abolished coming into being, introducing separation instead of coming into being. For he stupidly said that all things are mixed with each other, but are separated as they grow. For in the same seed [γονῇ] there are hairs, nails, veins, arteries, sinews, and bones; it so happens that they are imperceptible because they consist of small particles, but as they grow they gradually become distinct and separate. 'For how', he says, 'could hair come to be out of not hair, and flesh out of not flesh?' He said these things not only of bodies but also of colours. According to him there is black in white and white in black. And he laid down the same doctrine with respect to weights, holding that the light is mixed with the heavy and vice versa. All of which is false. For how will opposites coexist with opposites?

This text is often taken as pretty decisive evidence that it was chiefly reflection upon the biological phenomena of growth which led Anaxagoras to advance his doctrine of everything in everything and to formulate the argument for it adumbrated here.[66] Both the argument and the central concern with growth which the scholiast ascribes to Anaxagoras are also attributed to him by other sources. But the beauty of the scholium is thought to lie in its reporting (in the repudiating question) a fragment of the *ipsissima verba* in which Anaxagoras couched what we might call the biological argument. By preserving the philosopher's own words it seems to remove all shadow of doubt from the Aristotelian interpretation of Anaxagoras. For it is above all Aristotle who holds that Anaxagoras derived his thesis that in everything there is a portion of everything from the two premises: (i) anything can come out of anything, and (ii) strictly speaking nothing can come to be except from something of the same sort as itself.[67] And it is Aristotle who invariably suggests as examples of the sort of entity Anaxagoras had in mind when he advanced his theory of matter various kinds of animal tissue - flesh, blood, bone.[68] Aristotle's interpretation seems to have been taken over by Theophrastus, for the same general view of Anaxagoras is found - and expressed in language at one point very reminiscent of the scholium - in Aëtius and in a text of Simplicius which closely resembles Aëtius's report.[69]

Is the scholiast's repudiating question authentically Anaxagorean, as Diels announced (without argument)? The plain fact is: we do not and cannot (failing new evidence) know. The words which Diels takes to be a quotation have no distinctively antique or Ionian characteristics, nor are they reassuringly set in an extended authentic context. The repudiating question they constitute undoubtedly enlivens the scholiast's account: why should he not, appreciating this, have invented it himself and then fathered it on Anaxagoras? This hypothesis is surely no more nor less likely than Diels's view that we have here a genuine Anaxagorean tag: although if genuine, it is perhaps surprising that it should not have survived among the portions of Anaxagoras's book known to Simplicius,[70] at any rate if it formed part of a major and general argument for the central doctrine, such as would naturally belong in the first few pages of the book whence Simplicius's fragments derive.

Even if Fragment 10 is indeed a fragment, that would not in itself lend any extra credence to the Aristotelian interpretation. We already knew from Aristotle himself that, according to Anaxagoras, 'flesh from food is added to flesh [in the body]' (GA I 18, 723a10-11: Ἀναξαγόρας μὲν γὰρ εὐλόγως φησὶ σάρκας ἐκ τῆς τροφῆς προσιέναι ταῖς σαρξίν). What would increase the probability of Aristotle's account of the rationale of the doctrine of everything in everything is independent evidence that he did not merely apply it to the phenomena of growth, but that reflection on those phenomena was crucial to both his reasoning in favour of the thesis and the interpretation he wanted the thesis to receive. Yet although the scholium implies that such reflection was indeed crucial to Anaxagoras's conception of universal mixture, its testimony on the point is very probably dependent on Aristotle, and gives his interpretation rather weaker support than scholars have tried to extract from it. I have argued the case fully elsewhere,[71] so here I present just its main points.

The most important fact about the scholium is that it is, to all appearances, a paraphrase or a revised version of the passage in Book I of Aristotle's *Physics* where an explanation is offered of why Anaxagoras believed the elements of things to consist of ὁμοιομερῆ, homoeomerous stuffs, and opposites, and to be infinite in number (*Phys.* I 4, 187a21-b7). This becomes immediately clear when one looks at the passage. Aristotle has divided physicists into two groups, those who produce the world by positing variations in a single fundamental substance, and those who take the original stuff of the world to be from the beginning a plurality. In the latter group he places

ὅσοι δ' ἓν καὶ πολλά φασιν εἶναι, ὥσπερ Ἐμπεδοκλῆς καὶ Ἀναξαγόρας· ἐκ τοῦ μίγματος γὰρ καὶ οὗτοι ἐκκρίνουσι τἆλλα.

διαφέρουσι δὲ ἀλλήλων τῷ τὸν μὲν περίοδον ποιεῖν τούτων, τὸν
δ' ἅπαξ, καὶ τὸν μὲν ἄπειρα, τά τε ὁμοιομερῆ καὶ τἀναντία, τὸν
δὲ τὰ καλούμενα στοιχεῖα μόνον. ἔοικε δὲ 'Αναξαγόρας ἄπειρα
οὕτως οἰηθῆναι διὰ τὸ ὑπολαμβάνειν τὴν κοινὴν δόξαν τῶν φυσικῶν
εἶναι ἀληθῆ, ὡς οὐ γιγνομένου οὐδενὸς ἐκ τοῦ μὴ ὄντος· διὰ
τοῦτο γὰρ οὕτω λέγουσιν, ἦν ὁμοῦ πάντα, καὶ τὸ γίγνεσθαι
τοιόνδε καθέστηκεν ἀλλοιοῦσθαι, οἱ δὲ σύγκρισιν καὶ διάκρισιν
(ἔτι δ' ἐκ τοῦ γίγνεσθαι ἐξ ἀλλήλων τἀναντία· ἐνυπῆρχεν ἄρα).
εἰ γὰρ πᾶν μὲν τὸ γιγνόμενον ἀνάγκη γίγνεσθαι ἢ ἐξ ὄντων ἢ ἐκ
μὴ ὄντων, τούτων δὲ τὸ μὲν ἐκ μὴ ὄντων γίγνεσθαι ἀδύνατον (περὶ
γὰρ ταύτης ὁμογνωμονοῦσι τῆς δόξης ἅπαντες οἱ περὶ φύσεως), τὸ
λοιπὸν ἤδη συμβαίνειν ἐξ ἀνάγκης ἐνόμισαν, ἐξ ὄντων μὲν καὶ
ἐνυπαρχόντων γίγνεσθαι, διὰ μικρότητα δὲ τῶν ὄγκων ἐξ
ἀναισθήτων ἡμῖν. διό φασι πᾶν ἐν παντὶ μεμῖχθαι, διότι πᾶν ἐκ
παντὸς ἑώρων γιγνόμενον· φαίνεσθαι δὲ διαφέροντα καὶ προσ-
αγορεύεσθαι ἕτερα ἀλλήλων ἐκ τοῦ μάλισθ' ὑπερέχοντος διὰ πλῆθος
ἐν τῇ μίξει τῶν ἀπείρων· εἰλικρινῶς μὲν γὰρ ὅλον λευκὸν ἢ μέλαν
ἢ γλυκὺ ἢ σάρκα ἢ ὀστοῦν οὐκ εἶναι, ὅτου δὲ πλεῖστον ἕκαστον
ἔχει, τοῦτο δοκεῖν εἶναι τὴν φύσιν τοῦ πράγματος.

those who say that it is both one and many, like Empedocles and
Anaxagoras. For they too separate the other things out from
the mixture. But they differ from one another, in that Empedocles makes a cycle of these things [sc. separation and mix-
ture], whereas Anaxagoras posits a single separation, and
Anaxagoras makes the elements unlimited, consisting both of
homoeomerous stuffs and of opposites, whereas Empedocles posits
only the so called elements.

Anaxagoras seems to have thought of the elements in this
way as unlimited through accepting as true the opinion held in
common among the physicists, that nothing comes to be out of
what is not. For it is on this ground that they say things
like: 'All things were together', and 'to come-to-be such and
such is to be altered' (or, as some say, 'coming together and
separation'). (Moreover, it was also a consideration that
opposites come to be out of one another: they must, it seemed,
have been in there.)[72] For if it is necessary that everything
which comes to be come to be either from things which are or
from things which are not, but of these alternatives coming to

be from things which are not is impossible (for on this opinion
all writers on nature are agreed), they thought that the remaining alternative must necessarily follow: that things come
to be from things which are and which are already in there,
but from things which are imperceptible to us because of the
smallness of their particles.

They say that everything is mixed in everything because
they saw everything coming to be from everything; but that they
appear different and are called different from one another in
consequence of the numerical preponderance [sc. of a certain
ingredient or ingredients] in the mixture of the unlimited
[particles] - for there is no whole object which is purely
white, black, sweet, flesh or bone, but whatever each has most
of is thought to be the nature of the thing.

The scholium follows this passage from the *Physics* in all its
main points, as will appear from the comparison which I now make.
(a) *Empedocles*. Both texts associate Anaxagoras and Empedocles
with a doctrine of universal mixture. Both treat Empedocles
first, and briefly. And although the scholium does not make
this at all clear, it is presumably referring to the same doctrine of the cosmic cycle which Aristotle mentions.[73] (b) *The
ancient doctrine*. Both texts suppose that fundamental to
Anaxagoras's position is the doctrine, regarded as 'common' or
'ancient', that nothing comes to be out of nothing. Both
associate with this Anaxagoras's substitution of some other
notion for 'come to be' - whether 'alter' or 'separate/become
distinct' (διακρίνεσθαι). (c) *Mixture*. Aristotle states, and
the scholiast implies, that Anaxagoras held the doctrine of
universal mixture because he thought this would explain why all
manner of substances (both authors mention animal tissue)
emerge from all sorts of other substances (e.g. seeds, to take
the scholiast's example). (d) *Latency, emergence, and preponderance*. Both authors agree that before things 'come to be',
they exist in the substance from which they emerge imperceptible to us, because they are present in the form of very small
particles. If a certain substance emerges from another, it
does so because its particles have grown more numerous (scholiast): if something appears to be of a certain sort, it does so

because it contains a preponderant number of particles of that sort (Aristotle). (e) *Elements*. The items in the universal mixture are, for both authors, of two basic kinds: homoeomerous stuffs (perhaps only *living* stuffs),[74] and opposites.

There are, of course, great differences between the two texts. They can be summed up in the difference of ethos. Aristotle writes a dispassionate, careful exposition, attributing to Anaxagoras plenty of abstract arguments. The scholiast, by contrast, is much briefer and a much lighter read; he prefers examples to abstract ratiocination throughout (not just in the repudiating question); and he adopts a critical, indeed a dismissive, attitude to Anaxagoras,[75] which sinks to the level of knockabout comedy when he suggests that the philosopher 'discovered an ancient doctrine' (as it might be rummaging in his attic).

Did the scholiast's ultimate source know Anaxagoras's book directly? The examples cited in the presentation of the views both of Anaxagoras and of Empedocles certainly suggest a well-informed author;[76] and the scholium has a freshness and vigour altogether unusual in second- and third-hand doxographical reports. These may well be signs of independent acquaintance with Anaxagoras's work. Together with the scholium's reliance principally on Aristotle's *Physics*, rather than on Theophrastus, they point to an early Peripatetic writer, perhaps Eudemus. For we know that Eudemus ('the most authentically Aristotelian of Aristotle's associates', in Simplicius's opinion[77]) wrote a large work in several books on physics, which Wehrli characterizes thus:[78] 'From the fragments there emerges the picture of a shortened and revised version of Aristotle's *Physics*, which follows the original in its disposition and in its formulation of problems, and is independent only in details.' I submit that our scholium squares exactly with that description of Eudemus's work.

The ultimate author of the scholium may, then, preserve Anaxagoras's own words in his repudiating question; even if he does not, his account of Anaxagoras's theory of growth may be based in part upon his own consultation of Anaxagoras's book. But we cannot trust him automatically when he implies that Anaxagoras developed a principal argument for the general doctrine of everything in everything in terms of a biological example and as a consequence of reflection upon specifically biological phenomena. For he plainly read Anaxagoras (if he did read him) through Aristotelian spectacles, and he demonstrably follows Aristotle in such matters of *general* interpretation, just as did Theophrastus on this point (to judge from the report of Aëtius, at any rate) as elsewhere:[79]

Ἀναξαγόρας Ἡγησιβούλου ὁ Κλαζομένιος ἀρχὰς τῶν ὄντων τὰς ὁμοιομερείας ἀπεφήνατο. ἐδόκει γὰρ αὐτῷ ἀπορώτατον εἶναι, πῶς ἐκ τοῦ μὴ ὄντος δύναταί τι γίγνεσθαι ἢ φθείρεσθαι εἰς τὸ μὴ ὄν. τροφὴν γοῦν προσφερόμεθα ἁπλῆν καὶ μονοειδῆ, τὸν Δημήτριον καρπὸν ἐσθίοντες καὶ τὸ ὕδωρ πίνοντες, καὶ ἐκ ταύτης τρέφεται θρὶξ φλέψ ἀρτήρια σὰρξ νεῦρα ὀστᾶ καὶ τὰ λοιπὰ μόρια. τούτων οὖν γιγνομένων ὁμολογητέον ὅτι ἐν τῇ τροφῇ τῇ προσφερομένῃ πάντα ἐστὶ τὰ ὄντα, καὶ ἐκ τῶν ὄντων πάντα αὔξεται.

Anaxagoras of Clazomenae, son of Hegesibulus, declared the homoeomeries to be principles of the things that are. For it seemed to him a great difficulty, how anything could come into being from what is not or perish into what is not. At any rate, we take in sustenance which is simple and uniform, eating bread and drinking water, and from it hair, veins, arteries, flesh, sinews, bones and the remaining parts are nourished. Since, then, these things happen it must be agreed that all the things that are are in the sustenance we take in, and from the things that are all things are increased.

Yet although Theophrastus and the ultimate author of the scholium are not witnesses truly independent of Aristotle on the question of the rationale of interpretation of Anaxagoras's central doctrine, they are witnesses whose word it is unsafe to discount. If they partly echo Aristotle, they do so as intelligent men, who were able (the one certainly, the other quite probably) to verify his account for themselves by consulting Anaxagoras's book.

Should we therefore conclude that Anaxagoras supported his central doctrine of everything in everything with a *general argument* such as Aristotle attributes to him? In favour of this conclusion we might adduce the fact that in Fragment 6 Anaxagoras develops a subsidiary line of thought of great generality, which it is tempting, although (as we saw) not obligatory, to construe as an ancillary argument for the doctrine. Acceptance of the conclusion would require us to add some nuances to the characterization of his dogmatism which we offered in Chapter 1. There it was suggested that on the whole he eschewed argument on fundamental points when presenting his cosmogonical hypotheses about mind and the primordial mixture, content perhaps to rest his case on their evident explanatory virtues. Now we should have to add that when it came to the crucial thesis of his whole system, he realized that its vast and vastly counter-intuitive metaphysical claims could not be expected to win assent without the provision of some general reasoning in its support, supplemented by telling illustrations. At the point where his ideas became most Parmenidean and least Ionian, he will have come closest to abandoning Ionian dogmatism and to applying something like the Eleatic argumentative style to his enunciation of a fundamental doctrine.

On the other hand, it is perhaps safer to infer from the evidence we have reviewed in this section simply that Anaxagoras adduced some *examples* of change in connexion with his central doctrine. The scholiast's account is developed entirely in terms of examples, and Theophrastus seems to imply that the example of the growth of tissues bore the main burden of whatever argument Anaxagoras advanced. I prefer the conjecture that Anaxagoras did not himself explicitly formulate the generalization that anything can come out of anything as an abstract rationale of his central doctrine (that will have been due to Aristotle), but presented a list of σημεῖα or τεκμήρια, *specific* 'signs' or 'evidences' of its truth, such as we noted earlier in Diogenes of Apollonia and in early Hippocratic writers.[80] Chief among these, no doubt, was a description of the emergence of tissues from food (or, if we follow the scholiast, sperm), perhaps followed by the question: 'How could hair come to be out of not hair, and flesh out of not flesh?'; and an account of how the heavy comes to be from the light, and white from black (further doxographical notices suggest that Anaxagoras here adduced the formation of snow from water).[81] We should not assume that these σημεῖα reflected altogether accurately Anaxagoras's most deep-seated *reasons* for holding the doctrine of everything in everything. As was suggested in an earlier section of this chapter, Anaxagoras may have set more store by the reciprocal changes of basic pairs of opposites than by biological phenomena; and he may have thought the doctrine necessary to explain not only

why anything could come to be out of anything, but also why the
world does not disintegrate but remains - and will remain - a *single*
order of things. In the very listing of σημεῖα Anaxagoras shows
greater epistemological sensitivity than we were able to find him
exhibiting in the fragments with regard to his doctrines of mind,
or primordial mixture, and of unlimited smallness. The epistemological interest in question is one more characteristic of Ionian
philosophy and science than of the Eleatics (contrast the suggestion
made at the end of the previous paragraph apropos of the alternative
interpretation of the evidence with which we are concerned). Its
appearance at this point in Anaxagoras's work certainly does something to weaken one's impression of dogmatism on fundamental issues.
But one is left in doubt as to how far his citation of σημεῖα in
connexion with the doctrine of everything in everything is the
expression of a pure commitment to providing grounds for hypotheses,
or how far it springs from the skilful expositor's desire to season
assertion with appeal to evidence now and again, and to show the
reader how his central thesis unlocks the secret of every type of
change in the universe.

CONCLUSION

Aristotle and the scholiast write as though tissues and opposites
were perfectly coordinate and altogether unrelated principles of
Anaxagorean physics - as if the fact that something contains a portion of flesh had nothing to do with its possession of portions of
hard and soft, wet and dry, and as if the biological changes of
reproduction and growth were as fundamental to the theory of matter
as the physical changes of cosmogonic and meteorological separation.
If Aristotle suspected that Anaxagoras saw connexions and differences here, he did nothing to explore them. The present chapter, by
contrast, has attempted to articulate with some precision a connected, hierarchical system of principles, beginning with opposites and
constructing from them inanimate stuffs and finally seeds of animals
and plants and of their tissues. Aristotle is probably guilty of
ignoring nuances of differentiation in Anaxagoras's text. Our
account certainly squeezes more significance from them than Anaxagoras himself cared to make very explicit; and it has to admit that
in the reports of his arguments for his central doctrine there are

not even hints of the appropriate hierarchical differentiation. Once again we must retreat, half defeated by the fragmentariness of the evidence and by the indeterminacy of Anaxagoras's own prose, from the danger of writing 'a history of thoughts which no one ever actually succeeded in thinking, at a level of coherence which no one ever actually attained'.[82]

NOTES

Chapter 1. Mind

[1] The text from καὶ ὁποῖα to ἔσται is uncertain. It is quoted four times by Simplicius, each time differently (according to Diels's text). Since ὅσα (or ἄσσα) νῦν μὴ ἔστιν and ὅσα (or ὁπόσα) νῦν ἔστι seem to be variants, and since we plainly need the latter clause, I have followed Deichgräber (352, with n.11) in omitting the former. His observation that ἔμελλεν ἔσεσθαι is a blanket expression, covering past, present and future alike, has been overlooked by translators, who wrongly render καὶ ὁποῖα ἦν as 'and', as though it continued a list.

[2] My translation of the second paragraph follows closely that of Barnes.

[3] This makes it the more surprising that discussions of it and the other fragments on νοῦς in the modern literature are comparatively unrewarding: Anaxagoras's theory of matter has received the lion's share of discerning attention. Fortunately Barnes has now supplied an excellent account, particularly on the causal role of νοῦς and on the vexed question of how far Anaxagoras uses it as a teleological principle: topics which I have therefore left undiscussed. See also the useful treatment in Guthrie 272-9, and more stimulating observations in Hussey 138-41. The only recent article of any substance known to me is a disappointing one by von Fritz (2).

[4] But if, as I have argued elsewhere (Schofield 11), Simplicius knew only an anthology of passages from Anaxagoras's book - whether as quotations in a work of Theophrastus or otherwise - the sheer quotability of Frag. 12 may have helped to ensure that so much of it was preserved.

[5] Simplicius already observed: ὃν [sc. νοῦν] ἀξίως Ἀναξαγόρας ἐξύμνησε (in Phys. 176.32 Diels).

[6] Dover (2) 113.

[7] Ibid. 114.

[8] This interpretation of Anaxagoras has by now achieved canonical status. For a brief statement and defence of it consult Raven (2) 319, 368-9; see also Chapter 2, pp.63-4 above.

[9] DK 28B7, 5-6.

[10] in Phys. 152.11-16.

[11] *Ibid.* 152.16-21.

[12] See especially Deichgräber 347-53, to which many of my observations in the next few paragraphs are due.

[13] Ar. *Rhet.* III 9, 1409a24-35; cf., e.g., Norden (1) and (2) 367ff., Fränkel (1) 67-76.

[14] Lesky 489.

[15] His use of the indirect proof in so abstract a form may be further sign of Parmenidean influence on Anaxagoras. For as Diller (128-32) argues, the Eleatics were the pioneers of this form of argument in Greek philosophical and scientific work. On the other hand, it is a form of reasoning which, in informal guise, might naturally be used by any reflective person speculating about life or nature. Two Homeric instances, pointed out to me by Geoffrey Lloyd, are *Iliad* XXIV 563ff., and *Odyssey* XVI 194ff.; and he notes examples in *On the Sacred Disease* (VI 356.15ff. Littré (Ch.2), 358.11ff. (Ch.3), 364.20ff. (Ch.5)), whose Hippocratic author may never have read his Parmenides (Lloyd (2) 4, 8).

[16] Cf. Chadwick.

[17] I owe these examples to Fehling (1) 149 and to Colin Macleod (*per litteras*).

[18] See especially Deichgräber 357-61 (and, of course, Norden (2) 143-76).

[19] Denniston (2) 4.

[20] On καί...γε see Denniston (1) 157-8; as Deichgräber recognized (350) καὶ ὅσα γε ψυχήν κτλ. is thus closely linked with what precedes and no strong stop should be put after ἰσχύει μέγιστον. The absence of γε at the beginning of the sentence καὶ τῆς περιχωρήσιος κτλ. is likewise an indication that a strong stop should be placed after πάντων νοῦς κρατεῖ (contrary to Guthrie's translation (273)).

[21] Aristotle perhaps construed Anaxagoras as reasoning by analogy in this way: νοῦν δή τις εἰπὼν ἐνεῖναι, καθάπερ ἐν τοῖς ζῴοις, καὶ ἐν τῇ φύσει τὸν αἴτιον τοῦ κόσμου καὶ τῆς τάξεως πάσης... (*Metaph.* 984b15-17 = A58).

[22] Zeller 1222 n.1 (ἄμοιρον is suggested by the context, ἁπλόον by Ar. *de An.* 405a16-17 (= A100); cf. *Metaph.* 989b17 (= A61)). Deichgräber (348) suggested that we retain ἄπειρον, but take it not (as is usually done) as ἄπειρος (B) LSJ, but rather as the privative of πεῖρα 'without trial or experience', ἄπειρος (A) LSJ. This proposal has rightly not won support, but I think Aristotle may have construed ἄπειρον in this way. His description of Anaxagoras's νοῦς as ἁπλοῦν is probably derived from αὐτὸς ἐπ' ἑωυτοῦ in Frag. 12. But on three occasions he describes it also as ἀπαθές or ἀπαθῆ: e.g. 'Αναξαγόρας δὲ μόνος

ἀπαθῆ φησιν εἶναι τὸν νοῦν, καὶ κοινὸν οὐθὲν οὐθενὶ τῶν ἄλλων ἔχειν (de An. 405b19-21 (= A100); cf. ibid. 429b22-4, Phys. 256b24-5 (= A56)). Since this description is always coupled with the report that νοῦς is unmixed, I think it not fanciful to suppose that ἀπαθῆ must be based on something in Frag. 12, although admittedly it could have been αὐτοκρατές rather than ἄπειρον.

23 Cf. Jöhrens 42-3.

24 Lucr. I 72-4; see Jones on this motif in the Hellenistic period and in later antiquity.

25 DK 22B45. My reading of this fragment is close to that of Hussey 57.

26 Rep. 486A8-10.

27 Cf. Quine 98.

28 Cf. Aët. III 16.2 (A90). Supporters of this interpretation include Burnet 268 and Raven (1) 134-5. Anaxagoras also speaks at the end of Frag. 12 of 'greater and lesser mind'. This too may suggest a corporeal interpretation, although equally it may be interpreted as a compendious way of distinguishing between the minds of the greater and smaller animals mentioned in the first paragraph of the fragment.

29 Above all E. Med. 529.

30 Guthrie (276-8) provides a cautious and subtly argued statement of this view.

31 See de An. III 4.

32 So, e.g., Jaeger 161-4, Guthrie 279, Hussey 139.

33 Norden (2). Most of the examples cited below may be found either in his Hellenic section (143-76) or in Fehling (1) 201-2; cf. also Deichgräber 357-61.

34 Dover (1) xxxv.

35 See de An. 405a16-17, b19-21, 429a18-20 (= A100), 429b22-4.

36 Anaxagoras, of course, contrives only to *suggest* a connexion between knowledge and strength by the artifice of assonance in ἴσχει καὶ ἰσχύει.

37 Ar. PA IV 10, 687a7-10 (= A102).

38 Cf. Hussey 140.

39 My interpretation is close to that of Lanza (227). Alternatives: (i) The point of mentioning the fineness and purity of νοῦς is to explain why mixture with other things would prevent

its controlling things as it does in fact. After all, Anaxagoras's indirect proof that νοῦς exists on its own, unmixed, simply took it for granted that mixture would have this effect, so an explanation would not come amiss. The idea might be that the ability of νοῦς to know and control things, depending on its existing in a fine and pure condition, would become ineffective if νοῦς were mixed with grosser matter like flesh or earth, and as it were submerged by them. The nature of the dependence is obscure, but scholars have sometimes thought that it may be connected with the idea of penetration (e.g. Burnet 268, no doubt following Pl. *Crat.* 413C7 (= A55)): only a fine, pure substance could penetrate and so know and control things. Now Anaxagoras may have believed something like this, and it may be part of what he is meaning to convey here. But I do not think it can be his main point. As Jöhrens pointed out (46), ἔστι γάρ...καθαρώτατον is linked pretty tightly with καὶ γνώμην γε κτλ., yet clearly *that* clause cannot specify a reason why νοῦς could not control things in a mixed state; moreover, both clauses evidently say something very positive about νοῦς, yet on this interpretation the first, at least, seems to construe fineness and purity more as liabilities than as excellences. (ii) Jöhrens (46-7) takes the whole of ἔστι γάρ...πάντων νοῦς κρατεῖ as supporting [κρατεῖν]: 'Die Macht des Nus...ist...eine Folge seiner Reinheit und Feinheit und der dadurch ermöglichten γνωμη.' (Thus the idea of a dependence of knowledge and control on fineness and purity is retained from interpretation (i).) But against this: (a) surely there must be *some* connexion intended between being fine and pure and being unmixed; (b) καὶ γνώμην γε connects the second clause tightly with the first, but it does not actually indicate that it is entailed by it. Deichgräber (351) argues that a later writer would have written ὥστε *vel sim.*, but that Anaxagoras wished to retain the hymnic qualities of parataxis. Well, his indirect proof makes it highly probable that Anaxagoras *did* think knowledge and control depended on purity and fineness. But he is surely not asserting that dependence here, although he can use ὥστε when he wants to as well as the next man.

[40] Anaxagoras probably attributed ψυχή, and therefore νοῦς, to plants: cf. Plu. *Mor.* 911D (= A116).

[41] Cf. the difficulty in interpreting Anaxagoras's claim that νοῦς controls all animate things raised by Aristotle, *de An.* I 2, 404b3-6. It is hard to credit the claim of [Ar.] *Plant.* 815 a15-20 (A117) that according to Anaxagoras plants have feelings, emotions and desires; on the other hand, if n.40 was correct, the author may draw on a sound source when he reports as Anaxagorean the idea that they have *intellectum intellegentiamque* (*ibid.* 815b16-17).

[42] Discussed e.g. by Heinimann 130-1.

[43] Timpanaro 68.

[44] Thesleff 94.

[45] On this topic see Kranz (1).

[46] Note the ancient judgements on the prose style of Anaximenes and Anaxagoras preserved in Diogenes Laertius (II 3 (DK 13A1), 6 (DK 59A1)), and the remark on choice of style with which Diogenes of Apollonia began his book (B1).

[47] S.E. *M* VII 140 (= Frag. 21a).

[48] Cf. Lloyd (1) 338-9.

[49] It is, of course, an inference that their writings had this narrative form, but one not open to much doubt. See e.g. Kahn 199-200.

[50] Vitr. 7 Pr. 12.

[51] Hp. *Aër.* Chs. 8 (*bis*), 9, 16, 21.

[52] Cf., e.g., Thesleff 98; and on appeals to evidence etc. in early Attic literature see Finley Ch. 1.

[53] Ar. *Cael.* II 13, 295b11-16.

[54] DK 28B8, 51-2 and 60.

[55] Pl. *Tim.* 29B-D.

[56] Lloyd (2) 7, 9-10.

[57] Fränkel (2) 257.

[58] Cf. Humphreys 225-6.

[59] His followers included Archelaus (DK 60A1-5) and Metrodorus of Lampsacus (DK 61A2,6). No doubt Pericles was not the only young aristocratic politician nor Euripides the only young poet to sit at his feet.

[60] On literacy at Athens see Harvey, especially 628-9, and Havelock 36-41.

[61] See, e.g., Schmalzriedt, especially Ch. 7. Anaxagoras is reported to have written only one σύγγραμμα, i.e. work intended for general circulation (D.L. I 16 = A37); but it is conceivable that he left, beside this work, some ὑπομνήματα on the physical questions which, as the A section of Diels-Kranz shows, he discussed in such detail. So Lanza 11.

[62] Fränkel (2) 257 n.9; cf. Schmalzriedt 74-5, West 5, Humphreys 223. There is surprisingly little reliable evidence of early philosophers reading their books to audiences. Pl. *Parm.* 127C-D, although fictional, is sufficient to show that it was a regular practice. Cf. also Ar. *Pol.* 1263b16, D.L. III 35, 37, IX 39 (cited by Ryle 24-5).

63 *Ibid.*

64 So, e.g., Harvey 587; cf. Goody 78.

65 Was reading a widely disseminated skill in fifth-century Athens? Most of Harvey's grounds for an affirmative answer relate to the latter part of the fifth century and to the fourth, and I incline to agree with Havelock (40) that we should suppose 'a stage, characteristic of the first two-thirds of the fifth century, which we may call semi-literacy, in which writing skills were gradually but rather painfully being spread through the population without any corresponding increase in fluent reading'. The strongest argument for a degree of literacy in the second quarter of the fifth century (i.e. the date of the composition of Anaxagoras's book) far more sophisticated than the mere ability to write one's name or identify letters is, of course, 'the costly engraving on marble (for ὁ βουλόμενος to read) of the transactions of the sovereign people' (Turner 9; cf., e.g., Harvey 598-601). But even if, with Havelock (*ibid.*; cf. Davison (2) 155) one accepts that 'one cannot build up a habit of popular literacy on a fund of inscriptions' and that there was not (at this period) 'the ready and copious supply of books or journals which alone makes fluent reading possible', it remains likely that an Athenian in the upper stratum of society who had an interest in intellectual matters would have acquired a habit of reading. Anaxagoras will presumably have hoped for readers like him both in Athens and in Ionia, where, of course, prose writing flourished (and so, presumably, did its readers).

66 Fränkel (1) 76; cf. van Groningen 11.

67 Cf. van Groningen 55: 'La littérature archaïque, destinée avant tout à la récitation, fait souvent appel à la collaboration intelligente du lecteur. Aussi ne faut-il pas s'étonner si les enchaînements et les insertions ne sont pas toujours aussi lucides qu'une logique inexorable n'aurait voulu.' We should remember this when we are tempted to charge Anaxagoras with 'obscure, sometimes barely intelligible, Greek' (Vlastos (3) 357).

68 Goody suggests (37) that 'writing, and more especially alphabetic literacy, made it possible to scrutinise discourse in a different kind of way [sc. from those available in purely oral cultures] by giving oral communication a semi-permanent form... It increased the potentialities of criticism because writing laid out discourse before one's eyes...The human mind was freed to study static "text" (rather than be limited by participation in the dynamic "utterance").'

69 Cf. Pfeiffer, esp. Ch. 2.

70 In many, although not all, respects I follow Taylor and Diano.

71 I follow Heinimann (170-209) in thinking *Aër.* earlier than *Morb.Sacr.* and to be dated *c.* 440-30.

[72] See DK 59A1-27.

[73] Cf., e.g., Raven (2) 362-3.

[74] Dover (3) 31; I refer to Davison (1).

[75] D.L. II 10 (A1); cf. A11-12.

[76] Hippol. I 8.5 (A42); cf. A. *Supp.* 559-61, Fr. 300 Nauck^2.

[77] Ar. *GA* IV 1, 763b30-3 (A107); cf. A. *Eu.* 657-66. Both this and the texts mentioned in n.76 are discussed exhaustively by Rösler (1), Ch. 6. Is Aeschylus's explicit appeal to a τεκμήριον at 662 indirect evidence that Anaxagoras made much of τεκμήρια or σημεῖα?

[78] E.g. D.L. II 12 (A1), Isoc. XV 235 (A15), D.S. XII 39 (A17).

[79] See *OCD*^{2} s.v. Pericles.

[80] Pl. *Phd.* 97B-99C.

[81] *Ibid.* 96Aff..

[82] Pl. *Hp.Ma.* 281C, 282E-283B.

[83] Cf. Dover (1) xxxvi.

[84] See D.L. II 14-15 (A1), Ar. *Rhet.* 1398b15 (A23), Euseb. *Praep. Ev.* 10.14.13 (A7). On Epicurus as self-appointed reviver of the school see Sedley 53-4.

[85] Plu. *Per.* 32 (A17).

[86] Cf. Kahn 163-5, O'Brien.

[87] This question is discussed briefly in Chapter 3, pp.81-2.

Chapter 2. Primordial mixture

[1] Famous, however, in the order: ὁμοῦ πάντα χρήματα ἦν. For discussion of the original reading see Rösler (2).

[2] *FGH* 1 F1.

[3] See the excellent discussion in Schmalzriedt, Ch. 4; also Fehling (2).

[4] Hdt. I Pr.

[5] *FGH* 555 F2.

[6] DK 24B1.

7 Cf., e.g., Schmalzriedt 120 n.2; Kirk 36.

8 So Fehling (2) 62-4, Schmalzriedt 38 n.13.

9 Cf. Schmalzriedt *passim*.

10 *H.Ap.* 165-78; Diehl I^3 p.87; Th. II 103. On the notion of σφραγίς see Thgn. 19-23, Poll. IV 66, with *RE* III 2 (2nd series) 1757-8 and Kranz (2), to whom these examples are due.

11 In Frags. 4a and 12.

12 Frags. 4a (*ad init.*) and 5.

13 Cf. Schmalzriedt 121 n.6, 122-3.

14 I follow Schmalzriedt 123, against West 9, in thinking that these *were* the very first words of his book.

15 DK 64B1.

16 Hp. *VM* 1-2.

17 Procl. *in Euc.* p.66, 4ff. [= DK 42A1].

18 DK 80B1.

19 So Gigon 7.

20 Fränkel (1) 287 n.1. Frag. 4c appears to conclude an argument for holding that the original mixture contained everything in our present world; but Frag. 4b, which it rounds off in Diels-Kranz, contains no such argument, but only one for the claim that the infinite number of seeds were all unlike each other (see p.127 above). Fränkel strangely denies Anaxagoras the prefatory words τούτων δὲ οὕτως ἐχόντων here, but appears to give him them back at 290 n.1.

21 So e.g. Furley (2) 71, Strang 372.

22 See Strang 377 n.13.

23 See Chapter 4, p.167 n.67 below.

24 On this difficult clause see Schofield 17 n.59.

25 I have been much helped by Philoponus (*in Phys.* 396.15-398.8), who is greatly superior to Simplicius *ad loc.* (cf. Schofield 9 n.36).

26 *Phys.* 203a3-4.

27 *Phys.* 203a4-16.

28 *Phys.* 203a16-18.

29 *Phys.* 203a18-19.

30 *Phys.* 203a19-21.

31 This seems to be the meaning of τῷ παντί here, *pace* Schofield 10 n.38.

32 Following Simp. *in Phys.* 460.12 (= A45).

33 Frag. 10.

34 Philoponus (*in Phys.* 397.27) thinks ἐκ τοῦ τοιούτου means ἐκ τοῦ ὁμοίου: from a body like itself; and holds that Aristotle thereby enunciates the 'like by like' principle referred to above (p.50 and nn. 32 and 33). As we have seen, this principle is certainly needed by Anaxagoras to derive the notion of mixture from the observation that anything comes to be from anything. But it is not relevant in the present argument. And it is most natural and fits the context well to take the expression as a precise reference back to the one sort of body which has been specified in the passage, viz. a μῖγμα (203a23). Cf. the remarks of Bernays on *Poet.* 1449b27-8 (also Lucas *ad loc.*).

35 This is a dangerous way of arguing for an origin to the world: for without restrictions on the generality of (P) and (Q), it is impossible to stop an infinite regress of self-applications of (Q).

36 It will be recalled that Aristotle is notoriously under suspicion 'of arguing [in *EN* I 2, 1094a18-22] that since every purposive activity aims at some end desired for itself there must be some end desired for itself at which every purposive activity aims' (Ackrill 14).

37 Sentence (iv) has already shown that Aristotle's Anaxagoras is aware of the need to distinguish between theses which could be confused through failure to interpret the scope of the existential and universal quantifiers correctly. And the addition of the words 'although not at the same time' (πλὴν οὐχ ἅμα) in (Q) indicates that there and in (R) 'coming to be' is to be interpreted according to the reading of the quantifiers implied by my formulation of (Q), i.e. the existential nested within the universal.

38 This reconstruction was inspired by and borrows heavily from Barnes's account of Anaxagoras, 28-33.

39 ὁμοιομερής is a technical Aristotelian term, which was in all probability not used by Anaxagoras, but coined by Aristotle himself, and applied by him to the living tissues which he thought elemental in Anaxagoras's system because in his own biological theory he invariably classifies tissues as the homoeomerous parts of the body (e.g. *PA* II 2, 647b10-17; Bonitz, *Index Aristotelicus* 510b34-42). A substance counts as homoeomerous for Aristotle if and only if it is divisible into

parts which are like each other and like the whole of which they are parts, where likeness is a matter of strict synonymy (*Cat.* 1, 1a6-12; *Top.* V 5, 135a20-b6; *GC* I 1, 314a20; *PA* II 9, 655b6). The role (or rather the absence of a role) for either the concept or the name ὁμοιομερής in Anaxagorean theory has been well discussed in recent years: see, e.g., Mathewson 77-81, Guthrie 282-4, 325-6, Furley (2) 69-71. There is a catalogue of ὁμοιομερῆ at *Meteor.* IV 10, 388a13-20. It includes metallic bodies and animal and vegetable tissues.

40 This principle is expressed in an over-simplified form (for example, Anaxagoras would presumably want to say that some substances come to be through *concentration* of some stuff extracted from many other substances; cf. Strang 363-4). But the formulation of (3) is adequate for present purposes.

41 On the difficult issue of Anaxagoras's criteria for discriminability see Chapter 3, p.155 n.6.

42 Notably *Cael.* III 3, 302a31-b3 (= A43); cf. also *Phys.* I 4, 187a36-b4.

43 Barnes 31.

44 Here I follow the standard view of modern commentators: e.g. Vlastos (1) 326-7, Guthrie 271-2, Furley (2) 61-76.

45 Aristotle assumed that a more basic task for mind was to initiate movement in the first place (this is implied by sentence (viii), 203a32-3; and see, e.g., *Phys.* VIII 1, 250b24-6). His assumption is shared by many modern commentators (e.g. Raven (2) 374, Guthrie 278). And, of course, it is a natural assumption on several counts, not least because one supposes that Anaxagoras would have described both the primordial mixture and the effects of mind differently had the mixture been in motion. Nonetheless, its correctness is open to doubt (cf. Hussey 140), just because he is so unexplicit on the question. Neither in Frag. 1 nor in Frag. 12, the most pertinent texts, does Anaxagoras commit himself on whether matter was at rest or in motion in its primordial condition; in particular, he does nothing in Frag. 12 to suggest that mind was responsible for motion above all else. The only text which makes mind the author of motion in so many words does not entail (although it may suggest) that it is the author of *all* motion: 'And after mind began to cause motion, separation began from all that was [? thus] moved. And whatever mind moved, that was all dispersed; but as things were being moved and dispersed, the rotation was making them disperse much more' (Frag. 13: καὶ ἐπεὶ ἤρξατο ὁ νοῦς κινεῖν, ἀπὸ τοῦ κινουμένου παντὸς ἀπεκρίνετο· καὶ ὅσον ἐκίνησεν ὁ νοῦς, πᾶν τοῦτο διεκρίθη· κινουμένων δὲ καὶ διακρινομένων ἡ περιχώρησις πολλῷ μᾶλλον ἐποίει διακρίνεσθαι). Conceivably Anaxagoras could see no way of deciding whether the primordial mixture was static or moving, and so made no pronouncement on the subject.

46 So Hussey 140.

47 Owen (2) 279.

48 *Ibid.*

49 So, e.g., Furley (2) 61-4.

50 So, e.g., Vlastos 326-7.

51 Owen (2) 276-7; cf. Raven (2) 368-9.

52 Cf., e.g., Procl. *El. Theol.* 103, with Dodds's magisterial note (254; cf. 346). The Neoplatonist commentators regularly formulate Anaxagoras's principles of everything in everything and of predominance (Theses 1 and 2 of p.108 above) in terms of variant forms of Porphyry's slogan: with τὸ πλεόναζον (Philop. *in Phys.* 87.21, 88.1, 95.26; Simp. *in Phys.* 177.21; cf., e.g., Olymp. *in Gorg.* 5.15-18) or τὸ ἐπικρατοῦν (Simp. *in Phys.* 27.7-8, 155.25, 163.3, 173.36; cf., e.g., Procl. *in Tim.* III 65.1-7). Their attitude is nicely summed up in a sentence of Olympiodorus (*in Alc.* 214 (= *SVF* III 302)): καὶ ὡς Ἀναξαγόρας ἔλεγε πάντα ἐν πᾶσιν, ἓν δὲ πλεονάζειν, οὕτω καὶ ἐπὶ τῶν θείων ἐροῦμεν ('And just as Anaxagoras used to say that all things are in all, but one predominates, so we shall say it of things divine too').

Chapter 3. Unlimited smallness

1 This is the view of Barnes (21-4, 37-9). So far as I know, he is the first scholar to have seen clearly that at least two alternative interpretations are possible.

2 This is the view of Raven (2) 369-70, 378; Guthrie 297-8. It seems to have been held by Aristotle: see *Cael.* III 3, 302a31-b3 (= A43); *Phys.* I 4, 187a36-b4.

3 On the word order see Chapter 2, pp.36-9 and n.1.

4 Choice of translation at this point turns on choice of overall interpretation.

5 This question has often exercised scholars: see, e.g., Jöhrens 9-10, Strang 376. I rather doubt whether Anaxagoras had a clear distinction between 'multitude' and 'magnitude' in mind here, for I fancy that 'multitude' is in this instance the noun from 'much', not 'many' (as perhaps in Frag. 2, where the 'surrounding stuff' (τὸ περιέχον) is said to be 'unlimited in its multitude'). But perhaps he means that there is *more* air or aither, measured by *weight*, than of any (or conceivably all) other substances, and that the *volume* of a given weight of air or aither is *greater* than that of the same weight of any other substance.

6 Cf. Thphr. *Sens.* 59 (= A70). No doubt Anaxagoras excepts air and aither from the scope of the assertion: 'nothing was

manifest on account of smallness'. For the explanation of this fact (that air and aither covered everything) cannot apply to them. Does he take them to be 'manifest', then? On the one hand, the picture of the world suggested by Frag. 1 certainly makes them perceptible in the way that mist and air *are* perceptible; and application of the principle of predominance enunciated at the end of Frag. 12 - that what something has most of, that it most manifestly is - would entail that the primordial mixture looks manifestly airy and misty if it looks manifestly anything. On the other hand, Frag. 4b suggests that Anaxagoras would not count air and aither as being manifest. There he says that in the primordial mixture 'not even any colour was manifest' (οὐδὲ χροιὴ ἔνδηλος ἦν οὐδεμία): as though absence of colour meant the absence of any manifest visible quality at all, and as though you could not expect any other manifest sensible qualities if even colour was missing. Anaxagoras seems to be making 'manifest' conditional upon the possibility of the sort of discriminations which are exemplified by the distinctions one makes between colours in one's visual field.

[7] Cf. Guthrie 297-8.

[8] Cf. Strang 361-2, and Chapter 4, pp.108-9 above.

[9] Cf. Vlastos (1) 350-1, who correctly observes: 'There would be trouble if, and only if, in order to characterize, identify, explain, etc. what happens at a given level we must have completed the process of characterizing, identifying, explaining, etc. what happens at all of the lower levels' - which is, as he says, 'a gratuitous supposition'. The particulate theory is criticized by Barnes (23) as follows: 'If *every* piece of S contains a particle of S^1, and if every piece of a piece of S is a piece of S, then every piece of S is wholly composed of particles of S^1 - which is absurd' (S and S^1 are defined as any pair of stuffs whatever). But (i) the particulate theorist would surely deny the second premiss or charge it with ambiguity; and (ii) the strongest conclusion which the conjunction of the premises appears to permit is that some particles of S^1 are pieces of S.

[10] Barnes 23.

[11] Cf. Jöhrens 7.

[12] So Ar. *Phys.* I 4, 187a25.

[13] So Barnes 22.

[14] Anaxagoras's principle of infinite divisibility has often been interestingly and incisively discussed. See Jöhrens 12-22, Raven (2) 270-2, Strang 365-8, Guthrie 288-90, Furley (2) 76-80, Barnes 35-7.

[15] Diels-Kranz print the textus receptus: τὸ γὰρ ἐὸν οὐκ ἔστι τὸ μὴ οὐκ εἶναι. But however this is construed it seems doubtful or strange Greek. (a) 'What is is not not being': here ἔστι is

taken as the sign of identity. But 'not being' would more
naturally be expressed by τὸ μὴ ἐόν. (b) 'It is not possible
for what is to be what is not' (sc. τὸ μὴ οὐκ ἐόν). But why,
again, the double negative? And why the confusing omission of
ἐόν? The proposer of this construal is forced to some far-
fetched speculation here (Moorhouse 73). (c) 'It is impossible
for what is not to be.' This is the usual interpretation,
adopted, e.g., by Raven (2) 370, Guthrie 289, according to
which Anaxagoras makes οὐκ ἔστι, 'it is impossible', govern not
an infinitive (μὴ οὐκ εἶναι), but an equivalent substantival
construction (τὸ μὴ οὐκ εἶναι), substituted for the infinitive.
Lanza (198) refers us to Kühner-Gerth II 2, 217-18, for
parallels. But against this: (i) If Anaxagoras wished to convey to us that οὐκ ἔστι is to be read in a modal fashion, why
follow it immediately with the τό-construction - which inevi-
tably suggests that οὐκ ἔστι is the negative copula or
identity-sign, here denying an equation (cf. (a) above).
(ii) More seriously, the parallels from Kühner-Gerth do not
suffice. Their instances of the substitution of τὸ μὴ οὐκ for
μὴ οὐκ are divided into two groups, corresponding to the two
types of construction with μὴ οὐκ, one used after negations of
verbs of *hindering*, *denying*, *avoiding*, etc., where the double
negative doubly negates, the other (the relevant one for us)
used after negations of verbs and phrases signifying *possibility*, *propriety*, *toleration*, etc. where it works as a single
negation only. Not unexpectedly, all Kühner-Gerth's examples
of both classes share the following feature: although the
substantival τὸ μὴ οὐκ + infinitive is for all semantic purposes equivalent to μὴ οὐκ + infinitive, it always works
syntactically as a substantival expression. As Moorhouse (*loc.
cit.*) says of the second use of τὸ μὴ οὐ: 'The construction is
varied, the τό-clause being equivalent to a noun-clause as
subject, as object, or adverbially in the accusative of
respect.' But just this feature is missing in construal (c):
τὸ μὴ οὐκ εἶναι does *not* function syntactically as a noun-
clause; it can *only* be read as a degenerate infinitive.

Zeller, followed, e.g., by Burnet 258 n.2, emended to τομῇ.
But even if we improve this by writing: τὸ γὰρ ἐὸν οὐκ ἔστι
τομῇ μὴ οὐκ εἶναι (with Jöhrens 19, Cornford (3) 56 n.1), the
proposal is unconvincing. As Jöhrens (20) points out, the
sense: 'what is cannot cease to be through cutting' would more
naturally be expressed otherwise - e.g. τομῇ οὐκ ἐὸν γενέσθαι,
or τομῇ μὴ οὐκ ἀπολέσθαι, or (since this bare use of τομή as
gerundive is in any case questionable) τέμνεσθαι εἰς τὸ μὴ ἐόν.

The simplest emendation is that adopted in the text which I
have printed.

[16] So, e.g., Raven (2) 370-2; Guthrie 289-90. This view is well
criticized by Strang 366-7, Furley (2) 76-80.

[17] Guthrie 289.

[18] On Zeno B1 and 2 see Furley (1) 63-9, (2) 78.

[19] Ar. GC I 2, 316a10-34, with Furley (1) 83-5. The relation of this argument to one ascribed by Porphyry to Parmenides (Simp. in Phys. 139.25-140.6) is unmistakable. But whether Porphyry's argument derives from Zeno or from Democritus or from some other source is an undecided question: see, e.g., Fränkel (3) 129 n.16 (who denies a Zenonian origin), Vlastos (2) 183 n.9 (who sees adaptation of an Eleatic, probably Zenonian, original), Owen (1) 163 n.10 (who supports a Zenonian origin, relating it - although I do not quite understand how - to the argument partially preserved in Zeno B1 and 2).

[20] So Strang 367.

[21] This is clear from Zeno B2 and Anaxagoras's supporting γάρ-clause.

[22] Sheer coincidence seems unlikely not so much because it is improbable that two thinkers at different ends of the Greek world should have had the same idea (why not?), but because it is hard to resist seeing an actual verbal echo of one philosopher by the other elsewhere. Anaxagoras (Frag. 5) says: τούτων δὲ οὕτω διακεκριμένων γινώσκειν χρὴ ὅτι πάντα οὐδὲν ἐλάσσω ἐστὶν οὐδὲ πλείω (οὐ γὰρ ἀνυστὸν πάντων πλείω εἶναι), ἀλλὰ πάντα ἴσα ἀεί ('These things having been thus made distinct, it is right to understand that all things are neither less nor more (since it is not possible that there be more than all), but all things are equal always'). Zeno (B3) says: εἰ πολλά ἔστιν, ἀνάγκη τοσαῦτα εἶναι ὅσα ἐστὶ καὶ οὔτε πλείονα αὐτῶν οὔτε ἐλάττονα ('If there are many things, then they must be just as many as they are, and neither more nor less than themselves'). For discussion see Raven (2) 371, Furley (2) 77-8. Zeno is making the point in order to argue that any plurality is necessarily finite, whereas Anaxagoras exploits it to defend the quite different principle of conservation of matter or kinds of matter through change. Neither need be deliberately adverting to the views of the other - which makes the verbal echo the more striking.

[23] So above all Furley (2) 76-80.

[24] Ibid. 79.

[25] See Chapter 2 above.

[26] Here I follow Strang 365.

[27] Aristotle supposes that Anaxagoras's universe is infinite in extent (Phys. III 5, 205b1-3 (= A50)); and probably this is the implication of the assertion in Frag. 2 that the surrounding element is unlimited in multitude (καὶ τό γε περιέχον ἄπειρόν ἐστι τὸ πλῆθος).

[28] So, e.g., Jöhrens 21, Strang 365-6, Barnes 35.

[29] So, e.g., Raven (2) 372, Guthrie 289.

[30] So, e.g., Jöhrens 22, Strang 366. Strang claims that 'Anaxagoras takes pains always to talk of larger and smaller, never of large and small (see B6 *ad fin.*; B12, 38.4, 39.4).' But he does pair 'large and small' at the beginning of Frag. 6, which seems to be no more than a stylistic variant for 'larger and smaller' at the end of the same fragment. Strang here extracts more from diction than is reasonable - or, of course, demonstrable.

[31] Strang 367; cf. Raven (2) 372, Guthrie 289 n.2.

[32] See n.15 above.

[33] Simp. *in Phys.* 164.20-2: 'For if everything is in everything and everything is separated out from everything, then from the putative least, too, something smaller than it will be separated out, and the putative biggest was separated out from something bigger than it.'

[34] Furley (2) 78-9; cf. also Barnes 33-4.

[35] Barnes 34.

[36] We cannot trust Simplicius, for probably he did not have Anaxagoras's book available to consult, only extracts from it: see Schofield 11.

[37] Furley (2) 78.

[38] Cf. Strang 366 (apropos of Frag. 3): 'Structural complexity is not, on Anaxagoras's theory, a function of size.'

[39] It is a considerable drawback to Barnes's account of the argument (35-7) that it gives no weight to this fact and indeed leaves it unexplained: as he himself recognizes.

[40] Both Barnes 36 and Strang 365-8 take (1) as more or less equivalent to (2), and then suppose that Anaxagoras means to derive the thesis from the conjunction of (2) and the hypothesis of primordial mixture. But although in sentence (ii) Anaxagoras refers to that hypothesis, there is no clear sign that it is meant to be a premiss of his argument.

[41] Why does Anaxagoras think that microscopic pure substances must be minima? Perhaps because of an idea about the conditions for *separating* them - as the language of (ii) suggests. The idea might be that no separating process could get a purchase on matter in such a way as to isolate pure stuffs unless such stuffs were made up of natural units or particles; and that the only natural units into which pure, simple substances could conceivably be broken down would be minima. This proposal brings a bonus. It would explain why Anaxagoras took it for granted that the non-existence of minima ensures not only that 'no pure substance could be arrived at by *division*', but also - what Strang (368) thought 'not obvious' - 'that a pure substance could not be arrived at by *redistribution*'. According

to my proposal, Anaxagoras assumes that any rearrangement of
matter resulting in pure stuffs requires particles to be rearranged;
if there are no particles of the right sort -
minima - there can be no redistribution whose outcome is the
separation of pure stuffs.

42 The translation of sentence (iii) is disputed. I follow
Barnes (35) in thinking it most natural to take καί as 'even',
making τῶν ἀποκρινομένων dependent on πολλά, and reading ὅσα as
in apposition to πολλά. Alternatively, one might follow Diels-Kranz
and Guthrie (289) in construing καί as 'and', and interpret
the sentence as chiastic in structure: 'In all things
there are many, and there is an equal number of the things that
are separating off in both the larger and the smaller.' Between
these two readings there is a difference only of nuance.
Much less probable is the popular interpretation (accepted by
Burnet 259 and Raven (2) 376), which takes καί again as 'and',
but construes τῶν ἀποκρινομένων as dependent on τοῖς μείζοσί τε
καὶ ἐλάσσοσι: 'In all things there are many, and an equal number
in both the greater and the smaller of the things that
are being separated off.' On each of the other two versions an
explanation of the position of τῶν ἀποκρινομένων in the sentence
is readily supplied; on this version it seems merely
awkward. I suppose Burnet and Raven were attracted by their
construal because it seemed to give good philosophical sense.
Anaxagoras will be making the point, crucial to his doctrine of
everything in everything, that even when a distinct object is
extracted from a prior mélange, it will contain portions of
every substance, no matter how large or small it is. A very
similar, although slightly less expected thought, emerges,
however, from the alternative versions. Anaxagoras's point is
this: In the world as it now is, there are many distinct substances
which have been separated, are being separated, and
will be separated off. But it remains the case that in everything,
however large or small, there is a portion of everything
- even of substances which collect together in distinct
concentrations. In short, all things are in everything, despite
separation. The old theme is repeated with a special
emphasis, hence the prominence given in the sentence to τῶν
ἀποκρινομένων.

The emphasis on τῶν ἀποκρινομένων is not the only element of
variation. Anaxagoras actually says not that all things are in
all, but that *many* things are in all. Plainly - in view of
sentences (i) and (ii) - he does not imply 'many *but not all*',
even though elsewhere (Frags. 11 and 12) he does qualify the
thesis to except νοῦς from its scope: such a qualification
would be quite unprepared for here. All that is involved is a
slight change of focus. Sentences (i) and (ii) have been concerned
with issues of high and complex Anaxagorean theory:
separation and the inherence of everything in everything. Sentence
(iii) states his position in a simpler way. It makes the
fundamental point, of which the full theory is a baroque elaboration,
that each stuff is not (as it might appear) one, but
many. Having put this point Anaxagoras can then make the sentence
concentrate on the thesis which it has been the object of

the fragment as a whole to establish: viz. that in this present world in which substances are continually being separated off, no less than at the beginning, size is irrelevant to structural complexity.

⁴³ This is also the interpretation of Burnet 262, Jöhrens 12, Raven (2) 377.

Chapter 4. Seeds, portions and opposites

¹ See especially Vlastos (1), Cornford (1), Guthrie 279-304, Raven (1) and (2), Strang, Kerferd, Furley (2) and Barnes 16-39.

² Furley (2) 72.

³ He has usually been thought to do so: see, e.g., Burnet 269-70, Strang 379 n.28 (innumerable worlds, contra Aristotle's pretty plain implication that Anaxagoras generated a single κόσμος: Phys. VIII 1, 250b18-27; cf. Simplicius, in Phys. 178.25-6, Aëtius II 1.2 (= A63)); Cornford (2) 6-8 (civilizations situated in different parts of the earth: a popular interpretation, endorsed, e.g., by Kahn 52-3, Guthrie 313-15). The principal objection against Cornford's interpretation is well put by Vlastos (3) 355: that Anaxagoras claims not merely that different civilizations would arise, but that 'the separation' would occur elsewhere - which must mean repetition of the whole process of cosmogony.

⁴ Fränkel (2) 284-93, Vlastos (3) 354-60; their view is endorsed by Furley (2) 73.

⁵ On which see Furley (2) 73 n.37, contra Strang 379 n.28.

⁶ Vlastos (3) 357, cf. 356.

⁷ Ar. Phys. I 4, 187b1-2; III 4, 203a23-4 (A45).

⁸ Frag. 10 (from PG XXXVI 911; cf. 521); NB also Aët. I 3.5 (A46), Simp. in Phys. 460.6-22 (A45).

⁹ But there is an interesting passage right at the end of his discussion of Phys. I 4 where he raises the possibility that it was just the simplest opposites which Anaxagoras made his elements, and not (as Aristotle held) substances such as earth (or - although he does not say this - other homoeomerous stuffs) which are in Aristotelian theory composite. See in Phys. 178.33-179.12, with Stokes 235-6 (whose criticism of Simplicius at 236-7 is, however, a little hasty).

¹⁰ That Frag. 16 is a text not about cosmogony but specifying a general pattern in meteorology is convincingly argued by Stokes 229-44.

11 Here I am indebted to Strang 361-2. I take it that Anaxagoras himself has a word for the concept of ingredient, viz. μοῖρα. But he has no word which unambiguously means *substance*, although as Strang says (362) his favourite way of referring to *substances* is to use the expression τὰ ἀποκρινόμενα. χρῆμα, which might have been taken for a likely candidate, is ambiguous as between *substance* and *ingredient*. What forces one to ascribe to him the concept of *substance* is just the theory constituted by Theses 1 and 2.

12 But since the regress can be construed as not vicious (cf. Chapter 3, pp.74-5 and n.9), this interpretation can claim the virtues only of elegance and - as we shall see shortly - explanatory power, not of necessity.

13 Strang 366.

14 This example is adapted from Kerferd 499.

15 Strang 362.

16 Frag. 8 supports the interpretation of μοῖραι (*ingredients*) as not in essence *substantial*. For Anaxagoras treats the opposites hot and cold as entities which it would be intelligible to conceive of as entirely separated from each other.

17 On this see Strang 363-4.

18 On the difference between these alternatives see Strang 362-4.

19 So Cornford (1) 302-3, Vlastos 334, Stokes 17. The precise force of πολλαὶ πολλῶν ('*many...of many*') is unclear.

20 Cornford was very ready to admit the charge of ambiguity ((1) 299-305); this is held to be the downfall of his reconstruction of Anaxagoras's theory of portions by Mathewson (71-3).

21 'The dense', understood as 'dense *substance*', can be readily distinguished from 'the rare', understood as 'rare *substance*': we may point to tables, chairs, books, on the one hand, and to cobwebs, feathers and the air itself on the other. The dense *ingredient* of a thing, on the other hand, is less easily distinguished from its rare, or indeed its hot, cold, wet or dry *ingredients*. One may point to its matter - e.g. flesh, gold, earth; but, of course, gold is both dense and cold. So the only way of making it clear what one has in mind by 'the dense' and 'the cold' as *ingredients* is to specify their powers - 'stuff which makes cold', 'stuff which condenses'. I take it that this is one point (if not the major point) which Cornford had in mind when he referred to them as 'quality-things' ((1) 314-15), and what Vlastos was thinking of when he wrote that they 'are conceived not as properties of Aristotelian substances, but as "quality-things" or, better still, as forms of energy or "power" (*dynamis*)' ((1) 329). Guthrie's discussion (284-6) is spoilt by a failure to distinguish between *substances* and *ingredients*.

[22] My account is much indebted to Cornford ((1) 299-305) and Vlastos ((1) 329-33).

[23] This obscure statement presumably has something to do with Anaxagoras's theory of the heavenly bodies: see, e.g., Guthrie 300-4.

[24] Mr David Sider's researches have established that Diels-Kranz were wrong to print γῆ as a conjectural supplement: it appears in all the MSS he has inspected. He suspects that Diels meant to print ⟨ἡ⟩ γῆ.

[25] With Cornford (1) 313. Cf. also Hp. *Vict.* I 4, which sets forth a heavily Anaxagorean theory of ingredients entirely in terms of opposites: water has in it not only wet and cold but dry and warm; NB also Hp. *Aër.* 8: ἔνεστι δὲ [ὑγρὸν] ἐν παντὶ χρήματι.

[26] *Contra*, e.g., Raven (2) 376, Guthrie 284-5.

[27] See the accounts of Cornford (1) 311-15, Burnet 263-4, Vlastos (1) 333.

[28] Perhaps earth can reasonably be thought of as naturally wet: but stones? Conceivably it is the dryness of stones which makes them more liable than water to be hurled to the periphery of the universe (Frag. 16; cf. n.23 above).

[29] Barnes 26; I am much indebted to his exploration of Anaxagoras's non-particulate theory of portions in what follows - although he takes the portions to be not opposites but homoeomerous stuffs.

[30] Cf. Strang 370: 'It is...the simple fleshiness of flesh and the simple wooliness of wool that seem to us to distinguish the two substances.' Simple in a way, of course: which is what gives some plausibility to Strang's claim that 'if we account for the difference by postulating E-flesh and E-wool [i.e. *ingredient* flesh and wool, as he thinks Anaxagoras did] we are merely importing into our theory the simplicity of our experience'. But Anaxagoras always goes out of his way to stress the extreme diversity and complexity of all our experience: 'seeds having forms and colours and savours of every kind' (Frag. 4a); 'of the other things [sc. other than the seeds] the one is in no way like the other' (Frag. 4b); 'nothing different [sc. from mind] is like anything else' (Frag. 12). As Strang himself argues, this apparently means that no two individuals of the same kind are altogether alike (364-5). There is no sign in the fragments that Anaxagoras worried about the problem of explaining why different complex sets of properties cohered to make up *substances* of different specific appearance: flesh, wool, and the like; so he does not appear to have the motive for introducing *ingredient* flesh or wool which Strang assumes he has.

[31] It is so construed by Vlastos (1) 338-9.

32 See Theophrastus, *Sens*. 27-30 (= A92).

33 Cf. Hussey 136-8.

34 Theophrastus seems to have seen that heaviness and lightness were the crucial principles here: see the accounts of Diogenes Laertius II 8 (= A1), and Hippolytus I 8.2 (= A42).

35 A point often enough noticed, although seldom pressed: e.g. Vlastos (1) 330, Furley (2) 66-7.

36 For this way of dividing Frag. 4 in Diels-Kranz see Fränkel (2) 287 n.1.

37 Furley (2) 71-2.

38 I quote Lloyd's formulation of the views ((1) 246; cf. Peck 114-15). Lloyd adds another possibility (which he himself rejects), viz. that a seed is conceived 'as a single natural substance, e.g. hair or gold, *and that alone*' (i.e. as satisfying the description of a μοῖρα or *ingredient* elaborated above). I have not included this as a separate option because, as we shall see, the conception of seed as *ingredient* is not incompatible with view (2).

39 As does Lloyd (1) 246-7; cf. also, e.g., Guthrie 298-300.

40 Vlastos (1) 324.

41 Here I am largely following the excellent remarks of Cornford (2) 7.

42 Hippolytus I 8.12 (= A42).

43 D.L. II 9 (= A1).

44 Thphr. *HP* III 1.4 (= A117); and as Furley (2) 73 notes: 'Another witness (Irenaeus II 14.2 (= A113)) extends the same theory to "animals" (perhaps maggots?).' He adds: 'These presumably would be the examples cited by Anaxagoras to make more plausible his theory of seeds lying latent where they might not be suspected.' But it is perhaps better to suppose that the remark about animals being created by seeds coming down to earth from heaven belongs actually to the zoogony, not to the evidence cited in support of it. Then we need not restrict its scope to maggots.

45 Cf. Guthrie 315-16, who notes Plutarch's attribution to Anaxagoras of the idea that plants are 'earthbound animals' (*Quaest. Nat.* 911D (= A116)).

46 Aët. II 8.1 (= A67).

47 Hippolytus I 8.12 (= A42); cf. Ar. *GA* IV 1, 763b30-764a1 (= A107), where the word σπέρμα is again used in reporting the same doctrine.

⁴⁸ With Peck 114-16, Furley (2) 71-6.

⁴⁹ Vlastos (1) 324.

⁵⁰ Let alone artifacts.

⁵¹ Aristotle knows a view about the nature of animal 'germ' (γονή), which makes it a πανσπερμία, or like a πανσπερμία; this theory might conceivably have construed hair, flesh, etc. as σπέρματα within the germ, although it must remain doubtful whether such an implication could be pressed. The theory (see GA IV 3, 769a28-b3) is ascribed by Aristotle simply to τινες, 'some people', but Vlastos (1) 344a22 and Furley (2) 74 think it is probably in essence Anaxagoras's. The difficulty with their identification is that the theory attributes some ingredients in the germ to one parent, some to the other (it says: 'For the offspring is like in appearance to that one of its parents from whom most enters into its composition', in support of the idea that the germ is a mixture containing unequal amounts of its ingredients). Aristotle has already told us that according to Anaxagoras *only* the male parent contributes seed (GA IV 1, 763b30-764a1 (= A107)). Vlastos attempts to make the sentence translated above *not* imply that both parents contribute to the germ, but in doing so he makes nonsense of the reasoning in the passage. His argument that 'the coderivation of the semen from male and female is the theory of Empedocles and Democritus to which the present theory is contrasted' is invalid. Aristotle's contrast seems to be between a theory which makes the germ a *unity* (albeit containing diversity) - the πανσπερμία theory - and the idea that there are *two* germs or seeds of the same sort, one contributed by the male parent, the other by the female (GA IV 3, 769a9-26; cf. 1, 764a10-11, b3-20). He prefers the view that makes the germ a unity, but in some unspecified respects finds it obscure and fanciful (3, 769a26-8, 36). Kember acknowledges the conflict between 769a28-b3 (construed as Anaxagorean) and 763b30-764a1, but decides that it is the former, not the latter, passage which faithfully reports Anaxagoras, despite Aristotle's explicit statement.

⁵² Vlastos (1) 343 n.17.

⁵³ Here I follow the interpretation of Jöhrens 36-7, Furley (2) 72.

⁵⁴ I do not think we should infer that Anaxagoras himself used the word πανσπερμία (cf. also n.51 above). Aristotle more usually associates it with the physical theory of Democritus: Phys. III 4, 203a21 (in contrast with Anaxagoras), Cael. III 4, 303a16, de An. I 2, 404a4. But 'it may well have been Anaxagoras who put the *idea* into the atomists' heads' (Guthrie 414 n.2; my italics).

⁵⁵ See, e.g., Vlastos (1) 352 n.80, Strang 372; *contra* Cornford (1) 316 n.11, Raven (2) 384.

⁵⁶ This alternative is made very probable by Aristotle's words a little further on (*Cael*. III 4, 302b13-17), where having said that Anaxagoras made all the ὁμοιομερῆ elemental, he argues that this is a mistake, since various 'mixed' bodies are homoeomerous - e.g. flesh, bone, wood, and *stone*. (At 302b2-3 the Oxford Classical Text ascribes to Aristotle the sentence: εἶναι γὰρ ἑκάτερον αὐτῶν ἐξ ἀοράτων τῶν ὁμοιομερῶν πάντων ἠθροισμένον, 'for each of them is collected together from *all the* ὁμοιομερῆ in invisible form'. This is surely doubtful Greek; and the manuscripts strongly favour ἠθροισμένων (read by Bekker, Prantl, Stocks and Guthrie). I guess that Aristotle wrote (in reminiscence of Frag. 1): ἐξ ἀοράτων ἠθροισμένων, 'from invisible particles collected together'; and that τῶν ὁμοιομερῶν πάντων is a scribal gloss, based upon πάντα τὰ ὁμοιομερῆ, 302b13.)

⁵⁷ Thphr. *CP* I 5.2.

⁵⁸ Barnes 21.

⁵⁹ Lloyd objected to the interpretation of σπέρματα as pure μοῖραι (i) that 'the term σπέρμα does not appear to have been used either as a synonym for μοῖρα or for the μοῖραι of natural substances'; (ii) that because seeds have all sorts of forms and colours and tastes (Frag. 4a), 'some at least of the opposites (e.g. bright and dark) are actually ingredients in the seeds' ((1) 246 and n.1). But (i) on the non-particulate interpretation of seeds we have been developing, σπέρματα (in Frags. 4a and 4b) is not *synonymous* with μοῖραι. Rather the word is used to refer to certain μοῖραι (viz. those of living substances and of their tissues, as I should suppose) under their dynamic aspect as that from which things will grow. Not all μοῖραι (on my view) are principles of growth; and it is no part of the essence of any μοῖρα as such that it be a principle of growth. Again, (ii) the best way of interpreting Anaxagoras's remark about seeds in Frag. 4a is to take it as a tacit acknowledgement that portions or *ingredients* of living substances or of their tissues are not simple but complexes of opposites. See p.133 above.

Is it a consequence of the non-particulate interpretation that when in Frag. 4b Anaxagoras speaks of 'seeds unlimited in number' he is committed to asserting the existence of an infinite number of kinds of living thing (cf. Strang 375)? Not necessarily. For his implicit criteria of numeration of seeds may be determined by the criteria he assumes for counting the individual *substances* which will grow from the seeds (cf. p.127 above).

⁶⁰ Leibniz, *Monadology* 67-8.

⁶¹ With most scholars (e.g. Guthrie 295 and n.1, Stokes 16) I take καὶ γῆς πολλῆς κτλ. as a genitive absolute.

⁶² D.L. VI 73. On the reliability of this evidence consult the tolerably sanguine discussion of von Fritz (1) 54-60.

[63] *PG* XXXVI 911; cf. 521.

[64] Diels 3-4.

[65] For defence of this reading see Schofield 15 n.58.

[66] See, e.g., Jaeger 239 n.9, Vlastos (1) 32-41, Guthrie 272 (but note the reservation at 286 n.1).

[67] See *Phys*. I 4, 187a26-b7 (= A52), quoted and translated below; III 4, 203a23-4 (= A45), quoted and translated in Chapter 2. Premiss (ii) is not made explicit by Aristotle (unless, following Furley (2) 68 and n.18, we translate 187a28-9 as: 'nothing comes to be from what *it* is not' - which seems improbable in the light of 187a32ff.). But the commentators see that his analysis assumes it: see Philoponus, *in Phys*. 396.25-7; Simplicius, *in Phys*. 460.12, with Schofield 10, 13.

[68] See, e.g., *Phys*. I 4, 187b5; III 4, 203a25-6; *Cael*. III 3, 302 a32 (= A43); *GC* I 1, 314a19-20 (= A46), a27-8.

[69] Aëtius I 3.5 (= A46), translated by Raven (2) 385 and in part below; Simplicius, *in Phys*. 460.15-19, translated by Schofield 8-9. Both texts are discussed by Schofield 2-13.

[70] Cf. Schofield 11.

[71] Schofield 14-24.

[72] For this punctuation see Schofield 22 n.71.

[73] The reference to the generation specifically of animals does not put this in doubt. For notoriously Empedocles speaks of a cycle of birth and death of 'mortal things' in the context of a general account of his cosmic cycle (B17, 3-5).

[74] Aristotle only once instances any others, and then hardly as though he were sticking close to Anaxagoras's own words: *Cael*. III 4, 302b17.

[75] Aristotle, of course, proceeds to an elaborate and less boisterous critique of Anaxagoras at 187b7ff.

[76] Moreover, his contention that Anaxagoras substituted the notion of 'separation' or 'distinction' (διακρίνεσθαι) for 'coming to be' is more accurate, at any rate as an account of Anaxagoras's general practice in the fragments and of his programmatic remark in Frag. 17, than Aristotle's assertion that the concept he preferred was 'alteration' (ἀλλοιοῦσθαι).

[77] Simp. *in Phys*. 411.15-16 (= Frag. 59 Wehrli); cf. *ibid*. 133.21-2 (= Frag. 44 Wehrli).

[78] Wehrli 87.

[79] Aët. I 3.5. On Theophrastus's relation to Aristotle in general

see e.g. Kahn 17-22.

80 DK 64B4; Hp. Aër. 8, 9, 16, 21; VM 8, 17 (cf. Chapter 1, pp.25-6). Of course, Eleatics spoke of σημεῖα too: see Parmenides B8.2 (σήματα), Melissus B8.1; but they had in mind purely abstract metaphysical arguments.

81 S.E. PH I 33, Cic. Acad. II 31, 100 (A97).

82 Skinner 18.

BIBLIOGRAPHY

Extensive bibliographies of Anaxagoras, now a little old, are to be found in the books of Lanza (see below) and of D.E. Gershenson and D.A. Greenberg: *Anaxagoras and the Birth of Physics* (New York 1964). For details of more recent publications consult the annual reports of *L'Année Philologique*. The present list is not a critical one, except in the sense that it includes all and only the works to which I have thought it helpful or amusing to refer the reader in the notes.

Ackrill, J.L. 'Aristotle on *eudaimonia*', *Proceedings of the British Academy* 60 (1974), 339-59

Allen, R.E. and Furley, D.J. (eds.) *Studies in Presocratic Philosophy*, Vol. 2 (London 1975)

Barnes, J. *The Presocratic Philosophers*, Vol. 2 (London 1979)

Bernays, J. 'Aristotle on the effect of tragedy', in *Articles on Aristotle*, Vol. 4: *Psychology and Aesthetics*, ed. J. Barnes, M. Schofield, and R. Sorabji (London 1979)

Burnet, J. *Early Greek Philosophy* (4th edn, London 1930)

Chadwick, J. 'The Berezan lead letter', *Proceedings of the Cambridge Philological Society* n.s.19 (1973), 35-7

Cornford, F.M. (1) 'Anaxagoras' theory of matter', in Allen and Furley

(2) 'Innumerable worlds in Presocratic philosophy', *Classical Quarterly* 28 (1934), 1-16

(3) *Plato and Parmenides* (London 1939)

Davison, J.A. (1) 'Protagoras, Democritus, and Anaxagoras', *Classical Quarterly* n.s.3 (1953), 33-45

(2) 'Literature and literacy in ancient Greece', *Phoenix* 16 (1962), 141-56, 219-33

Deichgräber, K. 'Hymnische Elemente in der philosophischen Prosa der Vorsokratiker', *Philologus* 88 (1933), 347-61

Denniston, J.D. (1) *The Greek Particles* (2nd edn, Oxford 1954)

(2) *Greek Prose Style* (Oxford 1952)

Diano, C. 'La data di pubblicazione della Syngraphē di Anassagora', *Giornale Critico della Filosofia Italiana* 51 (1972), 499-515

Diels, H. 'Atacta', *Hermes* 13 (1878), 1-9

Diller, H. 'ὄψις ἀδήλων τὰ φαινόμενα', in *Kleine Schriften zur antiken Literatur*, ed. H.-J. Newiger and H. Seyffert (Munich 1971)

Dodds, E.R. *Proclus: The Elements of Theology* (2nd edn, Oxford 1963)

Dover, K.J. (1) *Aristophanes: Clouds*, ed. with introd. and comm. (Oxford 1968)

(2) *Aristophanic Comedy* (London 1972)

(3) 'The freedom of the intellectual in Greek society', *Talanta*: Proceedings of the Dutch Archaeological and Historical Society 7 (1975), 24-54

Fehling, D. (1) *Die Wiederholungsfiguren und ihr Gebrauch bei den Griechen vor Gorgias* (Berlin 1969)

(2) 'Zur Funktion und Formgeschichte des Prooimiums in der älteren griechischen Prosa', in ΔΩPHMA: Hans Diller zum 70. Geburtstag ('Ελληνικὴ 'Ανθρωπιστικὴ 'Εταιρεία, 2nd series 27: Athens 1975)

Finley, J.H. *Three Essays on Thucydides* (Cambridge, Mass. 1967)

Fränkel, H. (1) *Wege und Formen frühgriechischen Denkens* (2nd edn, Munich 1960)

(2) *Early Greek Poetry and Philosophy*, translated by M. Hadas and J. Willis (Oxford 1975)

(3) 'Zeno of Elea's attacks on plurality', in Allen and Furley

von Fritz, K. (1) *Quellenuntersuchungen zu Leben und Philosophie des Diogenes von Sinope*, Philologus Supplementband 18.2 (1926)

(2) 'Der ΝΟΥΣ des Anaxagoras', in *Grundprobleme der Geschichte der antiken Wissenschaft* (Berlin and New York 1971)

Furley, D.J. (1) *Two Studies in the Greek Atomists* (Princeton 1967)

(2) 'Anaxagoras in response to Parmenides', *Canadian Journal of Philosophy* Suppl. Vol. 2 (1976), 61-85

Gigon, O. 'Zu Anaxagoras', *Philologus* 91 (1936-7), 1-41

Goody, J. *The Domestication of the Savage Mind* (Cambridge 1977)

van Groningen, B.A. *La Composition littéraire archaïque grecque*, Verhandelingen der k. Akadamie van Wetenschappen, Afd. Letterk. n.s. 65.2 (Amsterdam 1958)

Guthrie, W.K.C. *A History of Greek Philosophy*, Vol. 2 (Cambridge 1965)

Harvey, F.D. 'Literacy in the Athenian democracy', *Revue des Études Grecques* 79 (1966), 585-635

Havelock, E.A. *Preface to Plato* (Oxford 1963)

Heinimann, F. *Nomos und Physis*, Schweizerische Beiträge zur Altertumswissenschaft 1 (Basel 1945)

Humphreys, S.C. *Anthropology and the Greeks* (London 1978)

Hussey, E.L. *The Presocratics* (London 1972)

Jaeger, W. *The Theology of the Early Greek Philosophers* (Oxford 1947)

Jöhrens, O. *Die Fragmente des Anaxagoras*, diss. Göttingen (Bochum-Langendreer 1939)

Jones, R.M. 'Posidonius and the flight of the mind through the universe', *Classical Philology* 21 (1926), 97-113

Kahn, C.H. *Anaximander and the Origins of Greek Cosmology* (New York and London 1960)

Kember, O. 'Anaxagoras' theory of sex differentiation and heredity', *Phronesis* 18 (1973), 1-14

Kerferd, G.B. 'Anaxagoras and the concept of matter before Aristotle', in Mourelatos

Kirk, G.S. *Heraclitus: the Cosmic Fragments* (Cambridge 1954)

Kranz, W. (1) 'Das Verhältnis des Schöpfers zu seinem Werk in der althellenischen Literatur', *Neue Jahrbücher für das klassische Altertum* 27 (1924), 65-86

(2) 'Sphragis', *Rheinisches Museum für Philologie* 104 (1961), 3-46, 97-124

Kühner, R. and Gerth, B. *Ausführliche Grammatik der griechischen Sprache*, Vol. 2 (3rd edn, Hanover and Leipzig 1904)

Lanza, D. *Anassagora: Testimonianze e Frammenti* (Florence 1966)

Lesky, A. *A History of Greek Literature*, transl. J. Willis and C. de Heer (London 1966)

Lloyd, G.E.R. (1) *Polarity and Analogy* (Cambridge 1966)

(2) 'Aspects of the interrelations of medicine, magic and philosophy in ancient Greece', *Apeiron* 9 (1975), 1-16

Lucas, D.W. *Aristotle: Poetics* (Oxford 1968)

Mathewson, R. 'Aristotle and Anaxagoras: an examination of F.M. Cornford's interpretation', *Classical Quarterly* n.s.8 (1958), 67-81

Moorhouse, A.C. 'The construction with MH OY', *Classical Quarterly* 34 (1940), 70-7

Mourelatos, A.P.D. (ed.) *The Pre-Socratics* (Garden City, New York 1974)

Norden, E. (1) *Die antike Kunstprosa* (5th impression, Stuttgart 1958)

(2) *Agnostos Theos* (4th impression, Stuttgart 1956)

O'Brien, D. 'The relation of Anaxagoras and Empedocles', *Journal of Hellenic Studies* 88 (1968), 93-113

Owen, G.E.L. (1) 'Zeno and the mathematicians', in Allen and Furley

(2) 'Plato and Parmenides on the timeless present' in Mourelatos

Peck, A.L. 'Anaxagoras: predication as a problem in physics', *Classical Quarterly* 25 (1931), 27-37 and 112-20

Pfeiffer, R. *History of Classical Scholarship: from the beginnings to the end of the Hellenistic age* (Oxford 1968)

Quine, W.V.O. *Word and Object* (Cambridge, Mass. 1960)

Raven, J.E. (1) 'The basis of Anaxagoras's cosmology', *Classical Quarterly* n.s.4 (1954), 123-37

(2) 'Anaxagoras of Clazomenae', in G.S. Kirk and J.E. Raven, *The Presocratic Philosophers* (Cambridge 1957)

Rösler, W. (1) *Reflexe vorsokratischen Denkens bei Aischylos*, Beiträge zur klassischen Philologie 37 (Meisenheim an Glan 1970)

(2) 'ΟΜΟΥ ΧΡΗΜΑΤΑ ΠΑΝΤΑ ΗΝ', *Hermes* 99 (1971), 246-8

Ryle, G. *Plato's Progress* (Cambridge 1966)

Schmalzriedt, E. ΠΕΡΙ ΦΥΣΕΩΣ: *zur Frühgeschichte der Buchtitel* (Munich 1970)

Schofield, M. 'Doxographica Anaxagorea', *Hermes* 103 (1975), 1-24

Sedley, D.N. 'Epicurus and the mathematicians of Cyzicus', *Cronache Ercolanesi* 6 (1976), 23-54

Skinner, Q. 'Meaning and understanding in the history of ideas', *History and Theory* 8 (1969), 3-53

Stokes, M.C. 'On Anaxagoras', *Archiv für Geschichte der Philosophie*

47 (1965), 1-19 and 217-250

Strang, C. 'The physical theory of Anaxagoras', in Allen and Furley

Taylor, A.E. 'On the date of the trial of Anaxagoras', *Classical Quarterly* 11 (1917), 81-7

Thesleff, H. 'Scientific and technical style in early Greek prose', *Arctos* 4 (1966), 89-113

Timpanaro, S. *The Freudian Slip* (London 1976)

Turner, E.G. *Athenian Books in the Fifth and Fourth Centuries B.C.* (London 1952)

Vlastos, G. (1) 'The physical theory of Anaxagoras', in Allen and Furley

(2) 'A Note on Zeno B1', *ibid.*

(3) 'One world or many in Anaxagoras?', *ibid.*

Wehrli, F. *Eudemos von Rhodos*, Vol. 8 in *Die Schule des Aristoteles* (2nd edn, Basel and Stuttgart 1969)

West, M.L. *Early Greek Philosophy and the Orient* (Oxford 1971)

Zeller, E. *Die Philosophie der Griechen*, 1st pt. 2nd half, ed. W. Nestle (6th edn, Leipzig 1920)

INDEXES

I   INDEX OF PASSAGES

This index collects all Anaxagorean and Aristotelian texts which are discussed, touched upon, or used as evidence in text or notes. References to other authors are collected in the *General Index*.

   Anaxagoras is cited according to the numeration of testimonies and fragments in Diels-Kranz (6th and later editions), Aristotle according to page, column and line of Bekker's edition. For the division of Anaxagoras B4 into three, see p. 152 n. 20 and p. 164 n. 36.

ANAXAGORAS

A1	(6) 149 n.6;		n.8 (Aëtius);
	(8) 164 n.34;		154 n.39,167
	(9) 108,124;		n.68 (Aris-
	(10) 151 n.75;		totle)
	(12) 151 n.78;	A50	158 n.27
	(14-15) 151	A52	43-5,55,58,
	n.84		137-40
A7	151 n.84	A55	148 n.39
A11	151 n.75	A56	147 n.22
A12	151 n.75	A58	146 n.21
A15	151 n.78	A61	146 n.22
A17	151 n.78 (Dio-	A63	161 n.3
	dorus); 151	A67	125 (with n.46)
	n.85 (Plutarch)	A70	155 n.6
A23	151 n.84	A90	11-12 (with
A37	149 n.61		n.28)
A42	(2) 164 n.34;	A92	115,120 (with
	(5) 151 n.76;		n.32)
	(11) 108;	A97	168 n.81
	(12) 124,126	A100	146 n.22,147
A43	128-9,154 n.42,		n.35
	155 n.2,167	A102	16 (with n.37)
	n.68	A107	34 (with n.77),
A45	45-59,161 n.7,		164 n.47,165
	167 n.67 (Aris-		n.51
	totle); 136	A113	164 n.44
	(with n.69),	A116	148 n.40,164
	152 n.25,153		n.45
	n.32,161 n.8,	A117	125 (with n.44)
	167 n.67 (Sim-		(Theophrastus);
	plicius)		148 n.41
A46	136 (with		(ps.-Aristotle)
	n.69),141,161		

Index of passages

ANAXAGORAS *(cont.)*

B1	Ch.2 (esp. 36-40,41-2,64-6), Ch.3 (esp. 68-79,94-7),107-8, 151 n.1,154 n.45,155 nn.5 and 6
B2	114,125,155 n.5,158 n.27
B3	41, Ch.3, esp. 80-9,90,94-7, 156 n.15
B4a	38 (with nn. 11 and 12), 101-4,122-33, 161 n.3,163 n.30,164 n.36, 166 n.59
B4b	42,74,122-33, 152 n.20,156 n.6,163 n.30, 164 n.36,166 n.59
B4c	42-3,65-6, 152 n.20
B5	38 (with n.12), 42-3,65-6,158 n.22
B6	61, Ch.3 (esp. 68-70,84,87, 89-99),101, 104-5,108-9, 113,141,159-61
B8	63,105,108, 113,162 n.16
B10	50,106,129, 135-43
B11	13,18,22,108, 160 n.42
B12	Ch.1 (esp. 3-22),38 (with n.11),40-1,76, 107-8,110-16, 125,145 n.1, 146 nn.20-2, 147 nn.28,36 and 39,154 n. 45,156 n.6,159 n.30,160 n.42, 163 n.30
B13	40,108,154 n.45
B14	11,40
B15	107-8,113,114-15,163 n.24
B16	108,113-16, 132,161 n.10, 163 n.28
B17	44-5,63,72, 111,167 n.76
B21a	24-5

ARISTOTLE

Categoriae

1	
1a6-12	154 n.39

Topica

V 5	
135a20-b6	154 n.39

Physica

I 4	
187a25	156 n.12
187a26-b7	136 (with n.67),137-40
187a26-31	43-5,55,58 167 n.67
187a28-9,32ff.	
187a32,37	115
187a36-b4	155 n.2
187b1-2	106
187b5	136 (with n.68)
187b7ff.	167 n.75
III 4	
203a3-23	46
203a21	165 n.54
203a23-33	45-59,153
203a23-4	106,136 (with n.67)
203a25-6	167 n.68
203a33-b2	46-7
III 5	
205b1-3	158 n.27
VIII 1	
250b18-27	161 n.3
VIII 5	
256b24-5	147 n.22

Index of passages

De Caelo

II 13
295b11-16   26,63

III 3
302a31-b3   128-9,155 n.2
302a32   167 n.68
302b2-3   166 n.56

III 4
302b13-17   166 n.56
302b17   167 n.74
303a16   165 n.54

De Generatione et Corruptione

I 1
314a19-20,27-8   167 n.68
314a20   154 n.39
314a28-b1   128-9

I 2
316a10-34   80-1 (with n.19)

Meteorologica

IV 10
388a13-20   154 n.39

De Anima

I 2
404a4   165 n.54
404b3-6   148 n.41
405a16-17   146 n.22, 147 n.35
405b19-21   147 nn.22 and 35

III 4   11-12,14
429a18-20   147 n.35
429b22-4   147 nn.22 and 35

De Partibus Animalium

II 2
647b10-17   153 n.39

II 9
655b6   154 n.39

IV 10
687a7-10   16

De Generatione Animalium

I 18
723a10-11   129,137

IV 1
763b30-764a1   34,164 n.47, 165 n.51
764a10-11   165 n.51
764b3-20   165 n.51

IV 3
769a9-26   165 n.51
769a26-8,36   165 n.51
769a28-b3   165 n.51

Metaphysica

I 3
984b15-17   146 n.21

I 8
989b17   146 n.22

Ethica Nicomachea

I 2
1094a18-22   153 n.36

Ethica Eudemia

I 4
1215b6-8   23

I 5
1216a10-14   23

Politica

II 5
1263b16   149 n.62

Index of passages

Rhetorica

III 9
1409a24-35   7

Poetica

6
1449b27-8   153 n.34

II INDEX OF GREEK TERMS

ἄπειρον, reading and meaning in Frag. 12,10-11 (with n.22)

ἀποκρινόμενα: A.'s favourite way of referring to *substances*, 110, 162 n.11; variant interpretations of introduction of notion in Frag. 6,160 n.42

ἀρχή: the infinite as principle of things, 46,48; ambiguity of term, 48,51

γάρ: obscurity of force, 9,11,47-8,82,89,94-7; frequent use in Frag. 1,41

γονή, term used in preference to σπέρμα for genetic carrier, 129, 135,165 n.51

διακρίνεσθαι, A.'s use of the term, 111 (with n.18),139,167 n.76

εἰκός, ἐοικός, principle of reasoning in science and cosmology, 26-8

ἔνδηλον: A.'s concept discussed, 155 n.6 (cf. 56,70-8); its use in his principle of predominance, 76,108,118-20

ἐνυπάρχειν, term used by Ar. and Theophrastus in expounding A.'s doctrine of portions, 115

ἱστορίη, Ionian, 26-7,36

κατεῖχεν, ambiguity of expression in Frag. 1,70 (with n.4; cf. 71, 76)

κοσμός: fundamental explanandum for A. and Plato, 61; possible reduplication, 102-4 (with n.3); unity, 63,105,121; permanence, 91

λεπτός, ambiguity of expression in Frag. 12,11-12,147 n.39

μοῖρα: term expresses concept of *ingredient*, 162 n.11; designates not *substances*, but proportions, 75,162 n.16; notion expressed by ἐνυπάρχειν in Ar. and Theophrastus, 115; connexion with notion of σπέρμα, 164 n.38, 166 n.59

νόησις, concept in Diogenes of Apollonia, 5-6,13,18

νοῦς, see mind

ὁμοιομερῆ: term explained, 153 n.39; Ar. puts them among A.'s 'elements', 43,47-50,128-9 (with n.56),135-41; but in this essay construed as logically posterior to opposites as *ingredients*, 107,117-18 (with n.30),120,133-4; Ar.'s identification with A.'s σπέρματα sceptically discussed, 123,128-32

πανσπερμία, neither term nor concept to be ascribed to A., *pace* Ar. and Vlastos, 123,127 (with n.51),128 (with n.54)

πᾶς, reiteration in Frag. 12,8; and in later Ionian philosophical prose, 13; range of application in doctrine of everything in everything, 115-16; and in idea of 'seeds of all things', 126-7

σημεῖον, in Diogenes of Apollonia, 6,142; in Eleatics, 168 n.80; perhaps in A., 48,142-3,151 n.77; *see also* τεκμήριον

σπέρμα: A.'s use of the term, 122-32,164 n.47,165 n.51,166 n.59; *see also* seeds

σύγγραμμα, A. writes only one, 149 n.61

σφραγίς, concept used and documented, 37-8 (with n.10)

τεκμήριον: in Hippocratic writers, 26,142 (with n.80); in Aeschylus, 151 n.77; perhaps in A., 48,142-3,151 n.77; *see also* σημεῖον

ὑπόμνημα, A. perhaps writes a number, 149 n.61

χρῆμα: indeterminacy of expression in A., 77,78,96-7,126-7,162 n.11; primary denotation accepted in this essay, 107,115-16

III GENERAL INDEX

Aeschylus: invokes Zeus, 12; perhaps draws on A., 34

Aëtius, his general interpretation of A., 136,141

air and aither: distinguished, 71 (with n.6); interpreted by Ar. as 'seed-conglomerates', 128; but in Frag. 1 better construed as *ingredients*, 131-2; their predominance, 41-2,70-8; their multitude and magnitude, 155 n.5; why unlimited, 71; whether ἔνδηλα, 155 n.6; role in cosmogony and meteorology, 107-8,114-15; in zoogony and plant reproduction, 125-6

Alcmaeon, exordium of his book, 36-8

ambiguity: in A., 1-2,10-22,32-3, Ch.3 *passim*, 100-1,112-13,144; in philosophy of archaic age, 24

Anaximander: author of cosmogonical narrative, 25; used argument from sufficient reason, 26,62-3; probably did not argue for the existence of an original source of genesis, 44; *see* Ionian, Milesians

Anaximenes: author of cosmogonical narrative, 26; prose style assessed, 149 n.46; *see* Ionian, Milesians

Antiochus (the logographer), exordium of his book, 36-8

'anything from anything', principle ascribed to A. by Ar., 47-50,51, 106,139,153 n.34; validity of ascription discussed, 141-3; possible role in A.'s system, 53-9,61-2,65-6

archaic: style in A., 6-10; age of philosophy, 22-3; 'rationality', 97-8

argument, its role in A.'s philosophy, 1-2, Ch.1 *passim* (esp. 3-10, 24-32), Ch.2 *passim*,94-9, Ch.4 *passim* (esp. 101,141-4)

Aristophanes, on philosophy, 4

Aristotle: on A.'s νοῦς, 11-12,14,146 nn.21-2,148 n.41,154; on A.'s thesis of primordial mixture, 43-61,153,155 n.2; on A.'s thesis of everything in everything, 45-8,106-7,121-2,132,134-43,167 nn. 67 and 75; on A.'s 'elements', 43-4,128-9,137-43,156 n.12, 166 n.56,167 n.74; on A.'s ὁμοιομερῆ, 128-9,137-43,153 n.39,166 n.56, 167 n.74; takes A.'s κοσμός to be unique, 161 n.3, and his universe infinite, 158 n.27; on A.'s genetics, 165 n.51; on A.'s explanation of human intelligence, 16; on Anaximander's view of the position of the earth, 26,62-3; attributes an argument against infinite divisibility to Democritus, 80-1 (with n.19); his mode of philosophizing contrasted with A.'s, 33,89,97

General index

Barnes, J.: formalization of A.'s system exploited, 153 n.38 (cf. 40); discussion of 'like from like' principle, 57-8, of 'on account of smallness', 76, of ingredients, 117, of seeds, 130-1, of particulate interpretation of A.'s primordial mixture, 130-1, 156 n.9, of Frag. 3, 87 (with nn.34-5)

Berezan lead letter, repetitious, 8

bibliographical information: on A.'s νοῦς, 145 n.3; on his primordial mixture, 155 nn.1-2; on his principle of infinite divisibility, 156 n.14; on his doctrine of everything in everything, 161 n.1

biography, of A., 33-5

biology, its bearing on the doctrine of everything in everything, 106-7,121-43

body, and mind, 16-17,21-2

books: their character and reception in the sixth and fifth centuries (esp. Presocratic books), 22-33,149-50; beginning of A.'s book, 36-40; number of books by A. discussed, 149 n.61; *see also* oral culture; style

causation: A.'s general conception, 107-21; universality of, 50-9, 61-2; role of mind, 9-10,12-22,50-63,102-4,145 n.3,146 n.21,147 n.39,148 n.41,154 n.45; zoogony and reproduction, 124,133-4

chronology, of A., 33-5,81-2

common: opinion, 24; experience, 24; sense, 28,53-4,59,104,109,120

Cornford, F.M., view of opposites in A.'s system endorsed, 163 n.22

cosmogony: A.'s grounds for and use of cosmogonical hypothesis, 51-2,53-61,65-6,142; role of mind, 9-10,19-20,40,51-2,53-61,145 n.3,146 n.21,154 n.45; its physical operation, 107-8,110,113-15, 120-1,124,133,143; its possible duplication, 102-4,161 n.3; zoogony, 124-6,130,133,164 n.44; in Parmenides and Plato, 27-8; cosmogonical narrative, 25,62

cosmology: contrasted with metaphysics, 5,27-8,31; connected with it, 52-67,121

Deichgräber, K., on A.'s style, 6-8,148 n.39

Democritus: his system assimilated by Ar. to Milesian monism, 46-8; notion of πανσπερμία, 165 n.54; argument against infinite divisibility, 81 (with n.19); genetic theory, 165 n.51; employment of solemn religious style, 13 didacticism, in A., 97-100

Diels, H., claims scholium on Gregory as fragment of A., 135-7

Diogenes of Apollonia: chronology of, 33,35; his respect for argument and evidence, 5-6,28,31-2,142; exordium of his book, 39,149 n.46; his concept of νόησις,5-6,13,18; his use of solemn religious style, 13, and of repetition, 8,13; echoed by Euripides, 21

Diogenes of Sinope, exploits a doctrine of A. in *Thyestes*, 134-5

dogmatism, in A., 1-2,3-10,23-32,39-40,64-7,74,82,89,100-1,142-3

Dover, K.J.: on Aristophanes and the Presocratics, 4-5; on personification, 13

doxographical evidence, for A.'s central doctrines, 106-7,117,121-2, 124-6,134,142; *see* Aëtius; scholiast; Simplicius; Theophrastus

earth: position of in A.'s system, 107; in Anaximander's, 26,62-3; involved in general pattern of cosmic change, 113-16; general character, 107,163 n.28; *ingredient* in primordial mixture, 131-2; role in zoogony and plant reproduction, 124-8

Empedocles: chronological relation with A., 35 (with n.86); character of his philosophy, 23-4,38; theory of elements contrasted with A.'s, 44-6,128,135,138-9,167 n.73; genetic theory, 165 n.51

empirical observation, role in A.'s system, 53-66; *see* sense experience; ἔνδηλον

epistemology: slight role in A.'s thought, 1,24-5,143; bulks larger in later Ionian authors, 28; 'epistemological exordium', 36-40; epistemological considerations on identity of A.'s μοῖραι, 117-20

Euripides: on mind and God, 21-2; sits at A.'s feet, 149 n.59

'everything in everything': interpretation of principle, 13,54-5,68, 74-5,107-21,130-43,155 n.52,160 n.42; A.'s arguments for it, 45-8,54-5, Ch.4 *passim*; relation to principle of unlimited smallness, 66-7,79-80,87-94; relation to thesis of primordial mixture, 56,68; paradoxical character, 29

evidence, its provision by A. and other Ionian prose writers, 6,19, 26,142-3

forces, A.'s μοῖραι interpreted as, 120-1,133

Fränkel, H.: on early Greek philosophy books, 30; on Frag. 4,42,102, 152 n.20,164 n.36

Furley, D.J.: on Frag. 3,81-2,87-8; on A.'s seeds, 164 n.44,165 n.51

Galen, on A.'s bereavement, 23

God, perhaps identified with mind by A., 12-13,19-22

growth, A.'s theory, 135-43,166 n.59

Hecataeus, exordium of his book, 36,38

Heraclitus: philosophical style and activity, 23-4,29,30; exordium of his book, 37-8; doctrine on soul, 11; influence on epistemology, 28

Herodotus: appeals to εἰκός, 26; exordium of his book, 36,38

Hesiod: contrasted with philosophers, 5,23,25; repetition in, 8; use of solemn predication, 12

Hippocrates of Chios, epistemological impetus behind his *Elements*, 39

Hippocratic treatises: chronological relation of *Aër.*, *Morb. Sacr.*, and *VM* to A.'s book, 33 (with n.71); *Aër.* and *Vict.* influenced by A., 163 n.25; dogmatism and argument in *Aër.*, 25-6,142; in *VM*, 28,142; and in *Morb. Sacr.* 28,146 n.15; epistemological impetus of *VM* and *Morb. Sacr.*, 28,39

Homer: solemn predication in, 12; his exordia, 39; indirect proof in, 146 n.15; σφραγίς, in *H.Ap.*, 37-8

homoeomerous, *see* ὁμοιομερῆ

hymn, style in A. and others, 4,8-10,21,148 n.39

indeterminacy, of A.'s thought and prose, 1,78,94-9,100-1,144

individuation, of minds, 16-17,21-2

infinite: divisibility, 79-94 (esp. 89-90); size of universe, 83-4, 158 n.27; as principle of things, 46-8; 'elements' ascribed to A. by Ar., 43-4,46,156 n.12; components of primordial mixture, 70-8; seeds, 73-4,166 n.59; regress, 74-5 (with n.9), 108-9 (with n. 12),153 n.35; *see* smallness, unlimited; ἄπειρον

ingredients, in A.'s physical theory, 74-5,108-21,123,130-4,162,163 nn.25 and 30,164 n.38,166 n.59; *see also* portions; μοῖρα

Ion of Samos, uses σφραγίς, 38

Ionian: philosophical and scientific tradition, 24-31,71,107,110, 132,142-3; prose exordium, 36-9

large, A.'s views on, 80-5,90-3,159 n.30; *see also* smallness

Leibniz, G.W.F., monadology compared with A.'s views, 18,132

Leucippus, chronological relation with A., 35

'like from like', principle ascribed to A. by Ar. and his commentators, 44,50,53-9,61,136 (with n.67),153 n.34

literacy, in sixth- and fifth-century Greece, 29-33,150; *see also* books; oral culture

Lloyd, G.E.R.: on argument in early Hippocratic treatises, 28,146 n.15; on seeds in A., 123 (with n.38),166 n.59

Lucretius: on the mind of Epicurus, 10; on soul atoms, 79

mass nouns, and A.'s theory of mind, 13-14, and of matter, 116-17

matter: homogeneous and unorganized nature, 59-67; ontology and theory of change, Ch.4 (esp. 108-21,128-33,143); contrasted with mind, 11-12,16-17,21-2,59-61,63

Melissus: chronological relation with A., 35; notion of σημεῖον, 168 n.80

metaphysics: contrasted and connected with cosmology, 5,27-8,31,52-67,121; general metaphysical principles in A., Ch.2 (esp. 52-67), 78-9,87-8,108-9,142-3

meteorology, 107-8 (with n.10),113-15,116,120-1,124,143

Milesians: transmission of ideas, 31; style of exordia conjectured, 39; A.'s system compared and contrasted, 46-7,132; *see also* Anaximander; Anaximenes; Ionian

mind, 2, Ch.1 (esp. 3-22),40-1,51-2,55,58-61,63,145-8,154 n.45

mixture: primordial, Ch.2 *passim*, 68-79,107-8,142,154 n.45,155 n.6; its contents, 56-7,68-79,125-33; mixtures constitute objects in present world, 47-8,89-94, Ch.4 (esp. 107-21,130-40),153 n.34; mind unmixed, 7-8,14,19 (with n.39)

natural powers, A.'s μοῖραι interpreted as, 120-1,131-3,162 n.21

Neoplatonists, their doctrines compared with A.'s, 15,18,67 (with n.52) *nihil ex nihilo*, principle ascribed to A. by Ar., 44-5,50,58,135-41, 167 n.67; *see also* 'like from like'

nutrition, A.'s theory of, 106-7,121,129-30,136-43

opposites, as principles of A.'s ontology and theory of change, 43, 105,107-21,132-3,135-40,142-3,161 n.9,162 nn.16 and 21,163 n.25, 166 n.59

oral culture, as context of A.'s work, 29-33,98-9,149 n.62,150

Owen, G.E.L.: on principle of sufficient reason, 62-3; on Frag. 1 as contradicting Parmenides, 64

Oxyrhyncus Papyrus, repetition in, 8

Parmenides: devotion to argument compared and contrasted with A.'s dogmatism, 5,24-5,26-8,142-3 (with n.80),146 n.15; A. convinced by his argument *nihil ex nihilo*, 5,26-7,58,60,72; A.'s attitude to other Parmenidean doctrines, 63-4,65,78-9,82; P.'s use of paradox, 5,29; form of his work, 23-4,38; influence on epistemology, 28; susceptibility to modern analytic method, 94

particles: perhaps components of primordial mixture, 70-9; or of mixtures in general, 134,139-40; as seeds, 130-2; not incompatible with general principles of A.'s ontology, 156 n.9; unless construed as elementary or minimal, 109,159 n.41

Pericles, association with A., 22-3,33-5

Philoponus: superior to Simplicius as exegete, 152 n.25; particular exegetical points discussed, 153 n.34,167 n.67

Plato: on the mind of the philosopher, 11; on νοῦς, 18; on intellectual status of cosmology, 27; cosmogony compared with A.'s, 61; view of A., 22-3; supplies evidence for A.'s chronology, 34-5

Porphyry: enunciates doctrines of everything in everything and of predominance, 67; on an argument against infinite divisibility, 158 n.19

portions: as contents of primordial mixture, 70-9; how interpreted in doctrine of everything in everything, 13-14,55,107-21,130-3; *see also ingredients*, μοῖρα

predominance, theory of, 76,87,107-21,139-40,155 n.52

proof, indirect, 7 (with n.15)

prose, in early philosophy and science, 25-6,32-3; *see also* books; style

Protagoras: influence on epistemology, 28; exordium contrasted with A.'s, 40

Pythagoras, use of paradox, 29

quantifiers, scope of, 15-16,20,49-50,51-2 (with nn.36-7)

regress, *see* infinite

repetition, in A.'s style, 6-8,9,97-9

reproduction: A.'s interest in, 106-7,124-6 (with n.44),129-30,131-2, 143; his theory, 165 n.51

revelation, as Presocratic technique, 5,23-4

rhetoric, in A.'s style, 10,19,88-9,97-9,102

scholiast, on Gregory of Nazianzus (Frag. 10), 50,106,129,135-43

seeds: A.'s theory of, 121-34,139,143,164 nn.38 and 44,165 n.51, 166 n.59; whether particulate, 74-5,130-2; *see also* γονή; πανσπερμία; σπέρμα

sense experience, 105,118-20,155 n.6; *see also* empirical observation; ἔνδηλον

separation, A.'s theory of, 50-62, Ch.4 *passim* (esp. 102-4 (with n.3),107-8,110-16,120-1,135-41,143),154 nn.40 and 45,159 n.41, 160 n.42,167 n.76

Sextus Empiricus, ascribes epistemological principle to A. (Frag. 21a),24-5

Sider, D., on text of Frag. 15,163 n.24

Simplicius: character of his evidence as reporter of A., 106-7 (with n.9); extent of knowledge of A., 137,145 n.4,159 n.36; inferiority to Philoponus as exegete, 152 n.25; transmits Theophrastus's account of A., 136; on A.'s style in Frag. 12,145 n.5; on Frag. 3,87 (with n.33); on principle of *nihil ex nihilo*, 167 n.67; on a Zenonian argument against plurality, 80; on Eudemus, 140

smallness, unlimited, 41,64,66-7, Ch.3 *passim*, 109,159 n.30,160 n.42

Sophists: epistemological concerns, 28,39; chronological relation to A., 33-5

Sophocles, solemn predication in, 13

Strang, C.: on interpretation of 'everything in everything', 74-5, 108-9 (with n.11),163 n.30; on Frag. 3,86

style, of A.'s prose, 6-10,19 (with n.39),23-4 (with n.46),31-3, 88-9,97-9,100,102,144

substances, in A.'s ontology, 108-121 (esp. 108-9 with n.11; cf. 74-5),123,130-3,162 nn.16 and 21,163 n.30,166 n.59

sufficient reason, principle of, 26,62-4,65,72-3

Theophrastus: accepts Ar.'s general interpretation of A.'s physics, 136,141-2 (with n.79); on A.'s zoology and zoogony, 124-6,129-30; attests opposites as among A.'s μοῖραι, 115; on principles of cosmic separation, 164 n.34; scholiast not dependent on him, 1; *see also* Aëtius; doxographical evidence; Simplicius

Thucydides, use of σφραγίς, 38

tissues, of plants and animals, 128-43,153 n.39,166 n.59

unlimited: mind, 10-11 (with n.22; but cf. 17); smallness, 41,64, 66-7, Ch.3 *passim*,109,159 n.30,160 n.42; *see also* infinite

Vlastos, G.: view on duplication of κοσμοί in A. endorsed, 102-3; likewise view on role of opposites in A.'s physics, 163 n.22; but interpretation of A.'s seeds rejected, 123,126-7 (with n.51)

Xenophanes, employs solemn predication, 12

Zeno: chronological relation of his book with A.'s, 35,81-2 (with n.22); conception of and arguments for infinite divisibility, 78, 80-2 (with nn.19 and 21),86,89; employment of paradox, 29,81; susceptibility to modern methods of analysis, 94

LIBRARY OF DAVIDSON COLLEGE